Lecture Notes in Economics and Mathematical Systems

(Vol. 1–15: Lecture Notes in Operations Research and Mathematical Economics, Vol. 16–59: Lecture Notes in Operations Research and Mathematical Systems) For information about Vols. 1–29, please contact your bookseller or Springer-Verlag

continuation on page 185

Lecture Notes
in Economics and
Mathematical Systems

Managing Editors: M. Beckmann and H. P. Künzi

187

Willi Hock
Klaus Schittkowski

Test Examples for
Nonlinear Programming Codes

Springer-Verlag
Berlin Heidelberg New York 1981

Authors

Willi Hock
Klaus Schittkowski
Institut für Angewandte Mathematik und Statistik, Universität Würzburg
Am Hubland, 8700 Würzburg, Federal Republic of Germany

AMS Subject Classifications: (1980): 65 K 05, 90 C 30

ISBN-13: 978-3-540-10561-9   e-ISBN-13: 978-3-642-48320-2
DOI: 10.1007/978-3-642-48320-2

2142/3140-543210

Preface
· ·

The performance of a nonlinear programming algorithm can only
be ascertained by numerical experiments requiring the collection
and implementation of test examples in dependence upon the desired
performance criterium. This book should be considered as an assistance for a test designer since it presents an extensive collection of nonlinear programming problems which have been used in
the past to test or compare optimization programs. He will be in-
formed about the optimal solution, about the structure of the
problem in the neighbourhood of the solution, and, in addition,
about the usage of the corresponding FORTRAN subroutines if he is
interested in obtaining them on a magnetic tape.

Chapter I shows how the test examples are documented. In particular, the evaluation of computable information about the solution of a problem is outlined. It is explained how the optimal
solution, the optimal Lagrange-multipliers, and the condition
number of the projected Hessian of the Lagrangian are obtained.
Furthermore, a classification number is defined allowing a formal
description of a test problem, and the documentation scheme is
described which is used in Chapter IV to present the problems.
Chapter II contains detailed information about the usage of the
corresponding FORTRAN subroutines for all programmers who want to
receive them on a magnetic tape from the authors. A comprehensive
list of the test problems and some solution properties are given
in Chapter III. Furthermore, there is a list of the identification
numbers of some famous, frequently used test examples to simplify
their search. Together with their solution properties, all test
problems are presented then in Chapter IV using a common documentation scheme. Appendix A contains constant data for more extensive problems and the numerical test results computed by some
well-known optimization programs are listed in Appendix B. Some
further results are encluded in Appendix C where the optimal restriction function values and the corresponding Lagrange-multipliers are listed.

The coding of the test problem functions together with their gradients requires about 10,000 FORTRAN statements making it impossible to publish the corresponding listings. But the authors are willing to provide an interested user with all subroutines on a magnetic tape. An order form is included at the end of the book.

The authors would like to express their gratitude to the Rechenzentrum of the University of Würzburg for the generous support and to M. Bahr, R. Ruppert, and H. Megerle for their assistance when implementing and testing the programs.

Contents ....

DESCRIPTION OF THE DOCUMENTATION

This chapter shows how the information about the solution properties of the test problems are obtained, and the documentation scheme is described.

1. Introduction

The development of algorithms for solving the nonlinear programming problem

$$\min \quad f(x)$$

$$x \in \mathbb{R}^n: \quad \begin{aligned} g_j(x) &\geq 0 \ , \quad j=1,\ldots,m_1 \\ g_j(x) &= 0 \ , \quad j=m_1+1,\ldots,m \\ x_l &\leq x \leq x_u \end{aligned} \quad \text{(NLP)}$$

with continuously differentiable functions f and $g_1,\ldots,g_m$ requires the preparation of test examples. Our intention is to present an extensive collection of optimization problems which can be used by a test designer to choose from. All problems are found in the literature and have been used in the past to develop, test, or compare optimization software. There is no attempt to classify the problems in the sense of 'good' or 'bad' test examples, since this question depends on the performance profile of the test designer. It should be noted, however, that all problems have been executed to compare 26 optimization programs numerically, cf. Hock [31]. The same set of nonlinear programming codes was investigated by Schittkowski [55] in the scope of a comparative study based on randomly generated test problems with predetermined solutions.

Another intention is to provide a user with information about the structure of a test problem at the optimal solution to get more insight in the numerical behaviour of optimization codes. The fundamental tool is the Lagrange-function

$$L(x,u) := f(x) - \sum_{j=1}^{m} u_j g_j(x) \qquad (1)$$

defined for all $x \in \mathbb{R}^n$ and $u = (u_1,\ldots,u_m)^T \in \mathbb{R}^m$. The variables $u_1,\ldots,u_m$ are called 'Lagrange-multipliers'. To simplify the notation in this and the following section, let us assume that there are no bounds on the variables or, in other words, that they are formulated as general restrictions in the form

$$g_{m_1+i}(x) := x_i - x_{l_i}$$
$$g_{m_1+n+i}(x) := -x_i + x_{u_i} \qquad (2)$$

for $i=1,\ldots,n$, where $x = (x_1,\ldots,x_n)^T$, $x_l = (x_{l_1},\ldots,x_{l_n})^T$, $x_u = (x_{u_1},\ldots,x_{u_n})^T$. The Lagrange-function (1) allows to characterize the optimality conditions which can be stated in the following form, cf. McCormick [40].

<u>Theorem</u> (sufficient second order optimality condition): Let f and $g_1,\ldots,g_m$ be twice continuously differentiable functions. A point $x^* \in \mathbb{R}^n$ is an isolated local minimizer of (NLP), if there exists a vector $u^* = (u_1^*,\ldots,u_m^*)^T$ such that the following conditions are valid:

a) Kuhn-Tucker-conditions:

$$g_j(x^*) \geq 0, \quad j=1,\ldots,m_1$$
$$g_j(x^*) = 0, \quad j=m_1+1,\ldots,m$$
$$u_j^* \geq 0, \quad j=1,\ldots,m_1$$
$$u_j^* g_j(x^*) = 0, \quad j=1,\ldots,m_1$$
$$\nabla_x L(x^*,u^*) = 0 \qquad (3)$$

b) Second order condition: For every nonzero vector y with $y^T \nabla_x g_j(x^*) = 0$ for all j with $u_j^* > 0$, $j=1,\ldots,m_1$, and $y^T \nabla_x g_j(x^*) = 0$, $j=m_1,\ldots,m$, it follows that

$$y^T \nabla_x^2 L(x^*,u^*) y > 0. \qquad (4)$$

Under an additional assumption (constrained qualification), the reversal of the theorem is also valid. Since the Kuhn-Tucker-condition (3) indicates that the gradient of the objective function is a linear combination of the gradients of the restriction functions, we can consider the Lagrange-multipliers as a measure for the scaling or ascent properties of the restrictions at the optimal solution. In addition, a vanishing Lagrange-multiplier u_j^* with $g_j(x^*) = 0$ shows that the restriction g_j is redundant. In this situation, we say that a test problem is degenerate and the quotient of the absolutely greatest and absolutely smallest non-zero Lagrange-multipliers is called 'degree of degeneracy'.

The second order condition (4) is interpreted in the sense that the Lagrange-function projected on the subspace of the binding constraints is locally convex. A measure for the curvature of the Lagrangian in this subspace is given by the condition number of the Hesse-matrix, i.e. the quotient of the greatest and smallest eigenvalue. They are positive if and only if condition (4) is valid.

2. Computable information about a solution

This section describes the procedure which was used to compute an optimal solution and to check the optimality conditions (3) and (4). For many test examples, the exact solution x* of (NLP) is known a priori within machine precision. However, in all other cases, we have to approximate x* numerically, that means by an optimization code. But since none of the implemented optimization programs could solve all problems successfully, since different codes give different numerical solutions on return, and since, in particular, no optimization program can guarantee having found the global solution of (NLP), we executed the test problems by the routines of Table 1 which encludes the name of the author and the underlying mathematical method.

Code	Author	Method
VF02AD	Powell	Quadratic approximation
OPRQP	Bartholomew-Biggs	
GRGA	Abadie	Generalized reduced gradient
VF01A	Fletcher	Multiplier
FUNMIN	Kraft	
FMIN	Kraft, Lootsma	Penalty

Table 1: Optimization programs for evaluating the optimal solutions.

More detailed information about these programs is contained in Schittkowski [55]. The purpose of performing these test runs was not to compare the efficiency of the programs (has been done separately, cf. Hock [31]), but only to compute one solution as precise as possible. Therefore, the programs were executed with very low stopping tolerances and a decision was made which of the obtained results could be accepted and published as a solution of the test problem. This choice has been based on the objective function value $f(x^*)$ and the sum of constrained violations $r(x^*)$, i.e. of

$$ r(x^*) := -\sum_{j=1}^{m_1} \min(0, g_j(x^*)) + \sum_{j=m_1+1}^{m} |g_j(x^*)| \, , \tag{5} $$

where x^* denotes the current computed approximation of the exact, but unknown solution. A numerical solution was considered to be the best one which had the lowest objective function value among all results with a constraint violation below a tolerance of 10^{-7}.

The procedure described so far yielded for each test problem of this collection the data x^*, $f(x^*)$, and $r(x^*)$, where x^* is considered now to be the optimal solution of the optimization problem. But these results give too less information about the structure of the problem in the neighbourhood of the solution x^*. In particular, one has to determine the active constraints allowing a computation of the optimal Lagrange-multipliers u^*, i.e. of the index set

$$I(x^*) := \{ j : g_j(x^*) = 0 , 1 \le j \le m_1 \} .$$ (6)

However, we cannot expect in practice that $g_j(x^*)$ vanishes within machine precision. Since we do not know whether any small value of $g_j(x^*)$ indicates an active constraint or a small function value of a non-active constraint, we proceed from a tolerance ϵ ($\epsilon := 1$), determine the active constraints with respect to ϵ, and compute the corresponding Lagrange-multipliers as described subsequently. This procedure is repeated with $\epsilon := .1\epsilon$, until the norm of the Kuhn-Tucker-vector

$$e(x^*) := \| \nabla_x L(x^*, u^*) \|$$ (7)

increases significantly.

Next, we consider the problem to obtain the optimal Lagrange-multipliers u^* given a solution x^* and the active constraint set

$$I(x^*) = (j_1, \ldots, j_\mu) .$$

Since

$$\nabla_x L(x^*, u^*) = \nabla_x f(x^*) - \sum_{j=1}^{m} u_j^* \nabla_x g_j(x^*) ,$$ (8)

and $u_j^* = 0$ for all $j \le m_1$, $j \notin I(x^*)$, we write the Kuhn-Tucker-condition (3) in the form

$$f^* - G^* v^* = 0 ,$$

where $f^* := \nabla_x f(x^*)$ and

$$G^* := (\nabla_x g_{j_1}(x^*), \ldots, \nabla_x g_{j_\mu}(x^*), \nabla_x g_{m_1+1}(x^*), \ldots, \nabla_x g_m(x^*)) .$$

The calculation of u^* is therefore equivalent to the solution of the linear least squares problem

$$\min \| G^* v - f^* \|$$
$$v = (v_1, \ldots, v_{\mu+m_2})^T \in \mathbb{R}^{\mu+m_2} : v_j \ge 0 , j=1,\ldots,\mu ,$$ (9)

where $m_2 := m - m_1$ is the number of all equality constraints in (NLP). If v^* denotes the solution of (9), we obtain u^* by expanding v^* with zeros for all indices defined by the non-active inequality constraints. In addition, we get a measure for the degree of degeneracy of a test problem by considering the quotient of the absolutely largest and absolutely smallest multipliers, i.e. of

$$|v^*_{max}|/|v^*_{min}| \tag{10}$$

For examining the second order condition (4), first we have to project the Lagrangian on the tangent plane determined by the active constraints. The factorization

$$G^* = Q \begin{pmatrix} R \\ 0 \end{pmatrix} \tag{11}$$

with an orthogonal matrix Q and an upper triangular matrix R allows to write the condition $y^T \nabla_x g_j(x^*) = 0$ for $j \in I(x^*) \cup \{m_1+1,\ldots,m\}$ in the form

$$y^T G^* = y^T Q \begin{pmatrix} R \\ 0 \end{pmatrix} = (v^T : w^T) \begin{pmatrix} R \\ 0 \end{pmatrix} = v^T R = 0$$

with $\begin{pmatrix} v \\ w \end{pmatrix} := Q^T y$ if and only if $v = 0$ or

$$y = Q \begin{pmatrix} 0 \\ w \end{pmatrix} \quad , \quad w \in \mathbb{R}^{n-\mu-m_2} \tag{12}$$

Since

$$y^T \nabla_x^2 L(x^*,u^*)y = y^T Q Q^T \nabla_x^2 L(x^*,u^*) Q Q^T y$$

$$= (0 : w^T) Q^T \nabla_x^2 L(x^*,u^*) Q \begin{pmatrix} 0 \\ w \end{pmatrix}$$

$$= w^T H^* w$$

with an $(n-\mu-m_2)$ by $(n-\mu-m_2)$ matrix H^* given by

$$Q^T \nabla_x^2 L(x^*,u^*) Q =: \begin{pmatrix} * & : & * \\ * & : & H^* \end{pmatrix} ,$$

the second order condition (4) is equivalent to

$$w^T H^* w > 0 \tag{13}$$

for all $w \in \mathbb{R}^{n-\mu-m_2}$. H^* is symmetric and the eigenvalues λ^*_i of H^* give the information if H^* is positive definite or not. In addition, the quotient of the largest and smallest eigenvalue, i.e. of

$$\lambda^*_{max}/\lambda^*_{min} \quad , \tag{14}$$

determines the condition number of H^* which can be considered as a measure for the degree of difficulty of a test problem.

To sum up, the optimality analysis described so far gives
the following information about the solution of a test problem:

Solution : $\quad\quad x^*$

Minimal objective function value : $\quad f(x^*)$

Sum of constraint violation (5) : $\quad r(x^*)$

Norm of Kuhn-Tucker-vector (7) : $\quad e(x^*)$

Number of active constraints : $\quad \mu$

Active constraint set (6) : $\quad I(x^*)$

Degree of degeneracy (10) : $\quad u^*_{max}/u^*_{min}$
$$(:= |v^*_{max}|/|v^*_{min}|)$$

Condition number of projected
$\quad\quad\quad\quad\quad$ Hessian (14) : $\quad \lambda^*_{max}/\lambda^*_{min}$.

These data allow a quantitative measure whether the optimality
conditions are satisfied, and give an impression about the in-
fluence of the constraints and the curvature of the Lagrangian
in the neighbourhood of the solution.

The solution of the linear least squares problem (9) was
obtained by the program published in Lawson, Hanson [39]. G^*
and f^* are known precisely besides round-off errors since all
test problems are programmed together with their analytical
first derivatives. However, the Hessian matrix $\nabla_x^2 L(x^*,u^*)$ of
the Lagrangian had to be approximated numerically by a five
point central difference formula. The decomposition (11) was
performed by numerically stable Householder-transformations,
and the eigenvalues of the submatrix H^* have been evaluated by
subroutine RS of the EISPACK-system.

In most cases, the Lagrange-multipliers could be computed
successfully leading to a considerably small norm of the Kuhn-
Tucker-vector. Only in one test problem (no. 99), scaling difficulties were observed in the objective function so that it
appeared advisable to divide $e(x^*)$ by $\|\nabla f(x^*)\|$.

3. The classification number

The classification scheme of Bus [16] is slightly extended to give more detailed information about the problem and consists of a sequence of letters and numbers like

OCD-Kr-s .

The following lists give all possible abbreviations which could replace the letters O, C, D, and K.

O	Information about objective function
C	Constant objective function
L	Linear objective function
Q	Quadratic objective function
S	Sum of squares
P	Generalized polynomial objective function
G	General objective function

C	Information about constraint functions
U	Unconstrained problem
B	Upper and lower bounds only
L	Linear constraint functions
Q	Quadratic constraint functions
P	Generalized polynomial constraint functions
G	General constraint functions

D	Regularity of the problem
R	Regular problem
I	Irregular problem

K	Information about the solution
T	Exact solution known ('theoretical' problem)
P	Exact solution not known ('practical' problem)

A problem is called a regular one, if the first and second derivatives of all problem functions exist in the feasible region, otherwise an irregular one. K = P means that the solution of the problem can be obtained only numerically (sometimes called 'real life' problem).

The number r gives the information which partial derivatives are calculated analytically in the corresponding subroutine package. Since in our case, the user is always provided with the first derivatives, we have r = 1 for all problems. Finally, the number s is replaced by the current serial number within the the class of test problems identified by OCD-Kr.

To give an example, consider the problem

$$\min \quad (x_1-1)^2 + (x_2-2)^2 + (x_3-3)^2 + (x_4-4)^2$$
$$x_1 - 2 = 0 \qquad\qquad\qquad\qquad (15)$$
$$x_3^2 + x_4^2 - 2 = 0 .$$

Since the exact solution is given by $(2 , 2 , .6\sqrt{2} , .8\sqrt{2})$ and since it is the 10-th problem of its class, we classify this problem by

$$QQR-T1-10 .$$

4. The documentation scheme

We propose a documentation scheme providing the user with the following information about the test problem:

PROBLEM: Here we find the problem number and, if available, the name of the problem or its practical background in brackets. If there are several problems distinguished only by some parameters, all corresponding problem numbers are listed.

CLASSIFICATION: Using the classification scheme of the last section, the problem is identified in the form OCD-Kr-s. If several problems are distinguished only by some parameters not changing the classification scheme, we present this number in the form OCD-Kr-$(s_1,...,s_k)$.

SOURCE: Some references indicate where the problem has been found and where additional information or test results are given.

NUMBER OF VARIABLES: Contains the dimension of the problem n.

NUMBER OF CONSTRAINTS: Contains the number of all inequality constraints m_1, of all equality constraints $m-m_1$, and of all upper and lower bounds of the variables b. If there are linear restrictions, their number is presented in brackets behind m_1 or $m-m_1$, respectively.

OBJECTIVE FUNCTION: The objective function f(x) is defined.

CONSTRAINTS: The restrictions are described in the form

$$g_1(x) \geq 0$$
$$\vdots$$
$$g_{m_1}(x) \geq 0$$
$$g_{m_1+1}(x) = 0$$
$$\vdots$$
$$g_m(x) = 0$$
$$x_l \leq x \leq x_u \quad .$$

If the description of the problem functions requires an extensive set of constant data, then they are summarized in Appendix A.

START: The starting point x_o and the corresponding objective function value $f(x_o)$ are presented together with the information, whether x_o is feasible or not.

SOLUTION: This part of the documentation scheme contains the computable results about the solution of a test problem as described in Section 2 of Chapter I:

    x^* :   Optimal solution (exact or computed)

    $f(x^*)$:   Objective function value

r(x*) : Sum of constraint violations, cf. (5)

e(x*) : Norm of Kuhn-Tucker-vector, cf. (7)

μ : Number of active constraints

I(x*) : Active constraint set, cf. (6)

u^*_{max}/u^*_{min} : Degree of degeneracy, cf. (10)

$\lambda^*_{max}/\lambda^*_{min}$: Condition number of projected Hessian of the Lagrangian, cf. (14) .

To give an example, consider the optimization problem (15) of the last section. Since it is the 42-th problem within our series and the 10-th problem of the class QQR-T1, we describe it in the following format:

PROBLEM:	42
CLASSIFICATION:	QQR-T1-10
SOURCE:	Brusch [14]
NUMBER OF VARIABLES:	$n = 4$
NUMBER OF CONSTRAINTS:	$m_1 = 0$, $m-m_1 = 2(1)$, $b = 0$

OBJECTIVE FUNCTION:

$$f(x) = (x_1 - 1)^2 + (x_2 - 2)^2 + (x_3 - 3)^2 + (x_4 - 4)^2$$

CONSTRAINTS:

$$x_1 - 2 = 0$$

$$x_3^2 + x_4^2 - 2 = 0$$

START: x_0 = (1 , 1 , 1 , 1)   (not feasible)

$f(x_0)$ = 14

SOLUTION: x^* = $(2 , 2 , .6\sqrt{2} , .8\sqrt{2})$

$f(x^*)$ = $28 - 10\sqrt{2}$

$r(x^*)$ = 0

$e(x^*)$ = .2E-23

μ = 0

$I(x^*)$ = –

u^*_{max}/u^*_{min} = 2.5355/2 = 1.26

$\lambda^*_{max}/\lambda^*_{min}$ = 7.07/2 = 3.54

USAGE OF THE FORTRAN SUBROUTINES

This chapter describes the organization of the FORTRAN subroutines and informs the user about the way how to execute the
test problems. Since it is assumed that at least a subset of the
problems is used within a series of test runs for different
optimization programs, the problems are coded in a very flexible
manner. For example, it is possible to execute an arbitrary subset of the restrictions. To distinguish between linear and nonlinear constraints, we have to define a fixed succession of the
restrictions in the following way:

$$g_j(x) \geq 0 \ , \quad j=1,\ldots,m_{11} \ , \qquad \text{linear functions} \ ,$$

$$g_j(x) \geq 0 \ , \quad j=m_{11}+1,\ldots,m_1 \ , \qquad \text{nonlinear functions} \ ,$$

$$g_j(x) = 0 \ , \quad j=m_1+1,\ldots,m_{21} \ , \qquad \text{linear functions} \ ,$$

$$g_j(x) = 0 \ , \quad j=m_{21}+1,\ldots,m \ , \qquad \text{nonlinear functions} \ .$$

A test problem is set up by

call TPno(MODE) ,

where no is replaced by the actual problem number. The parameter
MODE describes the five possible operations of the subroutine:

MODE = 1 :   The driving program will be provided with all infor-
             mation necessary to initialize an optimization program
             for the solution of the test problem, i.e. dimension,
             type and number of constraints, upper and lower bounds,
             starting point, derivatives of the linear constraints,
             and, in particular, the exact or computed optimal
             solution.

MODE = 2 :   The objective function f(x) is computed at a current
             iterate x.

MODE = 3 : The gradient of the objective function will be computed.

MODE = 4 : A predetermined subset of the constraints $g_1(x),\ldots,$
$g_m(x)$ is evaluated at the iterate x.

MODE = 5 : The gradients of a predetermined subset of the nonlinear constraints are computed.

The information about the test problem are delivered in the
following common-blocks which have to be defined in the driving
program with appropriate array dimensions:

COMMON/L1/N,NILI,NINL,NELI,NENL : A call of TPno(1) gives on
return the data:
    N   Dimension of the problem, i.e. n.
    NILI   Number of linear inequalities, i.e. m_{11}.
    NINL   Number of nonlinear inequalities, i.e. m_1-m_{11}.
    NELI   Number of linear equalities, i.e. $m_{21}-m_1$.
    NENL   Number of nonlinear equalities, i.e. $m-m_{21}$.

COMMON/L2/X(n) : For MODE = 1 , X will be set to the starting
point x_0. For MODE > 1 , X must contain the argument x for
which the problem functions or derivatives are to be computed.

COMMON/L3/G(m) : For all indices j with INDEX1(j) = .TRUE. ,
G(j) is set to the j-th constraint value $g_j(x)$. Action only
for MODE = 4 .

COMMON/L4/GF(n) : Contains the gradient of the objective function
on return, i.e. $GF(i) = \frac{\partial}{\partial x_i} f(x)$, i=1,...,n . Action only for
MODE = 3 .

COMMON/L5/GG(m,n) : For MODE = 1 , all constant partial derivatives are stored in GG. In particular, the rows $1,\ldots,m_{11}$ and
$m_1+1,\ldots,m_{21}$ of GG give the constant derivatives of the linear
constraints, if present. For MODE = 5 , the j-th row of GG
defined by INDEX2 = .TRUE. will be replaced by the gradient
of the j-th restriction, i.e. $GG(j,i) = \frac{\partial}{\partial x_i} g_j(x)$, if this term
is not constant. Since all array dimensions of the common blocks

are defined by the exact values of n or m, respectively, we
recommend to define GG as a one-dimensional array in the
driving program and to use it there in the form

$$GG((i-1) \cdot m+j) = \frac{\partial}{\partial x_i} g_j(x) \ .$$

COMMON/L6/FX : For MODE = 2 , FX contains the objective function value f(x) on return.

COMMON/L9/INDEX1(m) : The logical array INDEX1 has to be predetermined by the user before a call of TPno(4) and defines
  the restrictions which are to be computed in the case
  MODE = 4 . INDEX1 is not changed by the subroutine.

COMMON/L10/INDEX2(m) : The logical array INDEX2 has to be predetermined by the user before every call of TPno(5), and
  defines the gradients of the nonlinear restrictions which are
  to be computed in the case MODE = 5 . INDEX2 is not changed
  during a call of TPno.

COMMON/L11/LXL(n) : The logical array LXL informs about the
  existence of lower bounds. If there is a lower bound for the
  i-th variable, LXL(i) is set to .TRUE. during a call of TPno(1).
  Otherwise, we find LXL(i) = .FALSE. .

COMMON/L12/LXU(n) : Same for the existence of upper bounds.

COMMON/L13/XL(n) : If LXL(i) = .TRUE. , XL(i) is replaced by
  a lower bound for the i-th variable during a call of TPno(1).

COMMON/L14/XU(n) : If LXU(i) = .TRUE. , XU(i) is set to an upper
  bound for the i-th variable during a call of TPno(1).

COMMON/L20/LEX,NEX,FEX,XEX(NEX·n) : L20 gives information about
  the optimal solution of the problem and is set up during a
  call of TPno(1). If LEX = .FALSE. , a precise solution is
  not known a priori and x* has been computed as described in
  Section 2 of Chapter I. Otherwise, we have LEX = .TRUE. .
  NEX gives the number of all optimal solutions. NEX = -1 indicates that infinitely many solutions are present. FEX con-

tains the minimal objective function value and XEX the j-th
optimal solution in XEX(n·(j-1)+i), i=1,...,n, j=1,...,NEX.
In the case NEX = -1 , XEX contains only one arbitrary solution.

The user should be aware that some test problems require constant data and that in this case, additional storage capacity is
necessary to define auxiliary arrays in subroutine TPno. The
program package contains a subroutine GLEICH to find zeros of a
real function and is executed in TP88 to TP92. A parameter
EPS = .1E-8 is chosen according to the machine precision of
the Telefunken TR440 and should be adopted to the actual precision. Test problems TP68 and TP69 require the evaluation of the
normal distribution, i.e. of

$$\frac{1}{\sqrt{2\pi}} \int_0^x e^{-t^2/2} dt \ .$$

A function F68(t) is encluded for calculating the expression
$(\sqrt{2\pi})^{-1} e^{-t^2/2}$ and an internal function

$$AINTEG(F,A,B,EPS)$$

evaluates the integral $\int_a^b f(x) \, dx$ subject to the accuracy EPS.
This subroutine has to be provided by the user, in addition.
Using the instructions given above, the test problem (15) of
the previous chapter is compiled now to give an example:

```
SUBROUTINE TP42(MODE)
COMMON/L1/N,NILI,NINL,NELI,NENL
COMMON/L2/X(4)
COMMON/L3/G(2)
COMMON/L4/GF(4)
COMMON/L5/GG(2,4)
COMMON/L6/FX
COMMON/L9/INDEX1
COMMON/L10/INDEX2
COMMON/L11/LXL
COMMON/L12/LXU
COMMON/L13/XL(4)
COMMON/L14/XU(4)
COMMON/L20/LEX,NEX,FEX,XEX(4)
```

```
      LOGICAL LEX,LXL(4),LXU(4),INDEX1(2),INDEX2(2)
C
      GOTO(1,2,3,4,5),MODE
C
    1 N=4
      NILI = 0
      NINL = 0
      NELI = 1
      NENL = 1
      DO 6  I=1,4
      X(I) = 1.
      LXU(I) = .FALSE.
    6 LXL(I) = .FALSE.
      GG(1,1) = 1.
      GG(1,2) = 0.
      GG(1,3) = 0.
      GG(1,4) = 0.
      GG(2,1) = 0.
      GG(2,2) = 0.
      LEX = .TRUE.
      NEX = 1
      FEX = 28. - 10.*SQRT(2.)
      XEX(1) = 2.
      XEX(2) = 2.
      XEX(3) = SQRT(.72)
      XEX(4) = SQRT(1.28)
      RETURN
C
    2 FX = (X(1)-1.)**2 + (X(2)-2.)**2 + (X(3)-3.)**2
     1                                 + (X(4)-4.)**2
      RETURN
C
    3 DO 7  I=1,4
    7 GF(I) = 2.*(X(I) - FLOAT(I))
      RETURN
C
    4 IF (INDEX1(1))  G(1) = X(1) - 2.
      IF (INDEX1(2))  G(2) = X(3)**2 + X(4)**2 - 2.
      RETURN
C
    5 IF (.NOT.INDEX2(2))  GOTO 8
      GG(2,3) = 2.*X(3)
      GG(2,4) = 2.*X(4)
    8 RETURN
      END
```

Chapter III . . . .

CONDENSED INFORMATION ABOUT THE TEST PROBLEMS

To give a first survey of the test examples and their solution
properties, we present a comprehensive list of all problems in
Table 2. Beside the current problem number and the classification
number OCD-Kr-s as described in Section 3 of Chapter I, we report
the dimension n, the number of all inequality constraints m_1, the
number of all equality constraints $m-m_1$, and the number of all
bounds b. If linear restrictions exist, their number is given in
the brackets behind m_1 or $m-m_1$, respectively. The column headed
by x_0 gives the information, whether the starting point x_0 is
feasible (T) or not (F). Some numerical data obtained by the
analysis described in Section 2 of Chapter I are encluded. In
particular, the objective function value $f(x*)$, the sum of constraint violations $r(x*)$, the norm of the Kuhn-Tucker-vector
$e(x*)$, the number of active plus equality restrictions, i.e.
$\bar{\mu} := \mu + m - m_1$, the degree of degeneracy $u*_{max}/u*_{min}$, and the
condition number of the Hessian of the projected Lagrangian
$\lambda*_{max}/\lambda*_{min}$ are listed. A value of O. for $u*_{max}/u*_{min}$ indicates that
at least one multiplier $u*_j$ vanishes ($|u*_j| < .1E-5$) and that there
are redundant constraints, i.e. the problem is degenerate. By
$\lambda*_{max}/\lambda*_{min} = 0.$ we express that an eigenvalue $\lambda*_i$ of the Hessian
$H*$ of the projected Lagrangian is considered to be zero
($\lambda*_i < .1E-5$) implying that $H*$ becomes indefinite. In this case,
the problem is degenerate or the solution is not unique. Furthermore, some references and the corresponding page numbers are
given where more details about the test problems are found.

Some of the problems have frequently been executed in the past
to test or compare optimization software, e.g. the Colville-prob-
lems. To simplify their search, Table 3 gives a list of these
problems together with their names which are used in other pub-
lications. Information about the test problem classes are gathered
in Table 4 where for each test problem class defined by OCD, the
number of 'theoretical' (T) and 'practical' (P) problems are
listed together with the corresponding serial numbers.

No	OCD-Kr-s	n	m_1	$m-m_1$	b	x_0	$f(x^*)$	$r(x^*)$	$e(x^*)$	$\bar{u}$	u^*_{max}/u^*_{min}	$\lambda^*_{max}/\lambda^*_{min}$	Ref.	p.
1	PBR-T1-1	2	0	0	1	T	.0	.0	–	0	–	.25E4	[8]	24
2	PBR-T1-2	2	0	0	1	F	.5043E-1	.0	.1E-7	1	.10E1	.10E1	[8]	25
3	QBR-T1-1	2	0	0	1	T	.0	.0	.0	1	.10E1	.10E1	[56]	26
4	PBR-T1-3	2	0	0	2	T	.2666E1	.0	.0	2	.40E1	–	[1]	27
5	GBR-T1-1	2	0	0	4	T	-.1913E1	.0	–	0	–	.23E1	[41]	28
6	QQR-T1-1	2	0	1	0	F	.0	.0	.0	1	.0	.10E1	[8]	29
7	GPR-T1-1	2	0	1	0	F	-.1723E1	.0	.2E-24	1	.10E1	.10E1	[44,45]	30
8	CQR-T1-1	2	0	2	0	F	-.1000E1	.0	.0	2	.0	–	[8]	31
9	GLR-T1-1	2	0	1(1)	0	T	-.5000	.0	.7E-12	1	.10E1	.10E1	[44]	32
10	LQR-T1-1	2	1	0	0	F	-.1000E1	.0	.9E-11	1	.10E1	.10E1	[10]	33
11	QQR-T1-2	2	1	0	0	F	-.8498E1	.0	.2E-9	1	.10E1	.10E1	[10]	34
12	QQR-T1-3	2	1	0	0	T	-.3000E2	.0	.8E-10	1	.10E1	.10E1	[46]	35
13	QPR-T1-1	2	1	0	2	F	.1000E1	.0	.2E1	2	.0	–	[8,38]	36
14	QQR-T1-4	2	1	1(1)	0	F	.1393E1	.0	.0	2	.12E1	–	[13,29]	37
15	PQR-T1-1	2	2	0	1	F	.3065E3	.0	.0	2	.25E1	–	[8]	38
16	PQR-T1-2	2	2	0	3	F	.2500	.0	.0	1	.10E1	.10E1	[8]	39
17	PQR-T1-3	2	2	0	3	F	.1000E1	.0	.0	2	.0	–	[8]	40
18	QQR-T1-5	2	2	0	4	F	.5000E1	.0	.2E-9	1	.10E1	.10E1	[8]	41
19	PQR-T1-4	2	2	0	4	F	-.6962E4	.0	.0	2	.11E1	–	[8,27]	42
20	PQR-T1-5	2	3	0	2	F	.3820E2	.0	.0	2	.27E1	–	[8]	43
21	QLR-T1-1	2	1(1)	0	4	F	-.9996E2	.0	.0	1	.10E1	.10E1	[8]	44
22	QQR-T1-6	2	2(1)	0	0	F	.1000E1	.0	.0	2	.10E1	–	[13,29,57]	45
23	QQR-T1-7	2	5(1)	0	4	F	.2000E1	.0	.0	2	.10E1	–	[8]	46
24	PLR-T1-1	2	3(3)	0	2	T	-.1000E1	.0	.0	2	.17E1	–	[8,12]	47
25	SBR-T1-1	3	0	0	6	T	.0	.0	–	0	–	.70E7	[29,32]	48
26	PPR-T1-1	3	0	1	0	T	.0	.0	.0	1	.0	.0	[34,43]	49
27	PQR-T1-6	3	0	1	0	F	.4000E-1	.0	.0	1	.10E1	.25E2	[44,45]	50
28	QLR-T1-2	3	0	1(1)	0	T	.0	.0	.0	1	.0	.65E1	[34]	51
29	PQR-T1-7	3	1	0	0	T	-.2263E2	.0	.2E-9	1	.10E1	.22E1	[10]	52
30	QQR-T1-8	3	1	0	6	T	.1000E1	.0	.0	2	.0	.10E1	[8]	53
31	QQR-T1-9	3	1	0	6	T	.6000E1	.0	.6E-10	1	.10E1	.25E1	[8]	54
32	QPR-T1-2	3	1	1(1)	3	T	.1000E1	.0	.0	3	.0	–	[25]	55
33	PQR-T1-8	3	2	0	4	T	-.4586E1	.0	.0	3	.62E2	–	[6,28]	56
34	LGR-T1-1	3	2	0	6	T	-.8340	.0	.0	3	.10E2	–	[24]	57
35	QLR-T1-3	3	1(1)	0	3	T	.1111	.0	.5E-10	1	.10E1	.23E1	[1,18,23,57]	58
36	PLR-T1-2	3	1(1)	0	6	T	-.3300E4	.0	.0	3	.20E1	–	[10]	59
37	PLR-T1-3	3	2(2)	0	6	T	-.3456E4	.0	.0	1	.10E1	.30E1	[8,12]	60
38	PBR-T1-4	4	0	0	8	T	.0	.0	–	0	–	.14E4	[20,29]	61

Table 2: Condensed list of all test examples and some solution properties (continued).

No	OCD-Kr-s	n	m_1	$m-m_1$	b	x_0	$f(x^*)$	$r(x^*)$	$e(x^*)$	$\bar{\mu}$	u^*_{max}/u^*_{min}	$\lambda^*_{max}/\lambda^*_{min}$	Ref.	p.
39	LPR-T1-1	4	0	2	0	F	-.1000E1	.0	.0	2	.10E1	.10E1	[44,45]	62
40	PPR-T1-2	4	0	3	·0	F	-.2500	.0	.8E-11	3	.14E1	.10E1	[6,35]	63
41	PLR-T1-4	4	0	1(1)	8	F	.1926E1	.0	.1E-10	2	.10E1	.30E1	[8,42]	64
42	QQR-T1-10	4	0	2(1)	0	F	.1386E2	.0	.2E-23	2	.13E1	.35E1	[14]	65
43	QQR-T1-11	4	3	0	0	T	-.4400E2	.0	.2E-9	2	.20E1	.11E1	[8,18,27,57]	66
44	QLR-T1-4	4	6(6)	0	4	T	-.1500E2	.0	.0	4	.70E1	-	[37]	67
45	PBR-T1-5	5	0	0	10	F	.1000E1	.0	.0	5	.50E1	-	[8,42]	68
46	PGR-T1-1	5	0	2	0	T	.0	.0	.0	2	.0	.0	[34,43]	69
47	PPR-T1-3	5	0	3	0	T	.0	.0	.0	3	.0	.39E1	[34,43]	70
48	QLR-T1-5	5	0	2(2)	0	T	.0	.0	.0	2	.0	.27E1	[34,43]	71
49	PLR-T1-5	5	0	2(2)	0	T	.0	.0	.0	2	.0	.0	[34]	72
50	PLR-T1-6	5	0	3(3)	0	T	.0	.0	.0	3	.0	.36E1	[34]	73
51	QLR-T1-6	5	0	3(3)	0	T	.0	.0	.0	3	.0	.18E1	[34]	74
52	QLR-T1-7	5	0	3(3)	0	F	.5327E1	.0	.1E-9	3	.27E1	.14E2	[44,45]	75
53	QLR-T1-8	5	0	3(3)	10	F	.4093E1	.0	.3E-9	3	.29E1	.18E1	[42,43]	76
54	GLR-T1-2	6	0	1(1)	12	F	-.9081	.0	.2E-10	1	.10E1	.0	[8,50]	77
55	GLR-T1-3	6	0	6(6)	8	F	.6333E1	.0	.0	8	-	-	[33]	78
56	PGR-T1-2	7	0	4	0	T	-.3456E1	.0	.7E-10	4	.0	.27E2	[15]	79
57	SQR-P1-1	2	1	0	2	T	.2846E-1	.0	.1E-8	1	.10E1	.10E1	[8,27]	80
59	GQR-P1-1	2	3	0	4	F	-.7804E1	.0	.3E-6	1	.10E1	.10E1	[3,29]	81
60	PPR-P1-1	3	0	1	6	F	.3257E-1	.2E-9	.4E-7	1	.10E1	.28E1	[8,42,44]	82
61	QQR-P1-1	3	0	2	0	F	-.1436E3	.3E-9	.2E-6	2	.20E1	.10E1	[26]	83
62	GLR-P1-1	3	0	1(1)	6	T	-.2627E5	.0	.2E-5	1	.10E1	.45E2	[8,50]	84
63	QQR-P1-2	3	0	2(1)	3	F	.9617E3	.0	.6E-5	2	.44E1	.10E1	[29,48,57]	85
64	PPR-P1-2	3	1	0	3	F	.6300E4	.0	.3E-4	1	.10E1	.23E1	[7]	86
65	QQR-P1-3	3	1	0	6	F	.9535	.0	.4E-6	1	.10E1	.12E1	[47]	87
66	LGR-P1-1	3	2	0	6	T	.5182	.6E-10	.9E-11	2	.33E1	.10E1	[24]	88
67	GGI-P1-1	3	14	0	6	T	-.1162E4	.0	.0	3	.47E2	-	[20,29]	89
68	GGR-P1-1	4	0	2	8	F	-.9204	.5E-7	.1E-4	2	.18E3	.26E3	[19]	90
69	GGR-P1-2	4	0	2	8	F	-.9567E3	.4E-10	.3E-4	2	.14E1	.13E4	[19]	90
70	SQR-P1-1	4	1	0	8	T	.7498E-2	.0	.0	0	-	.20E5	[29,30]	91
71	PPR-P1-3	4	1	1	8	F	.1701E2	.0	.5E-6	3	.67E1	.10E1	[4]	92
72	LPR-P1-1	4	2	0	8	F	.7277E3	.0	.1E-4	2	.54E1	.10E1	[13]	93
73	LGI-P1-1	4	2(1)	1(1)	4	F	.2989E2	.1E-9	.0	4	.75E2	-	[10,13]	94
74	PGR-P1-1	4	2(2)	3	8	F	.5126E4	.7E-7	.5E-7	3	.13E1	.10E1	[9]	95
75	PGR-P1-2	4	2(2)	3	8	F	.5174E4	.3E-7	.0	4	.75E3	-	[9]	95
76	QLR-P1-1	4	3(3)	0	4	T	-.4682E1	.8E-10	.2E-10	2	.38E1	.18E1	[47]	96
77	PGR-P1-3	5	0	2	0	F	.2415	.1E-9	.5E-7	2	.27E1	.52E1	[8,42,44,45]	97

Table 2: Condensed list of all test examples and some solution properties (continued).

No	OCD-Kr-s	n	m_1	$m-m_1$	b	x_0	$f(x^*)$	$r(x^*)$	$e(x^*)$	$\bar{\mu}$	u^*_{max}/u^*_{min}	$\lambda^*_{max}/\lambda^*_{min}$	Ref.	p.
78	PPR-P1-4	5	0	3	0	F	-.2920E1	.3E-9	.9E-5	3	.77E1	.10E1	[1,51]	98
79	PPR-P1-5	5	0	3	0	F	.7878E-1	.6E-9	.7E-10	3	.14E3	.29E1	[8,42,44,45]	99
80	GPR-P1-1	5	0	3	10	F	.5395E-1	.4E-9	.5E-6	3	.77E1	.10E1	[52]	100
81	GPR-P1-2	5	0	3	10	F	.5395E-1	.2E-9	.1E-5	3	.77E1	.10E1	[52]	101
83	QQR-P1-4	5	6	0	10	F	-.3067E5	.0	.0	5	.30E2	-	[20,22,29]	102
84	QQR-P1-5	5	6	0	10	T	-.5280E7	.0	.0	5	.37E5	-	[8,11,12,29]	103
85	GGI-P1-2	5	38(3)	0	10	T	-.1905E1	.0	.0	0	-	.12E4	[3,17,29]	104
86	PLR-P1-1	5	10(10)	0	5	T	-.3235E2	.7E-9	.9E-8	4	.11E3	.10E1	[20,29,47]	105
87	GGI-P1-3	6	0	4	12	F	.8928E4	.1E-6	.7E-6	5	.0	.10E1	[20,29]	106
88	QGR-P1-1	2	1	0	0	F	.1363E1	.4E-11	.1E-6	1	.10E1	.10E1	[54]	107
89	QGR-P1-2	3	1	0	0	F	.1363E1	.7E-11	.9E-7	1	.10E1	.20E2	[54]	107
90	QGR-P1-3	4	1	0	0	F	.1363E1	.0	.1E-3	1	.10E1	.65E8	[54]	107
91	QGR-P1-4	5	1	0	0	F	.1363E1	.4E-11	.1E-6	1	.10E1	.11E9	[54]	107
92	QGR-P1-5	6	1	0	0	F	.1363E1	.0	.2E-2	1	.10E1	.43E7	[54]	107
93	PPR-P1-6	6	2	0	6	T	.1351E3	.8E-7	.8E-6	2	.11E1	.56E3	[4]	108
95	LQR-P1-1	6	4	0	12	F	.1562E-1	.2E-9	.0	6	.21E5	-	[29,32]	109
96	LQR-P1-2	6	4	0	12	F	.1562E-1	.2E-9	.0	6	.21E5	-	[29,32]	109
97	LQR-P1-3	6	4	0	12	F	.3136E1	.0	.0	6	.80E3	-	[29,32]	109
98	LQR-P1-4	6	4	0	12	F	.3136E1	.0	.0	6	.80E3	-	[29,32]	109
99	GGR-P1-3	7	0	2	14	F	-.8311E9	.3E-7	.9E-7	2	.46E3	.60E1	[8]	110
100	PPR-P1-7	7	4	0	0	T	.6806E3	.9E-7	.4E-8	2	.31E1	.11E2	[1,18,59]	111
101	PPR-P1-8	7	6	0	14	F	.1810E4	.1E-10	.6E-6	3	.0	.85E2	[5,22]	112
102	PPR-P1-9	7	6	0	14	F	.9119E3	.3E-10	.1E-6	3	.10E3	.73E2	[5,22]	112
103	PPR-P1-10	7	6	0	14	F	.5637E3	.6E-11	.9E-7	4	.33E2	.52E1	[5,22]	112
104	PPR-P1-11	8	6	0	16	F	.3951E1	.6E-10	.3E-10	4	.73E1	.43E2	[22,53]	113
105	GLR-P1-2	8	1(1)	0	16	T	.1138E4	.0	.0	0	-	.92E6	[13]	114
106	LQR-P1-5	8	6(3)	0	16	F	.7049E4	.0	.2E-4	6	.61E6	.21E1	[2,22]	115
107	PGR-P1-4	9	0	6	8	F	.5055E4	.2E-9	.0	9	.0	-	[4]	116
108	QQR-P1-6	9	13	0	1	F	-.8660	.4E-9	.3E-11	9	.0	-	[29,49]	117
109	PGR-P1-5	9	4(2)	6	16	F	.5362E4	.4E-7	.0	9	.0	-	[9]	118
110	GBR-P1-1	10	0	0	20	T	-.4578E2	.0	.0	0	-	.11E1	[29,48]	119
111	GGR-P1-4	10	0	3	20	F	-.4776E2	.3E-9	.1E-3	3	.16E1	.16E3	[13,29,58]	120
112	GLR-P1-3	10	0	3(3)	10	F	-.4771E2	.2E-7	.4E-6	5	.57E5	.21E2	[13,29,58]	121
113	QQR-P1-7	10	8(3)	0	0	T	.2431E2	.1E-8	.5E-9	6	.84E2	.35E1	[1,18,59]	122
114	QGR-P1-6	10	8(4)	3(1)	20	F	-.1769E4	.0	.2E-5	9	.46E3	.10E1	[13]	123
116	LQR-P1-6	13	15(5)	0	26	F	.9759E2	.0	.0	14	.49E7	-	[21,22]	124
117	PQR-P1-1	15	5	0	15	T	.3235E2	.0	.4E-4	11	.25E3	.32E2	[20,29]	125
118	QLR-P1-2	15	29(29)	0	30	T	.6648E3	.0	.0	15	.61E2	-	[4]	126
119	PLR-P1-2	16	0	8(8)	32	F	.2449E3	.3E-9	.4E-8	13	.23E2	.16E1	[20,29]	127

Table 2: Condensed list of all test examples and some solution properties.

Name	No.	Page
Colville No.1 (Shell, Himmelblau No.10)	86	105
Colville No.2 (Shell Dual, Himmelblau No.18)	117	125
Colville No.3 (Proctor and Gamble, Himmelblau No.11)	83	102
Colville No.4 (Wood, Himmelblau No.8)	38	61
Colville No.6 (Himmelblau No.15)	87	106
Colville No.7 (Himmelblau No.19)	119	127
Colville No.8 (Himmelblau No.7)	67	89
Himmelblau No.1	14	37
Himmelblau No.3	59	81
Himmelblau No.4	112	121
Himmelblau No.4a	111	120
Himmelblau No.5	63	85
Himmelblau No.9	70	91
Himmelblau No.12	85	104
Himmelblau No.16	108	117
Himmelblau No.17	110	119
Himmelblau No.21	25	48
Himmelblau No.22	95-98	109
Himmelblau No.24	22	45
Beale	35	58
Rosen-Suzuki	43	66
Cattle Feed	73	94
Transformer Design	93	108

Table 3: List of some famous test problems.

OCD	T	P	No.
CQR	1		8
LQR	1	6	10,95,96,97,98,106,116
LPR	1	1	39,72
LGR	1	1	34,66
LGI		1	73
QBR	1		3
QLR	8	2	21,28,35,44,48,51,52,53,76,118
QQR	11	7	6,11,12,14,18,22,23,30,31,42,43, 61,63,65,83,84,108,113
QPR	2		13,32
QGR		6	88,89,90,91,92,114
SBR	1		25
SQR		2	57,70
PBR	5		1,2,4,38,45
PLR	6	2	24,36,37,41,49,50,86,119
PQR	8	1	15,16,17,19,20,27,29,33,117
PPR	3	11	26,40,47,60,64,71,78,79,93,100, 101,102,103,104
PGR	2	5	46,56,74,75,77,107,109
GBR	1	1	5,110
GLR	3	3	9,54,55,62,105,112
GQR		1	59
GPR	1	2	7,80,81
GGR		4	68,69,99,111
GGI		3	67,85,87

Table 4: Test problem classes.

THE TEST PROBLEMS

Using the documentation scheme as proposed in Section 4 of
Chapter I, we present a detailed description of 114 problems
for testing nonlinear programming algorithms. The corresponding
FORTRAN subroutines are available on request. Extensive lists
of constant data are shown in Appendix A.

Originally, a set of 126 test problems has been implemented.
But we could not solve 12 problems with the desired degree of
accuracy and check the optimality conditions at the computed
solution. In particular, we did not succeed in solving some big
problems with more than 20 variables. The underlying idea for
this collection of test problems is to present only those examples which could be implemented and solved successfully in the
sense that the Kuhn-Tucker and second order optimality conditions
are verified numerically.

In many test problems given in the literature, we find lower
bounds of the kind $x_i \geq 0$ together with a division by x_i in
one of the problem functions. In most of these cases, the zero
bounds are replaced by some small positive numbers without in-
fluencing the optimal solution. As a consequence, many irregular
problems are transformed into regular ones in the corresponding
subroutines.

For investigating the active sets $I(x*)$, the reader should pay
attention to the succession of the constraints which is defined in
the following form, cf. (2): Inequalities, lower bounds, upper
bounds, equalities. In case of several local optimal solutions $x*$,
the remaining data $f(x*)$, $r(x*)$, etc., are only presented for the
first one. If real numbers are given with one or two digits only,
it is assumed that this is the precise value, i.e. that all other
digits are zero. The optimal solutions are not always the same as
those found in the literature. We suppose that we got either another local solution or, more probably, that there are printing
errors in the source.

PROBLEM:	1

| CLASSIFICATION: | PBR-T1-1 |

| SOURCE: | Betts [8] |

| NUMBER OF VARIABLES: | $n = 2$ |

NUMBER OF CONSTRAINTS: $m_1 = 0$, $m-m_1 = 0$, $b = 1$

OBJECTIVE FUNCTION:

$$f(x) = 100(x_2 - x_1^2)^2 + (1 - x_1)^2$$

CONSTRAINTS:

$$-1.5 \le x_2$$

START: x_0 = $(-2 , 1)$ (feasible)

$f(x_0)$ = 909

SOLUTION: x^* = $(1 , 1)$

$f(x^*)$ = 0

$r(x^*)$ = 0

$e(x^*)$ = –

μ = 0

$I(x^*)$ = –

u_{max}^*/u_{min}^* = –

$\lambda_{max}^*/\lambda_{min}^*$ = .25E 4

| PROBLEM: | 2 |

| CLASSIFICATION: | PBR-T1-2 |

| SOURCE: | Betts [8] |

| NUMBER OF VARIABLES: | $n = 2$ |

NUMBER OF CONSTRAINTS: $m_1 = 0$, $m-m_1 = 0$, $b = 1$

OBJECTIVE FUNCTION:

$$f(x) = 100(x_2 - x_1^2)^2 + (1 - x_1)^2$$

CONSTRAINTS:

$$1.5 \leq x_2$$

START: $. x_o$ $= (-2 , 1)$ (not feasible)

          $f(x_o)$ $= 909$

SOLUTION: $x^* \quad = (2a \cos(\frac{1}{3} \arccos\frac{1}{b}) , 1.5)$

            $f(x^*) \quad = .05042\ 61879$

            $r(x^*) \quad = 0$ $a = (598/1200)^{1/2}$

            $e(x^*) \quad = .13E-7$ $b = 400\ a^3$

            $\mu \quad\quad = 1$

            $I(x^*) \quad = (1)$

            $u^*_{max}/u^*_{min} = .1833/.1833 = 1$

            $\lambda^*_{max}/\lambda^*_{min} = 200/200 = 1$

PROBLEM:	3
CLASSIFICATION:	QBR-T1-1
SOURCE:	Schuldt [56]
NUMBER OF VARIABLES:	$n = 2$
NUMBER OF CONSTRAINTS:	$m_1 = 0$, $m-m_1 = 0$, $b = 1$

OBJECTIVE FUNCTION:

$$f(x) = x_2 + 10^{-5}(x_2 - x_1)^2$$

CONSTRAINTS:

$$0 \leq x_2$$

START:

$x_0 = (10 , 1)$ (feasible)

$f(x_0) = 1.00081$

SOLUTION:

$x^* = (0 , 0)$

$f(x^*) = 0$

$r(x^*) = 0$

$e(x^*) = 0$

$\mu = 1$

$I(x^*) = (1)$

$u^*_{max}/u^*_{min} = 1.0000/1.0000 = 1$

$\lambda^*_{max}/\lambda^*_{min} = .20E-4/.20E-4 = 1$

PROBLEM:	4
CLASSIFICATION:	PBR-T1-3
SOURCE:	Asaadi [1]
NUMBER OF VARIABLES:	n = 2
NUMBER OF CONSTRAINTS:	$m_1 = 0$, $m-m_1 = 0$, b = 2

OBJECTIVE FUNCTION:

$$f(x) = \frac{1}{3} (x_1 + 1)^3 + x_2$$

CONSTRAINTS:

$$1 \leq x_1$$

$$0 \leq x_2$$

START:	x_0	=	(1.125 , .125)	(feasible)
	$f(x_0)$	=	3.323568	

SOLUTION:	x*	=	(1 , 0)
	f(x*)	=	8/3
	r(x*)	=	0
	e(x*)	=	0
	μ	=	2
	I(x*)	=	(1 , 2)
	u^*_{max}/u^*_{min}	=	4.0000/1.0000 = 4.00
	$\lambda^*_{max}/\lambda^*_{min}$	=	-

PROBLEM:	5
CLASSIFICATION:	GBR-T1-1
SOURCE:	McCormick [41]
NUMBER OF VARIABLES:	$n = 2$
NUMBER OF CONSTRAINTS:	$m_1 = 0$, $m-m_1 = 0$, $b = 4$

OBJECTIVE FUNCTION:

$$f(x) = \sin(x_1 + x_2) + (x_1 - x_2)^2 - 1.5x_1 + 2.5x_2 + 1$$

CONSTRAINTS:

$$-1.5 \leq x_1 \leq 4$$

$$-3 \leq x_2 \leq 3$$

START:	x_0	=	$(0 , 0)$	(feasible)
	$f(x_0)$	=	1	

SOLUTION:	x^*	=	$(-\frac{\pi}{3} + \frac{1}{2} , -\frac{\pi}{3} - \frac{1}{2})$
	$f(x^*)$	=	$-\frac{1}{2}\sqrt{3} - \frac{\pi}{3}$
	$r(x^*)$	=	0
	$e(x^*)$	=	$-$
	μ	=	0
	$I(x^*)$	=	$-$
	u^*_{max}/u^*_{min}	=	$-$
	$\lambda^*_{max}/\lambda^*_{min}$	=	$4.00/1.73 = 2.31$

PROBLEM:	6
CLASSIFICATION:	QQR-T1-1
SOURCE:	Betts [8]
NUMBER OF VARIABLES:	n = 2
NUMBER OF CONSTRAINTS:	$m_1 = 0$, $m-m_1 = 1$, $b = 0$

OBJECTIVE FUNCTION:

$$f(x) = (1 - x_1)^2$$

CONSTRAINTS:

$$10(x_2 - x_1^2) = 0$$

START:

x_0 = (-1.2 , 1)   (not feasible).

$f(x_0)$ = 4.84

SOLUTION:

$x*$ = (1 , 1)

$f(x*)$ = 0

$r(x*)$ = 0

$e(x*)$ = 0

μ = 0

$I(x*)$ = –

u^*_{max}/u^*_{min} = 0

$\lambda^*_{max}/\lambda^*_{min}$ = .40/.40 = 1

PROBLEM:	7

CLASSIFICATION:	GPR-T1-1

SOURCE:	Miele e.al. [44,45]

NUMBER OF VARIABLES:	$n = 2$

NUMBER OF CONSTRAINTS: $m_1 = 0$, $m-m_1 = 1$, $b = 0$

OBJECTIVE FUNCTION:

$$f(x) = \ln(1 + x_1^2) - x_2$$

CONSTRAINTS:

$$(1 + x_1^2)^2 + x_2^2 - 4 = 0$$

START: $x_0 = (2 , 2)$ (not feasible)

$f(x_0) = \ln 5 - 2$

SOLUTION: $x^* = (0 , \sqrt{3})$

$f(x^*) = -\sqrt{3}$

$r(x^*) = 0$

$e(x^*) = .21E-24$

$\mu = 0$

$I(x^*) = -$

$u^*_{max}/u^*_{min} = .2887/.2887 = 1$

$\lambda^*_{max}/\lambda^*_{min} = 3.15/3.15 = 1$

PROBLEM:	8
CLASSIFICATION:	CQR-T1-1
SOURCE:	Betts [8]
NUMBER OF VARIABLES:	$n = 2$
NUMBER OF CONSTRAINTS:	$m_1 = 0$, $m-m_1 = 2$, $b = 0$

OBJECTIVE FUNCTION:

$$f(x) = -1$$

CONSTRAINTS:

$$x_1^2 + x_2^2 - 25 = 0$$

$$x_1 x_2 - 9 = 0$$

START:

$x_0 = (2, 1)$ (not feasible)

$f(x_0) = -1$

SOLUTION:

$x^* = (a, \frac{9}{a}), (-a, -\frac{9}{a}), (b, \frac{9}{b}), (-b, -\frac{9}{b})$

$f(x^*) = -1$

$r(x^*) = 0$

$e(x^*) = 0$

$\mu = 0$

$I(x^*) = -$

$u^*_{max}/u^*_{min} = 0$

$\lambda^*_{max}/\lambda^*_{min} = -$

$$a = \sqrt{\frac{25 + \sqrt{301}}{2}}$$

$$b = \sqrt{\frac{25 - \sqrt{301}}{2}}$$

PROBLEM:	9
CLASSIFICATION:	GLR-T1-1
SOURCE:	Miele e.al. [44]
NUMBER OF VARIABLES:	$n = 2$
NUMBER OF CONSTRAINTS:	$m_1 = 0$, $m-m_1 = 1(1)$, $b = 0$

OBJECTIVE FUNCTION:

$$f(x) = \sin(\pi x_1/12) \cos(\pi x_2/16)$$

CONSTRAINTS:

$$4x_1 - 3x_2 = 0$$

START:

$x_0 \quad = (0 , 0)$ (feasible)

$f(x_0) \quad = 0$

SOLUTION:

$x^* \quad = (12k - 3 , 16k - 4)$, $k=0, \pm 1, \pm 2, \ldots$

$f(x^*) \quad = - .5$

$r(x^*) \quad = 0$

$e(x^*) \quad = .73E-12$

$\mu \quad = 0$

$I(x^*) \quad = -$

$u^*_{max}/u^*_{min} = .03272/.03272 = 1$

$\lambda^*_{max}/\lambda^*_{min} = .049/.049 = 1$

PROBLEM:	10
CLASSIFICATION:	LQR-T1-1
SOURCE:	Biggs [10]
NUMBER OF VARIABLES:	$n = 2$
NUMBER OF CONSTRAINTS:	$m_1 = 1$, $m-m_1 = 0$, $b = 0$

OBJECTIVE FUNCTION:

$$f(x) = x_1 - x_2$$

CONSTRAINTS:

$$-3x_1^2 + 2x_1x_2 - x_2^2 + 1 \geq 0$$

START:	x_0	$= (-10 , 10)$	(not feasible)
	$f(x_0)$	$= -20$	

SOLUTION:	$x*$	$= (0 , 1)$
	$f(x*)$	$= -1$
	$r(x*)$	$= 0$
	$e(x*)$	$= .92E-11$
	μ	$= 1$
	$I(x*)$	$= (1)$
	u_{max}^*/u_{min}^*	$= .5000/.5000 = 1$
	$\lambda_{max}^*/\lambda_{min}^*$	$= 1.00/1.00 = 1$

PROBLEM:	11

CLASSIFICATION:	QQR-T1-2

SOURCE:	Biggs [10]

NUMBER OF VARIABLES:	$n = 2$

NUMBER OF CONSTRAINTS: $m_1 = 1$, $m-m_1 = 0$, $b = 0$

OBJECTIVE FUNCTION:

$$f(x) = (x_1 - 5)^2 + x_2^2 - 25$$

CONSTRAINTS:

$$-x_1^2 + x_2 \geq 0$$

START: x_o $= (4.9 , .1)$. (not feasible)

$f(x_o)$ $= -24.98$

SOLUTION: x^* $= ((a - \frac{1}{a})/\sqrt{6} , (a^2 - 2 + a^{-2})/6)$

$f(x^*)$ $= -8.49846\ 4223$

$r(x^*)$ $= 0$

$\qquad a = 7.5\sqrt{6} + \sqrt{338.5}$

$e(x^*)$ $= .17E-9$

μ $= 1$

$I(x^*)$ $= (1)$

$u^*_{max}/u^*_{min} = 3.0493/3.0493 = 1$

$\lambda^*_{max}/\lambda^*_{min} = 2.86/2.86 = 1$

PROBLEM:	12
CLASSIFICATION:	QQR-T1-3
SOURCE:	Mine e.al. [46]
NUMBER OF VARIABLES:	n = 2
NUMBER OF CONSTRAINTS:	$m_1 = 1$, $m-m_1 = 0$, $b = 0$

OBJECTIVE FUNCTION:

$$f(x) = .5x_1^2 + x_2^2 - x_1 x_2 - 7x_1 - 7x_2$$

CONSTRAINTS:

$$25 - 4x_1^2 - x_2^2 \geq 0$$

START: x_0 = (0 , 0)   (feasible)

$f(x_0)$ = 0

SOLUTION: x^* = (2 , 3)

$f(x^*)$ = -30

$r(x^*)$ = 0

$e(x^*)$ = .81E-10

μ = 1

$I(x^*)$ = (1)

u_{max}^*/u_{min}^* = .5000/.5000 = 1

$\lambda_{max}^*/\lambda_{min}^*$ = 3.90/3.90 = 1

PROBLEM:	13
CLASSIFICATION:	QPR-T1-1
SOURCE:	Betts [8], Kuhn, Tucker [38]
NUMBER OF VARIABLES:	$n = 2$
NUMBER OF CONSTRAINTS:	$m_1 = 1$, $m - m_1 = 0$, $b = 2$

OBJECTIVE FUNCTION:

$$f(x) = (x_1 - 2)^2 + x_2^2$$

CONSTRAINTS:

$$(1 - x_1)^3 - x_2 \geq 0$$

$$0 \leq x_1$$

$$0 \leq x_2$$

START:	x_0	$= (-2 , -2)$	(not feasible)
	$f(x_0)$	$= 20$	

SOLUTION:	x^*	$= (1 , 0)$	
	$f(x^*)$	$= 1$	
	$r(x^*)$	$= 0$	
	$e(x^*)$	$= 2$	(constraint qualification
	μ	$= 2$	not satisfied)
	$I(x^*)$	$= (1,3)$	
	u^*_{max}/u^*_{min}	$= 0/0$	
	$\lambda^*_{max}/\lambda^*_{min}$	$= -$	

PROBLEM:	14

CLASSIFICATION:	QQR-T1-4

SOURCE:	Bracken, McCormick [13], Himmelblau [29]

NUMBER OF VARIABLES:	$n = 2$

NUMBER OF CONSTRAINTS: $m_1 = 1$, $m - m_1 = 1(1)$, $b = 0$

OBJECTIVE FUNCTION:

$$f(x) = (x_1 - 2)^2 + (x_2 - 1)^2$$

CONSTRAINTS:

$$-.25x_1^2 - x_2^2 + 1 \geq 0$$

$$x_1 - 2x_2 + 1 = 0$$

START: x_0 $= (2 , 2)$ (not feasible)

$f(x_0)$ $= 1$

SOLUTION: x^* $= (.5(\sqrt{7} - 1) , .25(\sqrt{7} + 1))$

$f(x^*)$ $= 9 - 2.875\sqrt{7}$

$r(x^*)$ $= 0$

$e(x^*)$ $= 0$

μ $= 1$

$I(x^*)$ $= (1)$

$u_{max}^*/u_{min}^* = 1.8466/1.5945 = 1.15$

$\lambda_{max}^*/\lambda_{min}^* = -$

PROBLEM:	15
CLASSIFICATION:	PQR-T1-1
SOURCE:	Betts [8]
NUMBER OF VARIABLES:	$n = 2$

NUMBER OF CONSTRAINTS:	$m_1 = 2$	, $m-m_1 = 0$	, $b = 1$

OBJECTIVE FUNCTION:

$$f(x) = 100(x_2 - x_1^2)^2 + (1 - x_1)^2$$

CONSTRAINTS:

$$x_1 x_2 - 1 \geq 0$$

$$x_1 + x_2^2 \geq 0$$

$$x_1 \leq .5$$

START: . x_0 = (-2 , 1)   (not feasible)

$f(x_0)$ = 909

SOLUTION: x^* = (.5 , 2)

$f(x^*)$ = 306.5

$r(x^*)$ = 0

$e(x^*)$ = 0

μ = 2

$I(x^*)$ = (1 , 3)

u^*_{max}/u^*_{min} = 1751/700 = 2.50

$\lambda^*_{max}/\lambda^*_{min}$ = -

PROBLEM:	16
CLASSIFICATION:	PQR-T1-2
SOURCE:	Betts [8]
NUMBER OF VARIABLES:	$n = 2$
NUMBER OF CONSTRAINTS:	$m_1 = 2$, $m-m_1 = 0$, $b = 3$

OBJECTIVE FUNCTION:

$$f(x) = 100(x_2 - x_1^2)^2 + (1 - x_1)^2$$

CONSTRAINTS:

$$x_1 + x_2^2 \geq 0$$

$$x_1^2 + x_2 \geq 0$$

$$-.5 \leq x_1 \leq .5$$

$$x_2 \leq 1$$

START:	x_0	$= (-2 , 1)$	(not feasible)
	$f(x_0)$	$= 909$	

SOLUTION:	x^*	$= (.5 , .25)$
	$f(x^*)$	$= .25$
	$r(x^*)$	$= 0$
	$e(x^*)$	$= 0$
	μ	$= 1$
	$I(x^*)$	$= (4)$
	u^*_{max}/u^*_{min}	$= 1.0000/1.0000 = 1$
	$\lambda^*_{max}/\lambda^*_{min}$	$= 200/200 = 1$

PROBLEM:	17
CLASSIFICATION:	PQR-T1-3
SOURCE:	Betts [8]
NUMBER OF VARIABLES:	$n = 2$
NUMBER OF CONSTRAINTS:	$m_1 = 2$, $m-m_1 = 0$, $b = 3$

OBJECTIVE FUNCTION:

$$f(x) = 100(x_2 - x_1^2)^2 + (1 - x_1)^2$$

CONSTRAINTS:

$$x_2^2 - x_1 \geq 0$$

$$x_1^2 - x_2 \geq 0$$

$$-.5 \leq x_1 \leq .5$$

$$x_2 \leq 1$$

START:
$x_0 = (-2 , 1)$ (not feasible)
$f(x_0) = 909$

SOLUTION:
$x^* = (0 , 0)$
$f(x^*) = 1$
$r(x^*) = 0$
$e(x^*) = 0$
$\mu = 2$
$I(x^*) = (1 , 2)$
$u^*_{max}/u^*_{min} = 2.0000/0$
$\lambda^*_{max}/\lambda^*_{min} = -$

PROBLEM:	18
CLASSIFICATION:	QQR-T1-5
SOURCE:	Betts [8]
NUMBER OF VARIABLES:	$n = 2$

NUMBER OF CONSTRAINTS: $m_1 = 2$, $m-m_1 = 0$, $b = 4$

OBJECTIVE FUNCTION:

$$f(x) = .01x_1^2 + x_2^2$$

CONSTRAINTS:

$$x_1 x_2 - 25 \geq 0$$

$$x_1^2 + x_2^2 - 25 \geq 0$$

$$2 \leq x_1 \leq 50$$

$$0 \leq x_2 \leq 50$$

START: x_o = (2 , 2) (not feasible)

$f(x_o)$ = 4.04

SOLUTION: x^* = $(\sqrt{250} , \sqrt{2.5})$

$f(x^*)$ = 5

$r(x^*)$ = 0

$e(x^*)$ = .24E-9

μ = 1

$I(x^*)$ = (1)

u^*_{max}/u^*_{min} = .2000/.2000 = 1

$\lambda^*_{max}/\lambda^*_{min}$ = .079/.079 = 1

PROBLEM:	19
CLASSIFICATION:	PQR-T1-4
SOURCE:	Betts [8], Gould [27]
NUMBER OF VARIABLES:	$n = 2$

NUMBER OF CONSTRAINTS: $m_1 = 2$, $m-m_1 = 0$, $b = 4$

OBJECTIVE FUNCTION:

$$f(x) = (x_1 - 10)^3 + (x_2 - 20)^3$$

CONSTRAINTS:

$$(x_1 - 5)^2 + (x_2 - 5)^2 - 100 \geq 0$$

$$-(x_2 - 5)^2 - (x_1 - 6)^2 + 82.81 \geq 0$$

$$13 \leq x_1 \leq 100$$

$$0 \leq x_2 \leq 100$$

START:

x_0 = (20.1 , 5.84)   (not feasible)

$f(x_0)$ = -1808.858296

SOLUTION:

x^* = (14.095 , .84296079)

$f(x^*)$ = -6961.81381

$r(x^*)$ = 0

$e(x^*)$ = 0

μ = 2

$I(x^*)$ = (1 , 2)

u^*_{max}/u^*_{min} = 1229.5/1097.1 = 1.12

$\lambda^*_{max}/\lambda^*_{min}$ = −

PROBLEM:	20
CLASSIFICATION:	PQR-T1-5
SOURCE:	Betts [8]
NUMBER OF VARIABLES:	$n = 2$

NUMBER OF CONSTRAINTS:	$m_1 = 3$	, $m-m_1 = 0$	, $b = 2$

OBJECTIVE FUNCTION:

$$f(x) = 100(x_2 - x_1^2)^2 + (1 - x_1)^2$$

CONSTRAINTS:

$$x_1 + x_2^2 \geq 0$$

$$x_1^2 + x_2 \geq 0$$

$$x_1^2 + x_2^2 - 1 \geq 0$$

$$-.5 \leq x_1 \leq .5$$

START:	x_0	$= (-2 , 1)$	(not feasible)
	$f(x_0)$	$= 909$	

SOLUTION:	x^*	$= (.5 , .5\sqrt{3})$
	$f(x^*)$	$= 81.5 - 25\sqrt{3}$
	$r(x^*)$	$= 0$
	$e(x^*)$	$= 0$
	μ	$= 2$
	$I(x^*)$	$= (3 , 5)$
	u^*_{max}/u^*_{min}	$= 195.34/71.132 = 2.75$
	$\lambda^*_{max}/\lambda^*_{min}$	$= -$

PROBLEM:	21
CLASSIFICATION:	QLR-T1-1
SOURCE:	Betts [8]
NUMBER OF VARIABLES:	$n = 2$
NUMBER OF CONSTRAINTS:	$m_1 = 1(1)$, $m-m_1 = 0$, $b = 4$

OBJECTIVE FUNCTION:

$$f(x) = .01x_1^2 + x_2^2 - 100$$

CONSTRAINTS:

$$10x_1 - x_2 - 10 \geq 0$$

$$2 \leq x_1 \leq 50$$

$$-50 \leq x_2 \leq 50$$

START: x_o = $(-1 , -1)$ (not feasible)

$f(x_o)$ = -98.99

SOLUTION: x^* = $(2 , 0)$

$f(x^*)$ = -99.96

$r(x^*)$ = 0

$e(x^*)$ = 0

μ = 1

$I(x^*)$ = (2)

u_{max}^*/u_{min}^* = $.04/.04 = 1$

$\lambda_{max}^*/\lambda_{min}^*$ = $-$

PROBLEM:	22

CLASSIFICATION: QQR-T1-6

SOURCE: Bracken, McCormick [13], Himmelblau [29], Sheela [57]

NUMBER OF VARIABLES: $n = 2$

NUMBER OF CONSTRAINTS: $m_1 = 2(1)$, $m-m_1 = 0$, $b = 0$

OBJECTIVE FUNCTION:

$$f(x) = (x_1 - 2)^2 + (x_2 - 1)^2$$

CONSTRAINTS:

$$-x_1 - x_2 + 2 \geq 0$$

$$-x_1^2 + x_2 \geq 0$$

START: $x_0 = (2 , 2)$ (not feasible)

$f(x_0) = 1$

SOLUTION: $x^* = (1 , 1)$

$f(x^*) = 1$

$r(x^*) = 0$

$e(x^*) = 0$

$\mu = 2$

$I(x^*) = (1 , 2)$

$u^*_{max}/u^*_{min} = .6666/.6666 = 1$

$\lambda^*_{max}/\lambda^*_{min} = -$

PROBLEM:	23
CLASSIFICATION:	QQR-T1-7
SOURCE:	Betts [8]
NUMBER OF VARIABLES:	$n = 2$

NUMBER OF CONSTRAINTS: $m_1 = 5(1)$, $m-m_1 = 0$, $b = 4$

OBJECTIVE FUNCTION:

$$f(x) = x_1^2 + x_2^2$$

CONSTRAINTS:

$$x_1 + x_2 - 1 \geq 0$$

$$x_1^2 + x_2^2 - 1 \geq 0$$

$$9x_1^2 + x_2^2 - 9 \geq 0$$

$$x_1^2 - x_2 \geq 0$$

$$x_2^2 - x_1 \geq 0$$

$$-50 \leq x_i \leq 50 \quad , \quad i=1,2$$

START:

x_o	=	$(3 , 1)$	(not feasible)
$f(x_o)$	=	10	

SOLUTION:

x^*	=	$(1 , 1)$
$f(x^*)$	=	2
$r(x^*)$	=	0
$e(x^*)$	=	0
μ	=	2
$I(x^*)$	=	$(4 , 5)$
u_{max}^*/u_{min}^*	=	$2/2 = 1$
$\lambda_{max}^*/\lambda_{min}^*$	=	$-$

PROBLEM:	24
CLASSIFICATION:	PLR-T1-1
SOURCE:	Betts [8], Box [12]
NUMBER OF VARIABLES:	n = 2
NUMBER OF CONSTRAINTS:	$m_1 = 3(3)$, $m-m_1 = 0$, $b = 2$

OBJECTIVE FUNCTION:

$$f(x) = \frac{1}{27\sqrt{3}} ((x_1 - 3)^2 - 9) x_2^3$$

CONSTRAINTS:

$$x_1/\sqrt{3} - x_2 \geq 0$$

$$x_1 + \sqrt{3}x_2 \geq 0$$

$$-x_1 - \sqrt{3}x_2 + 6 \geq 0$$

$$0 \leq x_1$$

$$0 \leq x_2$$

START: x_0 = (1 , .5) (feasible).

  $f(x_0)$ = -.01336459

SOLUTION: x^* = $(3 , \sqrt{3})$

  $f(x^*)$ = -1

  $r(x^*)$ = 0

  $e(x^*)$ = 0

  μ = 2

  $I(x^*)$ = (1 , 3)

  u^*_{max}/u^*_{min} = .86603/.5 = 1.73

  $\lambda^*_{max}/\lambda^*_{min}$ = -

PROBLEM:	25

CLASSIFICATION:	SBR-T1-1

SOURCE:	Holzmann [32], Himmelblau [29]

NUMBER OF VARIABLES:	$n = 3$

NUMBER OF CONSTRAINTS:	$m_1 = 0$	, $m-m_1 = 0$	, $b = 6$

OBJECTIVE FUNCTION:

$$f(x) = \sum_{i=1}^{99} (f_i(x))^2$$

$$f_i(x) = -.01i + \exp(-\frac{1}{x_1}(u_i - x_2)^{x_3})$$

$$u_i = 25 + (-50 \ln(.01i))^{2/3}$$

$$i = 1,\ldots,99$$

CONSTRAINTS:

$$.1 \leq x_1 \leq 100$$

$$0 \leq x_2 \leq 25.6$$

$$0 \leq x_3 \leq 5$$

START: $x_0 = (100 , 12.5 , 3)$	$f(x_0) = 32.835$ (feasible)

SOLUTION: $\quad\quad\quad\quad\quad\quad\quad\quad f(x^*) = 0$

$x^* = (50 , 25 , 1.5)$

$r(x^*) = 0 \quad\quad\quad\quad\quad\quad e(x^*) = -$

$\mu = 0 \quad\quad\quad\quad\quad\quad\quad I(x^*) = -$

$u^*_{max}/u^*_{min} = -$

$\lambda^*_{max}/\lambda^*_{min} = 94.7/.14E-4 = .70E7$

PROBLEM:	26
CLASSIFICATION:	PPR-T1-1
SOURCE:	Huang, Aggerwal [34], Miele e.al. [43]
NUMBER OF VARIABLES:	$n = 3$
NUMBER OF CONSTRAINTS:	$m_1 = 0$, $m-m_1 = 1$, $b = 0$

OBJECTIVE FUNCTION:

$$f(x) = (x_1 - x_2)^2 + (x_2 - x_3)^4$$

CONSTRAINTS:

$$(1 + x_2^2)x_1 + x_3^4 - 3 = 0$$

START: x_0 = $(-2.6 , 2 , 2)$ (feasible)

$f(x_0)$ = 21.16

SOLUTION: x^* = $(1 , 1 , 1)$, (a , a , a)

$f(x^*)$ = 0

$r(x^*)$ = 0 $\qquad a = \sqrt[3]{\alpha-\beta} - \sqrt[3]{\alpha+\beta} - 2/3$

$e(x^*)$ = 0 $\qquad \alpha = \sqrt{139/108}$

μ = 0 $\qquad \beta = 61/54$

$I(x^*)$ = $-$

u^*_{max}/u^*_{min} = 0

$\lambda^*_{max}/\lambda^*_{min}$ = $4/0$

PROBLEM:	27
CLASSIFICATION:	PQR-T1-6
SOURCE:	Miele e.al. [44,45]
NUMBER OF VARIABLES:	$n = 3$
NUMBER OF CONSTRAINTS:	$m_1 = 0$, $m-m_1 = 1$, $b = 0$

OBJECTIVE FUNCTION:

$$f(x) = .01(x_1 - 1)^2 + (x_2 - x_1^2)^2$$

CONSTRAINTS:

$$x_1 + x_3^2 + 1 = 0$$

START:	x_0	= $(2 , 2 , 2)$	(not feasible)
	$f(x_0)$	= 4.01	

SOLUTION:	x^*	= $(-1 , 1 , 0)$
	$f(x^*)$	= .04
	$r(x^*)$	= 0
	$e(x^*)$	= 0
	μ	= 0
	$I(x^*)$	= -
	u^*_{max}/u^*_{min}	= .04/.04 = 1
	$\lambda^*_{max}/\lambda^*_{min}$	= 2/.08 = 25

PROBLEM:	28
CLASSIFICATION:	QLR-T1-2
SOURCE:	Huang, Aggerwal [34]
NUMBER OF VARIABLES:	$n = 3$
NUMBER OF CONSTRAINTS:	$m_1 = 0$, $m-m_1 = 1(1)$, $b = 0$

OBJECTIVE FUNCTION:

$$f(x) = (x_1 + x_2)^2 + (x_2 + x_3)^2$$

CONSTRAINTS:

$$x_1 + 2x_2 + 3x_3 - 1 = 0$$

START:

$x_o = (-4, 1, 1)$ (feasible)

$f(x_o) = 13$

SOLUTION:

$x^* = (.5, -.5, .5)$

$f(x^*) = 0$

$r(x^*) = 0$

$e(x^*) = 0$

$\mu = 0$

$I(x^*) = -$

$u^*_{max}/u^*_{min} = 0$

$\lambda^*_{max}/\lambda^*_{min} = 2.72/.42 = 6.45$

PROBLEM:	29
CLASSIFICATION:	PQR-T1-7
SOURCE:	Biggs [10]
NUMBER OF VARIABLES:	n = 3
NUMBER OF CONSTRAINTS:	$m_1 = 1$, $m-m_1 = 0$, $b = 0$

OBJECTIVE FUNCTION:

$$f(x) = - x_1 x_2 x_3$$

CONSTRAINTS:

$$-x_1^2 - 2x_2^2 - 4x_3^2 + 48 \geq 0$$

START:

x_0 = (1 , 1 , 1)   (feasible)

$f(x_0)$ = -1

SOLUTION:

x^* = (a,b,c) , (a,-b,-c) , (-a,b,-c) ,

$f(x^*)$ = $-16\sqrt{2}$ (-a,-b,c)

$r(x^*)$ = 0   a = 4

$e(x^*)$ = .19E-9   b = $2\sqrt{2}$

μ = 1   c = 2

$I(x^*)$ = (1)

u^*_{max}/u^*_{min} = .7071/.7071 = 1

$\lambda^*_{max}/\lambda^*_{min}$ = 7.79/3.52 = 2.22

PROBLEM:	30
CLASSIFICATION:	QQR-T1-8
SOURCE:	Betts [8]
NUMBER OF VARIABLES:	$n = 3$
NUMBER OF CONSTRAINTS:	$m_1 = 1$, $m-m_1 = 0$, $b = 6$

OBJECTIVE FUNCTION:

$$f(x) = x_1^2 + x_2^2 + x_3^2$$

CONSTRAINTS:

$$x_1^2 + x_2^2 - 1 \geq 0$$

$$1 \leq x_1 \leq 10$$

$$-10 \leq x_2 \leq 10$$

$$-10 \leq x_3 \leq 10$$

START:	x_0	$= (1 , 1 , 1)$	(feasible)
	$f(x_0)$	$= 3$	

SOLUTION:	x^*	$= (1 , 0 , 0)$
	$f(x^*)$	$= 1$
	$r(x^*)$	$= 0$
	$e(x^*)$	$= 0$
	μ	$= 2$
	$I(x^*)$	$= (1 , 2)$
	u^*_{max}/u^*_{min}	$= 1/0$
	$\lambda^*_{max}/\lambda^*_{min}$	$= 2/2 = 1$

PROBLEM:	31
CLASSIFICATION:	QQR-T1-9
SOURCE:	Betts [8]
NUMBER OF VARIABLES:	$n = 3$

NUMBER OF CONSTRAINTS: $m_1 = 1$, $m-m_1 = 0$, $b = 6$

OBJECTIVE FUNCTION:

$$f(x) = 9x_1^2 + x_2^2 + 9x_3^2$$

CONSTRAINTS:

$$x_1 x_2 - 1 \geq 0$$

$$-10 \leq x_1 \leq 10$$

$$1 \leq x_2 \leq 10$$

$$-10 \leq x_3 \leq 1$$

START:

x_o $= (1 , 1 , 1)$ (feasible)

$f(x_o)$ $= 19$

SOLUTION:

$x*$ $= (1/\sqrt{3} , \sqrt{3} , 0)$

$f(x*)$ $= 6$

$r(x*)$ $= 0$

$e(x*)$ $= .57E-10$

μ $= 1$

$I(x*)$ $= (1)$

$u_{max}^*/u_{min}^* = 6/6 = 1$

$\lambda_{max}^*/\lambda_{min}^* = 18/7.2 = 2.5$

PROBLEM:	32
CLASSIFICATION:	QPR-T1-2
SOURCE:	Evtushenko [25]
NUMBER OF VARIABLES:	n = 3
NUMBER OF CONSTRAINTS:	$m_1 = 1$, $m-m_1 = 1(1)$, b = 3

OBJECTIVE FUNCTION:

$$f(x) = (x_1 + 3x_2 + x_3)^2 + 4(x_1 - x_2)^2$$

CONSTRAINTS:

$$6x_2 + 4x_3 - x_1^3 - 3 \geq 0$$

$$1 - x_1 - x_2 - x_3 = 0$$

$$0 \leq x_i , \quad i = 1,2,3$$

START: x_0 = (.1 , .7 , .2)   (feasible)

$f(x_0)$ = 7.2

SOLUTION: x^* = (0 , 0 , 1)

$f(x^*)$ = 1

$r(x^*)$ = 0

$e(x^*)$ = 0

μ = 2

$I(x^*)$ = (2 , 3)

u^*_{max}/u^*_{min} = 4/0

$\lambda^*_{max}/\lambda^*_{min}$ = -

PROBLEM:	33
CLASSIFICATION:	PQR-T1-8
SOURCE:	Beltrami [6], Hartmann [28]
NUMBER OF VARIABLES:	n = 3

NUMBER OF CONSTRAINTS: $m_1 = 2$, $m-m_1 = 0$, b = 4

OBJECTIVE FUNCTION:

$$f(x) = (x_1 - 1)(x_1 - 2)(x_1 - 3) + x_3$$

CONSTRAINTS:

$$x_3^2 - x_2^2 - x_1^2 \geq 0$$

$$x_1^2 + x_2^2 + x_3^2 - 4 \geq 0$$

$$0 \leq x_1$$

$$0 \leq x_2$$

$$0 \leq x_3 \leq 5$$

START:

$$x_0 = (0, 0, 3) \qquad \text{(feasible)}$$
$$f(x_0) = -3$$

SOLUTION:

$$x^* = (0, \sqrt{2}, \sqrt{2})$$
$$f(x^*) = \sqrt{2} - 6$$
$$r(x^*) = 0$$
$$e(x^*) = 0$$
$$\mu = 3$$
$$I(x^*) = (1, 2, 3)$$
$$u^*_{max}/u^*_{min} = 11/.17678 = 62.23$$
$$\lambda^*_{max}/\lambda^*_{min} = -$$

PROBLEM:	34
CLASSIFICATION:	LGR-T1-1
SOURCE:	Eckhardt [24]
NUMBER OF VARIABLES:	$n = 3$

NUMBER OF CONSTRAINTS: $m_1 = 2$, $m-m_1 = 0$, $b = 6$

OBJECTIVE FUNCTION:

$$f(x) = -x_1$$

CONSTRAINTS:

$$x_2 - \exp(x_1) \geq 0$$

$$x_3 - \exp(x_2) \geq 0$$

$$0 \leq x_1 \leq 100$$

$$0 \leq x_2 \leq 100$$

$$0 \leq x_3 \leq 10$$

START: x_0 $= (0 , 1.05 , 2.9)$ (feasible)

   $f(x_0)$ $= 0$

SOLUTION: x^* $= (\ln(\ln 10) , \ln 10 , 10)$

   $f(x^*)$ $= -\ln(\ln 10)$

   $r(x^*)$ $= 0$

   $e(x^*)$ $= 0$

   μ $= 3$

   $I(x^*)$ $= (1 , 2 , 8)$

   u^*_{max}/u^*_{min} $= .4343/.04343 = 10$

   $\lambda^*_{max}/\lambda^*_{min}$ $= -$

PROBLEM:	35 (Beale's problem)

CLASSIFICATION: QLR-T1-3

SOURCE: Asaadi [1], Charalambous [18], Dimitru [23], Sheela [57]

NUMBER OF VARIABLES: $n = 3$

NUMBER OF CONSTRAINTS: $m_1 = 1(1)$, $m-m_1 = 0$, $b = 3$

OBJECTIVE FUNCTION:

$$f(x) = 9 - 8x_1 - 6x_2 - 4x_3 + 2x_1^2 + 2x_2^2 + x_3^2$$
$$+ 2x_1x_2 + 2x_1x_3$$

CONSTRAINTS:

$$3 - x_1 - x_2 - 2x_3 \geq 0$$

$$0 \leq x_i \quad , \quad i=1,2,3$$

START: x_o = (.5 , .5 , .5) (feasible)

$f(x_o)$ = 2.25

SOLUTION: x^* = (4/3 , 7/9 , 4/9)

$f(x^*)$ = 1/9

$r(x^*)$ = 0

$e(x^*)$ = .49E-10

μ = 1

$I(x^*)$ = (1)

u^*_{max}/u^*_{min} = .2222/.2222 = 1

$\lambda^*_{max}/\lambda^*_{min}$ = 3.72/1.61 = 2.31

PROBLEM:	36
CLASSIFICATION:	PLR-T1-2
SOURCE:	Biggs [10]
NUMBER OF VARIABLES:	$n = 3$

NUMBER OF CONSTRAINTS: $m_1 = 1(1)$, $m-m_1 = 0$, $b = 6$

OBJECTIVE FUNCTION:

$$f(x) = - x_1 x_2 x_3$$

CONSTRAINTS:

$$72 - x_1 - 2x_2 - 2x_3 \geq 0$$

$$0 \leq x_1 \leq 20$$

$$0 \leq x_2 \leq 11$$

$$0 \leq x_3 \leq 42$$

START: x_0 = (10 , 10 , 10)   (feasible)

$f(x_0)$ = -1000

SOLUTION: x^* = (20 , 11 , 15)

$f(x^*)$ = -3300

$r(x^*)$ = 0

$e(x^*)$ = 0

μ = 3

$I(x^*)$ = (1 , 5 , 6)

u^*_{max}/u^*_{min} = 110/55 = 2

$\lambda^*_{max}/\lambda^*_{min}$ = -

PROBLEM:	37

CLASSIFICATION:	PLR-T1-3

SOURCE:	Betts [8], Box [12]

NUMBER OF VARIABLES:	$n = 3$

NUMBER OF CONSTRAINTS: $m_1 = 2(2)$, $m-m_1 = 0$, $b = 6$

OBJECTIVE FUNCTION:

$$f(x) = -x_1 x_2 x_3$$

CONSTRAINTS:

$$72 - x_1 - 2x_2 - 2x_3 \geq 0$$

$$x_1 + 2x_2 + 2x_3 \geq 0$$

$$0 \leq x_i \leq 42 \quad , \quad i=1,2,3$$

START: x_0 = (10 , 10 , 10)   (feasible)

$f(x_0)$ = -1000

SOLUTION: x^* = (24 , 12 , 12)

$f(x^*)$ = -3456

$r(x^*)$ = 0

$e(x^*)$ = 0

μ = 1

$I(x^*)$ = (1)

u^*_{max}/u^*_{min} = 144/144 = 1

$\lambda^*_{max}/\lambda^*_{min}$ = 24/8 = 3

PROBLEM:	38 (Colville No.4)
CLASSIFICATION:	PBR-T1-4
SOURCE:	Colville [20], Himmelblau [29]
NUMBER OF VARIABLES:	$n = 4$
NUMBER OF CONSTRAINTS:	$m_1 = 0$, $m-m_1 = 0$, $b = 8$

OBJECTIVE FUNCTION:

$$f(x) = 100(x_2 - x_1^2)^2 + (1 - x_1)^2 + 90(x_4 - x_3^2)^2 + (1-x_3)^2$$
$$+ 10.1((x_2 - 1)^2 + (x_4 - 1)^2) + 19.8(x_2 - 1)(x_4 - 1)$$

CONSTRAINTS:

$$-10 \leq x_i \leq 10 , \quad i=1,\ldots,4$$

START:

$x_0 = (-3 , -1 , -3 , -1)$ (feasible)

$f(x_0) = 19192$

SOLUTION:

$x^* = (1 , 1 , 1 , 1)$

$f(x^*) = 0$

$r(x^*) = 0$

$e(x^*) = -$

$\mu = 0$

$I(x^*) = -$

$u^*_{max}/u^*_{min} = -$

$\lambda^*_{max}/\lambda^*_{min} = .10E4/.72 = .14E4$

PROBLEM:	39
CLASSIFICATION:	LPR-T1-1
SOURCE:	Miele e.al. [44,45]
NUMBER OF VARIABLES:	n = 4

NUMBER OF CONSTRAINTS:	$m_1 = 0$	, $m-m_1 = 2$	, $b = 0$

OBJECTIVE FUNCTION:

$$f(x) = -x_1$$

CONSTRAINTS:

$$x_2 - x_1^3 - x_3^2 = 0$$

$$x_1^2 - x_2 - x_4^2 = 0$$

START:

$$x_o = (2, 2, 2, 2) \quad \text{(not feasible)}$$

$$f(x_o) = -2$$

SOLUTION:

$$x^* = (1, 1, 0, 0)$$

$$f(x^*) = -1$$

$$r(x^*) = 0$$

$$e(x^*) = 0$$

$$\mu = 0$$

$$I(x^*) = -$$

$$u^*_{max}/u^*_{min} = 1/1 = 1$$

$$\lambda^*_{max}/\lambda^*_{min} = 2/2 = 1$$

PROBLEM:	40
CLASSIFICATION:	PPR-T1-2
SOURCE:	Beltrami [6], Indusi [35]
NUMBER OF VARIABLES:	$n = 4$
NUMBER OF CONSTRAINTS:	$m_1 = 0$, $m-m_1 = 3$, $b = 0$

OBJECTIVE FUNCTION:

$$f(x) = - x_1 x_2 x_3 x_4$$

CONSTRAINTS:

$$x_1^3 + x_2^2 - 1 = 0$$

$$x_1^2 x_4 - x_3 = 0$$

$$x_4^2 - x_2 = 0$$

START: $\quad x_0 \quad = (.8 , .8 , .8 , .8) \quad$ (not feasible)

$f(x_0) \quad = -.4096$

SOLUTION: $\quad x^* \quad = (2^a , 2^{2b} , (-1)^1 2^c , (-1)^1 2^b)$

$f(x^*)$	$= -.25$	$i=1,2$
$r(x^*)$	$= 0$	$a = -1/3$
$e(x^*)$	$= .80E-11$	$b = -1/4$
μ	$= 0$	$c = -11/12$
$I(x^*)$	$= -$	
u^*_{max}/u^*_{min}	$= .5/.3536 = 1.41$	
$\lambda^*_{max}/\lambda^*_{min}$	$= 1.74/1.74 = 1$	

PROBLEM:	41
CLASSIFICATION:	PLR-T1-4
SOURCE:	Betts [8], Miele e.al. [42]
NUMBER OF VARIABLES:	$n = 4$
NUMBER OF CONSTRAINTS:	$m_1 = 0$, $m-m_1 = 1(1)$, $b = 8$

OBJECTIVE FUNCTION:

$$f(x) = 2 - x_1 x_2 x_3$$

CONSTRAINTS:

$$x_1 + 2x_2 + 2x_3 - x_4 = 0$$

$$0 \leq x_i \leq 1 \quad , \quad i=1,2,3$$

$$0 \leq x_4 \leq 2$$

START:	x_0	$= (2 , 2 , 2 , 2)$	(not feasible)
	$f(x_0)$	$= -6$	

SOLUTION:	x^*	$= (2/3 , 1/3 , 1/3 , 2)$
	$f(x^*)$	$= 52/27$
	$r(x^*)$	$= 0$
	$e(x^*)$	$= .13E-10$
	μ	$= 1$
	$I(x^*)$	$= (8)$
	u^*_{max}/u^*_{min}	$= .1111/.1111 = 1$
	$\lambda^*_{max}/\lambda^*_{min}$	$= .67/.22 = 3$

PROBLEM:	42
CLASSIFICATION:	QQR-T1-10
SOURCE:	Brusch [14]
NUMBER OF VARIABLES:	$n = 4$
NUMBER OF CONSTRAINTS:	$m_1 = 0$, $m-m_1 = 2(1)$, $b = 0$

OBJECTIVE FUNCTION:

$$f(x) = (x_1 - 1)^2 + (x_2 - 2)^2 + (x_3 - 3)^2 + (x_4 - 4)^2$$

CONSTRAINTS:

$$x_1 - 2 = 0$$

$$x_3^2 + x_4^2 - 2 = 0$$

START: $x_0 = (1 , 1 , 1 , 1)$ (not feasible)

 $f(x_0) = 14$

SOLUTION: $x^* = (2 , 2 , .6\sqrt{2} , .8\sqrt{2})$

 $f(x^*) = 28 - 10\sqrt{2}$

 $r(x^*) = 0$

 $e(x^*) = .2E-23$

 $\mu = 0$

 $I(x^*) = -$

 $u^*_{max}/u^*_{min} = 2.5355/2.0000 = 1.26$

 $\lambda^*_{max}/\lambda^*_{min} = 7.07/2.00 = 3.54$

PROBLEM:	43 (Rosen-Suzuki)

CLASSIFICATION:	QQR-T1-11

SOURCE: Betts [8], Charalambous [18], Gould [27], Sheela [57]

NUMBER OF VARIABLES: $n = 4$

NUMBER OF CONSTRAINTS: $m_1 = 3$, $m-m_1 = 0$, $b = 0$

OBJECTIVE FUNCTION:

$$f(x) = x_1^2 + x_2^2 + 2x_3^2 + x_4^2 - 5x_1 - 5x_2 - 21x_3 + 7x_4$$

CONSTRAINTS:

$$8 - x_1^2 - x_2^2 - x_3^2 - x_4^2 - x_1 + x_2 - x_3 + x_4 \geq 0$$

$$10 - x_1^2 - 2x_2^2 - x_3^2 - 2x_4^2 + x_1 + x_4 \geq 0$$

$$5 - 2x_1^2 - x_2^2 - x_3^2 - 2x_1 + x_2 + x_4 \geq 0$$

START:	x_0	$= (0 , 0 , 0 , 0)$	(feasible)
	$f(x_0)$	$= 0$	

SOLUTION:

x^*	$=$	$(0 , 1 , 2 , -1)$
$f(x^*)$	$=$	-44
$r(x^*)$	$=$	0
$e(x^*)$	$=$	$.21E-9$
μ	$=$	2
$I(x^*)$	$=$	$(1 , 3)$
u^*_{max}/u^*_{min}	$=$	$2/1 = 2$
$\lambda^*_{max}/\lambda^*_{min}$	$=$	$9/8.07 = 1.12$

PROBLEM:	44
CLASSIFICATION:	QLR-T1-4
SOURCE:	Konno [37]
NUMBER OF VARIABLES:	$n = 4$

NUMBER OF CONSTRAINTS: $m_1 = 6(6)$, $m-m_1 = 0$, $b = 4$

OBJECTIVE FUNCTION:

$$f(x) = x_1 - x_2 - x_3 - x_1 x_3 + x_1 x_4 + x_2 x_3 - x_2 x_4$$

CONSTRAINTS:

$$8 - x_1 - 2x_2 \geq 0$$

$$12 - 4x_1 - x_2 \geq 0$$

$$12 - 3x_1 - 4x_2 \geq 0$$

$$8 - 2x_3 - x_4 \geq 0$$

$$8 - x_3 - 2x_4 \geq 0$$

$$5 - x_3 - x_4 \geq 0 \quad , \quad 0 \leq x_i \quad , \quad i=1,\ldots,4$$

START: $x_o = (0 , 0 , 0 , 0)$ (feasible)

$f(x_o) = 0$

SOLUTION: $x^* = (0 , 3 , 0 , 4)$

$f(x^*) = -15$

$r(x^*) = 0$

$e(x^*) = 0$

$\mu = 4$

$I(x^*) = (3 , 5 , 7 , 9)$

$u^*_{max}/u^*_{min} = 8.75/1.25 = 7$

$\lambda^*_{max}/\lambda^*_{min} = -$

PROBLEM:	45
CLASSIFICATION:	PBR-T1-5
SOURCE:	Betts [8], Miele e.al. [42]
NUMBER OF VARIABLES:	n = 5

NUMBER OF CONSTRAINTS: $m_1 = 0$, $m-m_1 = 0$, b = 10

OBJECTIVE FUNCTION:

$$f(x) = 2 - \frac{1}{120} x_1 x_2 x_3 x_4 x_5$$

CONSTRAINTS:

$$0 \leq x_i \leq i \quad , \quad i=1,\ldots,5$$

START: x_o = (2 , 2 , 2 , 2) (not feasible)

$f(x_o)$ = 26/15

SOLUTION: x^* = (1 , 2 , 3 , 4 , 5)

$f(x^*)$ = 1

$r(x^*)$ = 0

$e(x^*)$ = 0

μ = 5

$I(x^*)$ = (6 , 7 , 8 , 9 , 10)

u_{max}^*/u_{min}^* = 1/.2 = 5

$\lambda_{max}^*/\lambda_{min}^*$ = -

PROBLEM:	46

CLASSIFICATION:	PGR-T1-1

SOURCE:	Huang, Aggerwal [34], Miele e.al. [43]

NUMBER OF VARIABLES:	$n = 5$

NUMBER OF CONSTRAINTS: $m_1 = 0$, $m-m_1 = 2$, $b = 0$

OBJECTIVE FUNCTION:

$$f(x) = (x_1 - x_2)^2 + (x_3 - 1)^2 + (x_4 - 1)^4$$
$$+ (x_5 - 1)^6$$

CONSTRAINTS:

$$x_1{}^2 x_4 + \sin(x_4 - x_5) - 1 = 0$$

$$x_2 + x_3{}^4 x_4{}^2 - 2 = 0$$

START: $x_o = (.5\sqrt{2} , 1.75 , .5 , 2 , 2)$ (feasible)

$f(x_o) = 5.8125 - 1.75\sqrt{2}$

SOLUTION: $x^* = (1 , 1 , 1 , 1 , 1)$

$f(x^*) = 0$

$r(x^*) = 0$

$e(x^*) = 0$

$\mu = 0$

$I(x^*) = -$

$u^*_{max}/u^*_{min} = 0/0$

$\lambda^*_{max}/\lambda^*_{min} = 2.97/.74E{-}7 = .40E8$

PROBLEM:	47
CLASSIFICATION:	PPR-T1-3
SOURCE:	Huang, Aggerwal [34], Miele e.al. [43]

NUMBER OF VARIABLES: $n = 5$

NUMBER OF CONSTRAINTS: $m_1 = 0$, $m-m_1 = 3$, $b = 0$

OBJECTIVE FUNCTION:

$$f(x) = (x_1 - x_2)^2 + (x_2 - x_3)^3 + (x_3 - x_4)^4 + (x_4 - x_5)^4$$

CONSTRAINTS:

$$x_1 + x_2^2 + x_3^3 - 3 = 0$$

$$x_2 - x_3^2 + x_4 - 1 = 0$$

$$x_1 x_5 - 1 = 0$$

START: x_o = $(2 , \sqrt{2} , -1 , 2-\sqrt{2} , .5)$ (feasible)

$f(x_o)$ = 12.4954368

SOLUTION: x^* = $(1 , 1 , 1 , 1 , 1)$

$f(x^*)$ = 0

$r(x^*)$ = 0

$e(x^*)$ = 0

μ = 0

$I(x^*)$ = −

u^*_{max}/u^*_{min} = 0/0

$\lambda^*_{max}/\lambda^*_{min}$ = 2.08/.53 = 3.92

PROBLEM:	48
CLASSIFICATION:	QLR-T1-5
SOURCE:	Huang, Aggerwal [34], Miele e.al. [43]
NUMBER OF VARIABLES:	$n = 5$
NUMBER OF CONSTRAINTS:	$m_1 = 0$, $m-m_1 = 2(2)$, $b = 0$

OBJECTIVE FUNCTION:

$$f(x) = (x_1 - 1)^2 + (x_2 - x_3)^2 + (x_4 - x_5)^2$$

CONSTRAINTS:

$$x_1 + x_2 + x_3 + x_4 + x_5 - 5 = 0$$

$$x_3 - 2(x_4 + x_5) + 3 = 0$$

START: x_0 = (3 , 5 , -3 , 2 , -2) (feasible)

$f(x_0)$ = 84

SOLUTION: x^* = (1 , 1 , 1 , 1 , 1)

$f(x^*)$ = 0

$r(x^*)$ = 0

$e(x^*)$ = 0

μ = 0

$I(x^*)$ = -

u^*_{max}/u^*_{min} = 0/0

$\lambda^*_{max}/\lambda^*_{min}$ = 4/1.49 = 2.69

PROBLEM:	49
CLASSIFICATION:	PLR-T1-5
SOURCE:	Huang, Aggerwal [34]
NUMBER OF VARIABLES:	n = 5
NUMBER OF CONSTRAINTS:	$m_1 = 0$, $m-m_1 = 2(2)$, $b = 0$

OBJECTIVE FUNCTION:

$$f(x) = (x_1 - x_2)^2 + (x_3 - 1)^2 + (x_4 - 1)^4 + (x_5 - 1)^6$$

CONSTRAINTS:

$$x_1 + x_2 + x_3 + 4x_4 - 7 = 0$$

$$x_3 + 5x_5 - 6 = 0$$

START: x_0 = (10 , 7 , 2 , -3 , .8) (feasible)

 $f(x_0)$ = 266

SOLUTION: x^* = (1 , 1 , 1 , 1 , 1)

 $f(x^*)$ = 0

 $r(x^*)$ = 0

 $e(x^*)$ = 0

 μ = 0

 $I(x^*)$ = -

 u^*_{max}/u^*_{min} = 0/0

 $\lambda^*_{max}/\lambda^*_{min}$ = 4/.70E-10 = .57E11

PROBLEM:	50
CLASSIFICATION:	PLR-T1-6
SOURCE:	Huang, Aggerwal [34]
NUMBER OF VARIABLES:	n = 5
NUMBER OF CONSTRAINTS:	$m_1 = 0$, $m-m_1 = 3(3)$, b = 0

OBJECTIVE FUNCTION:

$$f(x) = (x_1 - x_2)^2 + (x_2 - x_3)^2 + (x_3 - x_4)^4 + (x_4 - x_5)^2$$

CONSTRAINTS:

$$x_1 + 2x_2 + 3x_3 - 6 = 0$$

$$x_2 + 2x_3 + 3x_4 - 6 = 0$$

$$x_3 + 2x_4 + 3x_5 - 6 = 0$$

START:
x_o = (35 , -31 , 11 , 5 , -5) (feasible)
$f(x_o)$ = 17416

SOLUTION:
x^* = (1 , 1 , 1 , 1 , 1)
$f(x^*)$ = 0
$r(x^*)$ = 0
$e(x^*)$ = 0
μ = 0
$I(x^*)$ = -
u^*_{max}/u^*_{min} = 0/0
$\lambda^*_{max}/\lambda^*_{min}$ = 5.89/1.64 = 3.6

PROBLEM:	51
CLASSIFICATION:	QLR-T1-6
SOURCE:	Huang, Aggerwal [34]
NUMBER OF VARIABLES:	n = 5
NUMBER OF CONSTRAINTS:	$m_1 = 0$, $m-m_1 = 3(3)$, $b = 0$

OBJECTIVE FUNCTION:

$$f(x) = (x_1 - x_2)^2 + (x_2 + x_3 - 2)^2 + (x_4 - 1)^2 + (x_5 - 1)^2$$

CONSTRAINTS:

$$x_1 + 3x_2 - 4 = 0$$

$$x_3 + x_4 - 2x_5 = 0$$

$$x_2 - x_5 = 0$$

START:	x_0	= (2.5 , .5 , 2 , -1 , .5) (feasible)
	$f(x_0)$	= 8.5

SOLUTION:	x^*	= (1 , 1 , 1 , 1 , 1)
	$f(x^*)$	= 0
	$r(x^*)$	= 0
	$e(x^*)$	= 0
	μ	= 0
	$I(x^*)$	= -
	u^*_{max}/u^*_{min}	= 0/0
	$\lambda^*_{max}/\lambda^*_{min}$	= 3.49/1.90 = 1.84

PROBLEM:	52
CLASSIFICATION:	QLR-T1-7
SOURCE:	Miele e.al. [44,45]
NUMBER OF VARIABLES:	n = 5
NUMBER OF CONSTRAINTS:	$m_1 = 0$, $m-m_1 = 3(3)$, $b = 0$

OBJECTIVE FUNCTION:

$$f(x) = (4x_1 - x_2)^2 + (x_2 + x_3 - 2)^2 + (x_4 - 1)^2$$
$$+ (x_5 - 1)^2$$

CONSTRAINTS:

$$x_1 + 3x_2 = 0$$

$$x_3 + x_4 - 2x_5 = 0$$

$$x_2 - x_5 = 0$$

START:
x_0 = (2 , 2 , 2 , 2 , 2)   (not feasible)
$f(x_0)$ = 42

SOLUTION:
x^* = (-33 , 11 , 180 , -158 , 11)/349
$f(x^*)$ = 1859/349
$r(x^*)$ = 0
$e(x^*)$ = .14E-9
μ = 0
$I(x^*)$ = -
u^*_{max}/u^*_{min} = 7.7479/2.9054 = 2.6667
$\lambda^*_{max}/\lambda^*_{min}$ = 26.93/1.99 = 13.51

PROBLEM:	53
CLASSIFICATION:	QLR-T1-8
SOURCE:	Betts [8], Miele e.al. [42,43]
NUMBER OF VARIABLES:	$n = 5$
NUMBER OF CONSTRAINTS:	$m_1 = 0$, $m-m_1 = 3(3)$, $b = 10$

OBJECTIVE FUNCTION:

$$f(x) = (x_1 - x_2)^2 + (x_2 + x_3 - 2)^2 + (x_4 - 1)^2 + (x_5 - 1)^2$$

CONSTRAINTS:

$$x_1 + 3x_2 = 0$$

$$x_3 + x_4 - 2x_5 = 0$$

$$x_2 - x_5 = 0$$

$$-10 \leq x_i \leq 10 \quad , \quad i=1,\ldots,5$$

START:

$x_0 = (2 , 2 , 2 , 2 , 2)$ (not feasible)

$f(x_0) = 6$

SOLUTION:

$x^* = (-33 , 11 , 27 , -5 , 11)/43$

$f(x^*) = 176/43$

$r(x^*) = 0$

$e(x^*) = .28E-9$

$\mu = 0$

$I(x^*) = -$

$u^*_{max}/u^*_{min} = 5.9535/2.0465 = 1.84$

$\lambda^*_{max}/\lambda^*_{min} = 3.49/1.90 = 1.84$

PROBLEM:	54
CLASSIFICATION:	GLR-T1-2
SOURCE:	Betts [8], Picket [50]
NUMBER OF VARIABLES:	$n = 6$
NUMBER OF CONSTRAINTS:	$m_1 = 0$, $m-m_1 = 1(1)$, $b = 12$

OBJECTIVE FUNCTION:

$$f(x) = -\exp(-h(x)/2)$$

$$h(x) = ((x_1 - 1.E6)^2/6.4E7 + (x_1 - 1.E4)(x_2 - 1)/2.E4$$

$$+ (x_2 - 1)^2)(x_3 - 2.E6)^2/(.96 \cdot 4.9E13)$$

$$+ (x_4 - 10)^2/2.5E3 + (x_5 - 1.E-3)^2/2.5E-3$$

$$+ (x_6 - 1.E8)^2/2.5E17$$

CONSTRAINTS:

$$x_1 + 4.E3x_2 - 1.76E4 = 0$$

$$0 \leq x_1 \leq 2.E4 \quad -10 \leq x_2 \leq 10 \quad 0 \leq x_3 \leq 1.E7$$

$$0 \leq x_4 \leq 20 \quad -1 \leq x_5 \leq 1 \quad 0 \leq x_6 \leq 2.E8$$

START:	x_o	$= (6E3 , 1.5 , 4E6 , 2 , 3E-3 , 5E7)$
	$f(x_o)$	$= -.7651$ (not feasible)

SOLUTION:	x^*	$= (91600/7, 79/70, 2E6, 10, 1E-3, 1E8)$
	$f(x^*)$	$= -\exp(-27/280)$
	$r(x^*)$	$= 0$
	$e(x^*)$	$= .20E-10$
	μ	$= 0$
	$I(x^*)$	$= -$
	u^*_{max}/u^*_{min}	$= .4865E-4/.4865E-4 = 1$
	$\lambda^*_{max}/\lambda^*_{min}$	$= 362.9/.36E-17 = .10E21$

PROBLEM:	55
CLASSIFICATION:	GLR-T1-3
SOURCE:	Hsia [33]
NUMBER OF VARIABLES:	n = 6
NUMBER OF CONSTRAINTS:	$m_1 = 0$, $m-m_1 = 6(6)$, $b = 8$

OBJECTIVE FUNCTION:

$$f(x) = x_1 + 2x_2 + 4x_5 + \exp(x_1 x_4)$$

CONSTRAINTS:

$$x_1 + 2x_2 + 5x_5 - 6 = 0$$

$$x_1 + x_2 + x_3 - 3 = 0$$

$$x_4 + x_5 + x_6 - 2 = 0$$

$$x_1 + x_4 - 1 = 0$$

$$x_2 + x_5 - 2 = 0$$

$$x_3 + x_6 - 2 = 0$$

$$0 \le x_1 , \quad i=1,\ldots,6 , \quad x_1 \le 1 , \quad x_4 \le 1$$

START:
$x_0 = (1 , 2 , 0 , 0 , 0 , 2)$ (not feasible)
$f(x_0) = 6$

SOLUTION:
$x^* = (0 , 4/3 , 5/3 , 1 , 2/3 , 1/3)$
$f(x^*) = 19/3$
$r(x^*) = 0$
$e(x^*) = 0$
$\mu = 8$
$I(x^*) = (1 , 8)$
$u^*_{max}/u^*_{min} = -$
$\lambda^*_{max}/\lambda^*_{min} = -$

PROBLEM:	56
CLASSIFICATION:	PGR-T1-2
SOURCE:	Brusch [15]
NUMBER OF VARIABLES:	n = 7
NUMBER OF CONSTRAINTS:	$m_1 = 0$, $m-m_1 = 4$, $b = 0$

OBJECTIVE FUNCTION:

$$f(x) = -x_1 x_2 x_3$$

CONSTRAINTS:

$$x_1 - 4.2\sin^2 x_4 = 0$$

$$x_2 - 4.2\sin^2 x_5 = 0$$

$$x_3 - 4.2\sin^2 x_6 = 0$$

$$x_1 + 2x_2 + 2x_3 - 7.2\sin^2 x_7 = 0$$

START:

x_o = .(1 , 1 , 1 , a , a , a , b)

$f(x_o)$ = -1   (feasible)

SOLUTION:

x^*	= $(2.4, 1.2, 1.2, \pm c + j\pi, \pm d + k\pi, \pm d + l\pi, (r+.5)\pi)$	
$f(x^*)$	= -3.456	$a = \arcsin\sqrt{1/4.2}$
$r(x^*)$	= 0	$b = \arcsin\sqrt{5/7.2}$
$e(x^*)$	= .67E-10	$c = \arcsin\sqrt{4/7}$
μ	= 0	$d = \arcsin\sqrt{2/7}$
$I(x^*)$	= -	$j,k,l,r = 0, \pm 1, \pm 2, \ldots$
u^*_{max}/u^*_{min}	= 1.44/.68E-11 = .21E12	
$\lambda^*_{max}/\lambda^*_{min}$	= 20.74/.76 = 27.45	

PROBLEM:	57
CLASSIFICATION:	SQR-P1-1
SOURCE:	Betts [8], Gould [27]
NUMBER OF VARIABLES:	$n = 2$
NUMBER OF CONSTRAINTS:	$m_1 = 1$, $m-m_1 = 0$, $b = 2$

OBJECTIVE FUNCTION:

$$f(x) = \sum_{i=1}^{44} f_i(x)^2$$

$$f_i(x) = b_i - x_1 - (.49 - x_1)\exp(-x_2(a_i - 8))$$

$$i = 1, \ldots, 44$$

a_i, b_i: cf. Appendix A

CONSTRAINTS:

$$.49x_2 - x_1 x_2 - .09 \geq 0$$

$$.4 \leq x_1 , \quad -4 \leq x_2$$

START:	x_0	=	(.42 , 5)	(feasible)
	$f(x_0)$	=	.030798602	

SOLUTION:	x^*	=	(.419952675 , 1.284845629)
	$f(x^*)$	=	.02845966972
	$r(x^*)$	=	0
	$e(x^*)$	=	.98E-7
	μ	=	1
	$I(x^*)$	=	(1)
	u^*_{max}/u^*_{min}	=	.06671/.06671 = 1
	$\lambda^*_{max}/\lambda^*_{min}$	=	.23/.23 = 1

PROBLEM:	59
CLASSIFICATION:	GQR-P1-1
SOURCE:	Barnes [3], Himmelblau [29]

NUMBER OF VARIABLES: $n = 2$

NUMBER OF CONSTRAINTS: $m_1 = 3$, $m-m_1 = 0$, $b = 4$

OBJECTIVE FUNCTION:

$$f(x) = -75.196 + 3.8112x_1 + .0020567x_1^3 - 1.0345E\text{-}5x_1^4$$

$$+ 6.8306x_2 - .030234x_1x_2 + 1.28134E\text{-}3x_2x_1^2$$

$$+ 2.266E\text{-}7x_1^4x_2 - .25645x_2^2 + .0034604x_2^3 - 1.3514E\text{-}5x_2^4$$

$$+ 28.106/(x_2 + 1) + 5.2375E\text{-}6x_1^2x_2^2 + 6.3E\text{-}8x_1^3x_2^2$$

$$- 7E\text{-}10x_1^3x_2^3 - 3.405E\text{-}4x_1x_2^2 + 1.6638E\text{-}6x_1x_2^3$$

$$+ 2.8673\exp(.0005x_1x_2) - 3.5256E\text{-}5x_1^3x_2$$

CONSTRAINTS:

$$x_1x_2 - 700 \geq 0$$

$$x_2 - x_1^2/125 \geq 0 \qquad\qquad 0 \leq x_1 \leq 75$$

$$(x_2 - 50)^2 - 5(x_1 - 55) \geq 0 \qquad\qquad 0 \leq x_2 \leq 65$$

START:	x_0	= (90 , 10)	(not feasible)
	$f(x_0)$	= 86.878639	

SOLUTION:

x^* = (13.55010424 , 51.66018129)

$f(x^*)$ = -7.804226324

$r(x^*)$ = 0

$e(x^*)$ = .27E-6

μ = 1

$I(x^*)$ = (1)

u^*_{max}/u^*_{min} = .01142/.01142 = 1

$\lambda^*_{max}/\lambda^*_{min}$ = .13/.13 = 1

PROBLEM:	60
CLASSIFICATION:	PPR-P1-1
SOURCE:	Betts [8], Miele e.al. [42,44]

NUMBER OF VARIABLES:	$n = 3$		

NUMBER OF CONSTRAINTS: $m_1 = 0$, $m-m_1 = 1$, $b = 6$

OBJECTIVE FUNCTION:

$$f(x) = (x_1 - 1)^2 + (x_1 - x_2)^2 + (x_2 - x_3)^4$$

CONSTRAINTS:

$$x_1(1 + x_2^2) + x_3^4 - 4 - 3\sqrt{2} = 0$$

$$-10 \leq x_i \leq 10 \quad , \quad i=1,2,3$$

START: x_o $= (2 , 2 , 2)$ (not feasible)

$f(x_o)$ $= 1$

SOLUTION: x^* $= (1.104859024, 1.196674194, 1, 535262257)$

$f(x^*)$ $= .03256820025$

$r(x^*)$ $= .23E-9$

$e(x^*)$ $= .38E-7$

μ $= 1$

$I(x^*)$ $= (1)$

$u^*_{max}/u^*_{min} = .01073/.01073 = 1$

$\lambda^*_{max}/\lambda^*_{min} = 5.72/2.07 = 2.76$

PROBLEM:	61

CLASSIFICATION:	QQR-P1-1

SOURCE:	Fletcher, Lill [26]

NUMBER OF VARIABLES:	$n = 3$

NUMBER OF CONSTRAINTS:	$m_1 = 0$	, $m-m_1 = 2$	, $b = 0$

OBJECTIVE FUNCTION:

$$f(x) = 4x_1^2 + 2x_2^2 + 2x_3^2 - 33x_1 + 16x_2 - 24x_3$$

CONSTRAINTS:

$$3x_1 - 2x_2^2 - 7 = 0$$

$$4x_1 - x_3^2 - 11 = 0$$

START:

x_0 $= (0 , 0 , 0)$ (not feasible)

$f(x_0)$ $= 0$

SOLUTION:

x^* $= (5.326770157, -2.118998639, 3.210464239)$

$f(x^*)$ $= -143.6461422$

$r(x^*)$ $= .29E-9$

$e(x^*)$ $= .21E-6$

μ $= 0$

$I(x^*)$ $= -$

$u_{max}^*/u_{min}^* = 1.7378/.8877 = 1.96$

$\lambda_{max}^*/\lambda_{min}^* = 7.83/7.83 = 1$

PROBLEM:	62
CLASSIFICATION:	GLR-P1-1
SOURCE:	Betts [8], Picket [50]
NUMBER OF VARIABLES:	$n = 3$
NUMBER OF CONSTRAINTS:	$m_1 = 0$, $m-m_1 = 1(1)$, $b = 6$

OBJECTIVE FUNCTION:

$$f(x) = -32.174(255 \ln((x_1+x_2+x_3+.03)/(.09x_1+x_2+x_3+.03))$$

$$+ 280 \ln((x_2+x_3+.03)/(.07x_2+x_3+.03))$$

$$+ 290 \ln((x_3+.03)/(.13x_3+.03)))$$

CONSTRAINTS:

$$x_1 + x_2 + x_3 - 1 = 0$$

$$0 \leq x_i \leq 1 \; , \quad i=1,2,3$$

START:	x_o	$= (.7 , .2 , .1)$ (feasible)
	$f(x_o)$	$= -25698.3$

SOLUTION:	x^*	$= (.6178126908, .328202223, .5398508606E-1)$
	$f(x^*)$	$= -26272.51448$
	$r(x^*)$	$= 0$
	$e(x^*)$	$= .20E-5$
	μ	$= 0$
	$I(x^*)$	$= -$
	u^*_{max}/u^*_{min}	$= 6387/6387 = 1$
	$\lambda^*_{max}/\lambda^*_{min}$	$= .32E6/.72E4 = 44.9$

PROBLEM:	63

CLASSIFICATION:	QQR-P1-2

SOURCE:	Himmelblau [29], Paviani [48], Sheela [57]

NUMBER OF VARIABLES: $n = 3$

NUMBER OF CONSTRAINTS: $m_1 = 0$, $m-m_1 = 2(1)$, $b = 3$

OBJECTIVE FUNCTION:

$$f(x) = 1000 - x_1^2 - 2x_2^2 - x_3^2 - x_1 x_2 - x_1 x_3$$

CONSTRAINTS:

$$8x_1 + 14x_2 + 7x_3 - 56 = 0$$

$$x_1^2 + x_2^2 + x_3^2 - 25 = 0$$

$$0 \leq x_i \quad , \quad i=1,2,3$$

START: x_0 = (2 , 2 , 2) (not feasible)

$f(x_0)$ = 976

SOLUTION: x^* = (3.512118414,.2169881741,3.552174034)

$f(x^*)$ = 961.7151721

$r(x^*)$ = 0

$e(x^*)$ = .62E-5

μ = 0

$I(x^*)$ = -

u^*_{max}/u^*_{min} = 1.223/.2749 = 4.45

$\lambda^*_{max}/\lambda^*_{min}$ = 1.52/1.52 = 1

PROBLEM:	64
CLASSIFICATION:	PPR-P1-2
SOURCE:	Best [7]

NUMBER OF VARIABLES:	$n = 3$		

NUMBER OF CONSTRAINTS: $m_1 = 1$, $m-m_1 = 0$, $b = 3$

OBJECTIVE FUNCTION:

$$f(x) = 5x_1 + 50000/x_1 + 20x_2 + 72000/x_2$$
$$+ 10x_3 + 144000/x_3$$

CONSTRAINTS:

$$1 - 4/x_1 - 32/x_2 - 120/x_3 \geq 0$$

$$1.E-5 \leq x_i \quad , \quad i=1,2,3$$

START: x_0 = (1 , 1 , 1)   (not feasible)

$f(x_0)$ = 266035

SOLUTION: x^* = (108.7347175,85.12613942,204.3247078)

$f(x^*)$ = 6299.842428

$r(x^*)$ = 0

$e(x^*)$ = .28E-4

μ = 1

$I(x^*)$ = (1)

u^*_{max}/u^*_{min} = 2279/2279 = 1

$\lambda^*_{max}/\lambda^*_{min}$ = .21/.092 = 2.28

PROBLEM:	65
CLASSIFICATION:	QQR-P1-3
SOURCE:	Murtagh, Sargent [47]
NUMBER OF VARIABLES:	$n = 3$
NUMBER OF CONSTRAINTS:	$m_1 = 1$, $m-m_1 = 0$, $b = 6$

OBJECTIVE FUNCTION:

$$f(x) = (x_1 - x_2)^2 + (x_1 + x_2 - 10)^2/9 + (x_3 - 5)^2$$

CONSTRAINTS:

$$48 - x_1^2 - x_2^2 - x_3^2 \geq 0$$

$$-4.5 \leq x_i \leq 4.5 \quad , \quad i=1,2$$

$$-5 \leq x_3 \leq 5$$

START:

$x_0 = (-5 , 5 , 0)$ (not feasible)

$f(x_0) = 1225/9$

SOLUTION:

$x^* = (3.650461821, 3.65046168, 4.6204170507)$

$f(x^*) = .9535288567$

$r(x^*) = 0$

$e(x^*) = .40E-6$

$\mu = 1$

$I(x^*) = (1)$

$u^*_{max}/u^*_{min} = .08215/.08215 = 1$

$\lambda^*_{max}/\lambda^*_{min} = 1.95/1.68 = 1.16$

PROBLEM:	66
CLASSIFICATION:	LGR-P1-1
SOURCE:	Eckhardt [24]
NUMBER OF VARIABLES:	$n = 3$
NUMBER OF CONSTRAINTS:	$m_1 = 2$, $m-m_1 = 0$, $b = 6$

OBJECTIVE FUNCTION:

$$f(x) = .2x_3 - .8x_1$$

CONSTRAINTS:

$$x_2 - \exp(x_1) \geq 0$$

$$x_3 - \exp(x_2) \geq 0$$

$$0 \leq x_1 \leq 100$$

$$0 \leq x_2 \leq 100$$

$$0 \leq x_3 \leq 10$$

START:	x_o	= $(0 , 1.05 , 2.9)$	(feasible)
	$f(x_o)$	= .58	

SOLUTION:	x^*	= $(.1841264879, 1.202167873, 3.327322322)$
	$f(x^*)$	= .5181632741
	$r(x^*)$	= .58E-10
	$e(x^*)$	= .86E-11
	μ	= 2
	$I(x^*)$	= $(1 , 2)$
	u^*_{max}/u^*_{min}	= .6654/.2 = 3.33
	$\lambda^*_{max}/\lambda^*_{min}$	= .096/.096 = 1

PROBLEM:	67 (Colville No.8)
CLASSIFICATION:	GGI-P1-1
SOURCE:	Colville [20], Himmelblau [29]
NUMBER OF VARIABLES:	n = 3
NUMBER OF CONSTRAINTS:	$m_1 = 14$, $m-m_1 = 0$, $b = 6$

OBJECTIVE FUNCTION:

$$f(x) = -(.063y_2(x)y_5(x) - 5.04x_1 - 3.36y_3(x)$$
$$- .035x_2 - 10x_3)$$

$y_i(x)$: cf. Appendix A

CONSTRAINTS:

$$y_{i+1}(x) - a_i \geq 0 \quad , \quad i=1,\ldots,7$$

$$a_i - y_{i-6}(x) \geq 0 \quad , \quad i=8,\ldots,14$$

$$1.E-5 \leq x_1 \leq 2.E3$$

$$1.E-5 \leq x_2 \leq 1.6E4$$

$$1.E-5 \leq x_3 \leq 1.2E2$$

a_i : cf. Appendix A

START:
x_0 = (1745 , 12000 , 110)   (feasible)
$f(x_0)$ = 868.6458

SOLUTION:
x^* = (1728.371286,16000.00000,98.14151402)
$f(x^*)$ = -1162.036507
$r(x^*)$ = 0
$e(x^*)$ = 0
μ = 3
$I(x^*)$ = (9 , 11 , 19)
u^*_{max}/u^*_{min} = 1.5872/.03403 = 46.6
$\lambda^*_{max}/\lambda^*_{min}$ = -

PROBLEM:	68 , 69 (cost optimal inspection plan)
CLASSIFICATION:	GGR-P1-(1,2)
SOURCE:	Collani [19]

NUMBER OF VARIABLES:	n = 4

NUMBER OF CONSTRAINTS:	$m_1 = 0$	, $m-m_1 = 2$	, b = 8

OBJECTIVE FUNCTION:

$$f(x) = (a_i n_i - \frac{b_i(\exp(x_1) - 1) - x_3}{\exp(x_1) - 1 + x_4} x_4)/x_1 \quad , \quad i=1,2$$

No. 68 : $a_1 = .0001$, $b_1 = 1$, $d_1 = 1$, $n_1 = 24$

No. 69 : $a_2 = .1$, $b_2 = 1000$, $d_2 = 1$, $n_2 = 4$

CONSTRAINTS:

$$x_3 - 2\Phi(-x_2) = 0$$

$$x_4 - \Phi(-x_2 + d_i\sqrt{n_i}) - \Phi(-x_2 - d_i\sqrt{n_i}) = 0$$

$$\Phi(x) = \int_{-\infty}^{x} \exp(-y^2/2)/\sqrt{2\pi} \; dy$$

$.0001 \le x_1 \le 100$, $0 \le x_2 \le 100$, $0 \le x_3 \le 2$, $0 \le x_4 \le 2$

START:	x_0	= (1 , 1 , 1 , 1) (not feasible)
		- for both problems
	$f(x_0)$	= -.2618407 -631.3525

SOLUTION:

x^*	=	(.06785874,3.6461717,.00026617,.8948622)	
		(.02937141,1.1902534,.23394676,.7916678)	
$f(x^*)$	=	-.920425026	-956.71288
$r(x^*)$	=	.54E-7	.44E-10
$e(x^*)$	=	.14E-4	.33E-4
μ	=	0	0
$I(x^*)$	=	-	-
u^*_{max}/u^*_{min}	=	13.66/.0777 = 176	44.47/32.81 = 1.3
$\lambda^*_{max}/\lambda^*_{min}$	=	16.4/.062 = .26E3	.26E5/19.6 = .1E4

PROBLEM:	70
CLASSIFICATION:	SQR-P1-1
SOURCE:	Himmelblau [29,30]
NUMBER OF VARIABLES:	$n = 4$

NUMBER OF CONSTRAINTS: $m_1 = 1$, $m-m_1 = 0$, $b = 8$

OBJECTIVE FUNCTION:

$$f(x) = \sum_{i=1}^{19} (y_{i,cal} - y_{i,obs})^2$$

$$y_{i,cal} = (1 + \frac{1}{12x_2})[x_3 b^{x_2} (x_2/6.2832)^{.5}(c_i/7.685)^{x_2-1}$$

$$\exp(x_2 - bc_i x_2/7.658)] + (1 + \frac{1}{12x_1})[(1 - x_3)(b/x_4)^{x_1}$$

$$(x_1/6.2832)^{.5}(c_i/7.658)^{x_1-1} \exp(x_1 - bc_i x_1/(7.658x_4))]$$

$$b = x_3 + (1 - x_3)x_4$$

c_i, $y_{i,obs}$: cf. Appendix A

CONSTRAINTS:

$$x_3 + (1 - x_3)x_4 \geq 0$$

$$.00001 \leq x_i \leq 100 \quad , \quad i=1,2,4$$

$$.00001 \leq x_3 \leq 1$$

START:	x_0	$= (2 , 4 , .04 , 2)$	(feasible)
	$f(x_0)$	$= .9818596$	

SOLUTION:	x^*	$= (12.27695, 4.631788, .3128625, 2.029290)$
	$f(x^*)$	$= .007498464$
	$r(x^*)$	$= 0$
	$e(x^*)$	$= 0$
	μ	$= 0$
	$I(x^*)$	$= -$
	u^*_{max}/u^*_{min}	$= -$
	$\lambda^*_{max}/\lambda^*_{min}$	$= 18.1/.91E-3 = .20E5$

PROBLEM:	71
CLASSIFICATION:	PPR-P1-3
SOURCE:	Bartholomew-Biggs [4]
NUMBER OF VARIABLES:	n = 4
NUMBER OF CONSTRAINTS:	$m_1 = 1$, $m-m_1 = 1$, $b = 8$

OBJECTIVE FUNCTION:

$$f(x) = x_1 x_4 (x_1 + x_2 + x_3) + x_3$$

CONSTRAINTS:

$$x_1 x_2 x_3 x_4 - 25 \geq 0$$

$$x_1^2 + x_2^2 + x_3^2 + x_4^2 - 40 = 0$$

$$1 \leq x_i \leq 5 , \quad i=1,\ldots,4$$

START:

x_0 = (1 , 5 , 5 , 1) (feasible)

$f(x_0)$ = 16

SOLUTION:

x^* = (1 , 4.7429994 , 3.8211503 , 1.3794082)

$f(x^*)$ = 17.0140173

$r(x^*)$ = 0

$e(x^*)$ = .51E-6

μ = 2

$I(x^*)$ = (1 , 2)

u_{max}^* / u_{min}^* = 1.0879/.1615 = 6.74

$\lambda_{max}^* / \lambda_{min}^*$ = 1.18/1.18 = 1

PROBLEM:	72 (optimal sample size)
CLASSIFICATION:	LPR-P1-1
SOURCE:	Bracken, McCormick [13]
NUMBER OF VARIABLES:	$n = 4$

NUMBER OF CONSTRAINTS: $m_1 = 2$, $m-m_1 = 0$, $b = 8$

OBJECTIVE FUNCTION:

$$f(x) = 1 + x_1 + x_2 + x_3 + x_4$$

CONSTRAINTS:

$$.0401 - 4/x_1 - 2.25/x_2 - 1/x_3 - .25/x_4 \geq 0$$

$$.010085 - .16/x_1 - .36/x_2 - .64/x_3 - .64/x_4 \geq 0$$

$$.001 \leq x_i \leq (5 - i)E5 \quad , \quad i=1,\ldots,4$$

START: x_0 = (1 , 1 , 1 , 1)   (not feasible)

$f(x_0)$ = 5

SOLUTION: x^* = (193.4071,179.5475,185.0186,168.7062)

$f(x^*)$ = 727.67937

$r(x^*)$ = 0

$e(x^*)$ = .11E-4

μ = 2

$I(x^*)$ = (1 , 2)

u^*_{max}/u^*_{min} = .4147E5/.7693E4 = 5.39

$\lambda^*_{max}/\lambda^*_{min}$ = .011/.011 = 1.02

PROBLEM:	73 (cattle-feed)
CLASSIFICATION:	LGI-P1-1
SOURCE:	Biggs [10], Bracken, McCormick [13]

NUMBER OF VARIABLES: $n = 4$

NUMBER OF CONSTRAINTS: $m_1 = 2(1)$, $m-m_1 = 1(1)$, $b = 4$

OBJECTIVE FUNCTION:

$$f(x) = 24.55x_1 + 26.75x_2 + 39x_3 + 40.50x_4$$

CONSTRAINTS:

$$2.3x_1 + 5.6x_2 + 11.1x_3 + 1.3x_4 - 5 \geq 0$$

$$12x_1 + 11.9x_2 + 41.8x_3 + 52.1x_4 - 21$$

$$- 1.645(.28x_1^2 + .19x_2^2 + 20.5x_3^2 + .62x_4^2)^{1/2} \geq 0$$

$$x_1 + x_2 + x_3 + x_4 - 1 = 0$$

$$0 \leq x_i , \quad i=1,\ldots,4$$

START:

x_0 = (1 , 1 , 1 , 1) (not feasible)

$f(x_0)$ = 130.8

SOLUTION:

x^* = (.6355216,-.12E-11,.3127019,.05177655)

$f(x^*)$ = 29.894378

$r(x^*)$ = .99E-10

$e(x^*)$ = 0

μ = 3

$I(x^*)$ = (1 , 2 , 4)

u^*_{max}/u^*_{min} = 18.37/.2433 = 75.5

$\lambda^*_{max}/\lambda^*_{min}$ = -

PROBLEM:	74 , 75
CLASSIFICATION:	PGR-P1-(1,2)
SOURCE:	Beuneu [9]
NUMBER OF VARIABLES:	n = 4
NUMBER OF CONSTRAINTS:	$m_1 = 2(2)$, $m-m_1 = 3$, $b = 8$

OBJECTIVE FUNCTION:

$$f(x) = 3x_1 + 1.E-6x_1^3 + 2x_2 + \tfrac{2}{3}E-6x_2^3$$

CONSTRAINTS:

$$x_4 - x_3 + a_j \geq 0$$
$$x_3 - x_4 + a_j \geq 0$$
$$1000\sin(-x_3 - .25) + 1000\sin(-x_4 - .25) + 894.8 - x_1 = 0$$
$$1000\sin(x_3 - .25) + 1000\sin(x_3 - x_4 - .25) + 894.8 - x_2 = 0$$
$$1000\sin(x_4 - .25) + 1000\sin(x_4 - x_3 - .25) + 1294.8 = 0$$
$$0 \leq x_i \leq 1200 , \quad i=1,2$$
$$-a_j \leq x_i \leq a_j , \quad i=3,4$$

No. 74 : $a_1 = .55$ No.75 : $a_2 = .48$

START:	x_o	=	(0 , 0 , 0 , 0) (not feasible)
			— for both problems
	$f(x_o)$	=	0

SOLUTION:	x^*	=	(679.9453,1026.067,.1188764,−.3962336)	
			(776.1592,925.1949,.05110879, −.4288911)	
	$f(x^*)$	=	5126.4981	5174.4129
	$r(x^*)$	=	.75E-7	.30E-7
	$e(x^*)$	=	.52E-7	0
	μ	=	0	1
	$I(x^*)$	=	–	(1)
	u^*_{max}/u^*_{min}	=	5.46/4.11 = 1.33	2779/3.712 = 748.7
	$\lambda^*_{max}/\lambda^*_{min}$	=	.49E-2/.49E-2 = 1	–

PROBLEM:	76
CLASSIFICATION:	QLR-P1-1
SOURCE:	Murtagh, Sargent [47]
NUMBER OF VARIABLES:	n = 4
NUMBER OF CONSTRAINTS:	$m_1 = 3(3)$, $m-m_1 = 0$, $b = 4$

OBJECTIVE FUNCTION:

$$f(x) = x_1^2 + .5x_2^2 + x_3^2 + .5x_4^2 - x_1x_3 + x_3x_4$$

$$- x_1 - 3x_2 + x_3 - x_4$$

CONSTRAINTS:

$$5 - x_1 - 2x_2 - x_3 - x_4 \geq 0$$

$$4 - 3x_1 - x_2 - 2x_3 + x_4 \geq 0$$

$$x_2 + 4x_3 - 1.5 \geq 0$$

$$0 \leq x_i , \quad i=1,\ldots,4$$

START:	x_0	=	$(.5 , .5 , .5 , .5)$ (feasible)
	$f(x_0)$	=	-1.25

SOLUTION:	x^*	=	$(.2727273, 2.090909, -.26E-10, .5454545)$
	$f(x^*)$	=	-4.681818181
	$r(x^*)$	=	.84E-10
	$e(x^*)$	=	.15E-10
	μ	=	2
	$I(x^*)$	=	(1 , 6)
	u_{max}^*/u_{min}^*	=	1.7272/.4545 = 3.8
	$\lambda_{max}^*/\lambda_{min}^*$	=	1.83/1 = 1.83

PROBLEM:	77
CLASSIFICATION:	PGR-P1-3
SOURCE:	Betts [8], Miele e.al. [42,44,45]
NUMBER OF VARIABLES:	$n = 5$
NUMBER OF CONSTRAINTS:	$m_1 = 0$, $m-m_1 = 2$, $b = 0$

OBJECTIVE FUNCTION:

$$f(x) = (x_1 - 1)^2 + (x_1 - x_2)^2 + (x_3 - 1)^2$$
$$+ (x_4 - 1)^4 + (x_5 - 1)^6$$

CONSTRAINTS:

$$x_1^2 x_4 + \sin(x_4 - x_5) - 2\sqrt{2} = 0$$

$$x_2 + x_3^4 x_4^2 - 8 - \sqrt{2} = 0$$

START:	x_0	$= (2 , 2 , 2 , 2 , 2 , 2)$
	$f(x_0)$	$= 4$ (not feasible)

SOLUTION:	x^*	$= (1.166172, 1.182111, 1.380257, 1.506036,$
	$f(x^*)$	$= .24150513$ $.6109203)$
	$r(x^*)$	$= .12E-9$
	$e(x^*)$	$= .53E-7$
	μ	$= 0$
	$I(x^*)$	$= -$
	u^*_{max}/u^*_{min}	$= .08554/.03188 = 2.68$
	$\lambda^*_{max}/\lambda^*_{min}$	$= 3.92/.75 = 5.25$

PROBLEM:	78
CLASSIFICATION:	PPR-P1-4
SOURCE:	Asaadi [1], Powell [51]
NUMBER OF VARIABLES:	$n = 5$
NUMBER OF CONSTRAINTS:	$m_1 = 0$, $m-m_1 = 3$, $b = 0$

OBJECTIVE FUNCTION:

$$f(x) = x_1 x_2 x_3 x_4 x_5$$

CONSTRAINTS:

$$x_1^2 + x_2^2 + x_3^2 + x_4^2 + x_5^2 - 10 = 0$$

$$x_2 x_3 - 5 x_4 x_5 = 0$$

$$x_1^3 + x_2^3 + 1 = 0$$

START: x_0 = $(-2, 1.5, 2, -1, -1)$

$f(x_0)$ = -6 (not feasible)

SOLUTION: x^* = $(-1.717142, 1.595708, 1.827248, -.7636429,$

$f(x^*)$ = -2.91970041 $-.7636435)$

$r(x^*)$ = $.35E-9$

$e(x^*)$ = $.91E-5$

μ = 0

$I(x^*)$ = $-$

u_{max}^* / u_{min}^* = $.7444/.09681 = 7.69$

$\lambda_{max}^* / \lambda_{min}^*$ = $3.04/2.98 = 1.02$

PROBLEM:	79
CLASSIFICATION:	PPR-P1-5
SOURCE:	Betts [8], Miele e.al. [42,44,45]
NUMBER OF VARIABLES:	n = 5

NUMBER OF CONSTRAINTS: $m_1 = 0$, $m-m_1 = 3$, $b = 0$

OBJECTIVE FUNCTION:

$$f(x) = (x_1 - 1)^2 + (x_1 - x_2)^2 + (x_2 - x_3)^2$$
$$+ (x_3 - x_4)^4 + (x_4 - x_5)^4$$

CONSTRAINTS:

$$x_1 + x_2^2 + x_3^3 - 2 - 3\sqrt{2} = 0$$

$$x_2 - x_3^2 + x_4 + 2 - 2\sqrt{2} = 0$$

$$x_1 x_5 - 2 = 0$$

START: x_0 = (2 , 2 , 2 , 2 , 2)   (not feasible)

$f(x_0)$ = 1

SOLUTION: x^* = (1.191127,1.362603,1.472818,1.635017,

1.679081)

$f(x^*)$ = .0787768209

$r(x^*)$ = .58E-9

$e(x^*)$ = .71E-10

μ = 0

$I(x^*)$ = -

u_{max}^*/u_{min}^* = .3882E-1/.2873E-3 = 135.1

$\lambda_{max}^*/\lambda_{min}^*$ = 2.03/.70 = 2.88

PROBLEM:	80
CLASSIFICATION:	GPR-P1-1
SOURCE:	Powell [52]
NUMBER OF VARIABLES:	n = 5
NUMBER OF CONSTRAINTS:	$m_1 = 0$, $m-m_1 = 3$, $b = 10$

OBJECTIVE FUNCTION:

$$f(x) = \exp(x_1 x_2 x_3 x_4 x_5)$$

CONSTRAINTS:

$$x_1^2 + x_2^2 + x_3^2 + x_4^2 + x_5^2 - 10 = 0$$

$$x_2 x_3 - 5 x_4 x_5 = 0$$

$$x_1^3 + x_2^3 + 1 = 0$$

$$-2.3 \leq x_i \leq 2.3 \quad , \quad i=1,2$$

$$-3.2 \leq x_i \leq 3.2 \quad , \quad i=3,4,5$$

START:

x_0 = (-2 , 2 , 2 , -1 , -1) (not feasible)

$f(x_0)$ = 3.3546E-4

SOLUTION:

x^* = (-1.717143,1.595709,1.827247,-.7636413,

$f(x^*)$ = .0539498478   -.7636450)

$r(x^*)$ = .41E-9

$e(x^*)$ = .49E-6

μ = 0

$I(x^*)$ = -

u^*_{max}/u^*_{min} = .04016/.005222 = 7.69

$\lambda^*_{max}/\lambda^*_{min}$ = .16/.16 = 1.02

PROBLEM:	81
CLASSIFICATION:	GPR-P1-2
SOURCE:	Powell [52]
NUMBER OF VARIABLES:	$n = 5$
NUMBER OF CONSTRAINTS:	$m_1 = 0$, $m-m_1 = 3$, $b = 10$

OBJECTIVE FUNCTION:

$$f(x) = \exp(x_1 x_2 x_3 x_4 x_5) - .5(x_1^3 + x_2^3 + 1)^2$$

CONSTRAINTS:

$$x_1^2 + x_2^2 + x_3^2 + x_4^2 + x_5^2 - 10 = 0$$

$$x_2 x_3 - 5 x_4 x_5 = 0$$

$$x_1^3 + x_2^3 + 1 = 0$$

$$-2.3 \leq x_i \leq 2.3 , \quad i=1,2$$

$$-3.2 \leq x_i \leq 3.2 , \quad i=3,4,5$$

START:	x_o	= $(-2 , 2 , 2 , -1 , -1)$ (not feasible)
	$f(x_o)$	= $-.49966$

SOLUTION:	x^*	= $(-1.717142,1.159571,1.827248,-.7636474,$
	$f(x^*)$	= $.0539498478$ $-.7636390)$
	$r(x^*)$	= $.21E-9$
	$e(x^*)$	= $.11E-5$
	μ	= 0
	$I(x^*)$	= $-$
	u^*_{max}/u^*_{min}	= $.04016/.005223 = 7.69$
	$\lambda^*_{max}/\lambda^*_{min}$	= $.16/.16 = 1.02$

PROBLEM:	83 (Colville No.3)
CLASSIFICATION:	QQR-P1-4
SOURCE:	Colville [20], Dembo [22], Himmelblau [29]
NUMBER OF VARIABLES:	n = 5
NUMBER OF CONSTRAINTS:	$m_1 = 6$, $m-m_1 = 0$, b = 10

OBJECTIVE FUNCTION:

$$f(x) = 5.3578547x_3^2 + .8356891x_1x_5 + 37.293239x_1$$

$$- 40792.141$$

CONSTRAINTS:

$$92 \geq a_1 + a_2x_2x_5 + a_3x_1x_4 - a_4x_3x_5 \geq 0$$

$$20 \geq a_5 + a_6x_2x_5 + a_7x_1x_2 + a_8x_3^2 - 90 \geq 0$$

$$5 \geq a_9 + a_{10}x_3x_5 + a_{11}x_1x_3 + a_{12}x_3x_4 - 20 \geq 0$$

$$78 \leq x_1 \leq 102$$

$$33 \leq x_2 \leq 45$$

$$27 \leq x_i \leq 45 \quad , \quad i=3,4,5 \qquad a_i : \text{ cf. Appendix A}$$

START:

$$x_0 = (78 , 33 , 27 , 27 , 27) \quad \text{(not feasible)}$$
$$f(x_0) = -32217$$

SOLUTION:

$$x^* = (78,33,29.99526,45,36.77581)$$
$$f(x^*) = -30665.53867$$
$$r(x^*) = 0$$
$$e(x^*) = 0$$
$$\mu = 5$$
$$I(x^*) = (3 , 4 , 7 , 8 , 15)$$
$$u^*_{max}/u^*_{min} = 809.4/26.64 = 30.4$$
$$\lambda^*_{max}/\lambda^*_{min} = -$$

PROBLEM:	84
CLASSIFICATION:	QQR-P1-5
SOURCE:	Betts [8], Box [11,12], Himmelblau [29]

NUMBER OF VARIABLES: $n = 5$

NUMBER OF CONSTRAINTS: $m_1 = 6$, $m-m_1 = 0$, $b = 10$

OBJECTIVE FUNCTION:

$$f(x) = -a_1 - a_2 x_1 - a_3 x_1 x_2 - a_4 x_1 x_3 - a_5 x_1 x_4$$
$$-a_6 x_1 x_5$$

CONSTRAINTS:

$$294000 \geq a_7 x_1 + a_8 x_1 x_2 + a_9 x_1 x_3 + a_{10} x_1 x_4 + a_{11} x_1 x_5 \geq 0$$

$$294000 \geq a_{12} x_1 + a_{13} x_1 x_2 + a_{14} x_1 x_3 + a_{15} x_1 x_4 + a_{16} x_1 x_5 \geq 0$$

$$277200 \geq a_{17} x_1 + a_{18} x_1 x_2 + a_{19} x_1 x_3 + a_{20} x_1 x_4 + a_{21} x_1 x_5 \geq 0$$

$$0 \leq x_1 \leq 1000$$

$$1.2 \leq x_2 \leq 2.4$$

$$20 \leq x_3 \leq 60$$

$$9 \leq x_4 \leq 9.3$$

$$6.5 \leq x_5 \leq 7 \qquad a_i : \text{cf. Appendix A}$$

START: x_0 = (2.52 , 2 , 37.5 , 9.25 , 6.8)

$f(x_0)$ = -2351243.5 (feasible)

SOLUTION: x^* = (4.53743097 , 2.4 , 60 , 9.3 , 7)

$f(x^*)$ = -5280335.133

$r(x^*)$ = 0

$e(x^*)$ = 0

μ = 5

$I(x^*)$ = (6 , 13 , 14 , 15 , 16)

u^*_{max}/u^*_{min} = .7168E6/.1914E2 = .37E5

$\lambda^*_{max}/\lambda^*_{min}$ = -

PROBLEM:	85
CLASSIFICATION:	GGI-P1-2
SOURCE:	Barness [2], Caroll [17], Himmelblau [29]
NUMBER OF VARIABLES:	$n = 5$

NUMBER OF CONSTRAINTS: $m_1 = 38(3)$, $m-m_1 = 0$, $b = 10$

OBJECTIVE FUNCTION:

$$f(x) = -5.843E-7y_{17}(x) + 1.17E-4y_{14}(x) + 2.358E-5y_{13}(x)$$

$$+ 1.502E-6y_{16}(x) + .0321y_{12}(x) + .00423y_5(x)$$

$$+ 1.E-4c_{15}(x)/c_{16}(x) + 37.48y_2(x)/c_{12}(x) - .1365$$

CONSTRAINTS:

$1.5x_2 - x_3 \geq 0$ ..... $704.4148 \leq x_1 \leq 906.3855$

$y_1(x) - 213.1 \geq 0$ ..... $68.6 \leq x_2 \leq 288.88$

$405.23 - y_1(x) \geq 0$ ..... $0 \leq x_3 \leq 134.75$

$y_{j-2}(x) - a_{j-2} \geq 0$, $j=4,\ldots,19$ ..... $193 \leq x_4 \leq 287.0966$

$b_{j-18} - y_{j-18}(x) \geq 0$, $j=20,\ldots,35$ ..... $25 \leq x_5 \leq 84.1988$

$y_4(x) - .28/.72y_5(x) \geq 0$

$21 - 3496y_2(x)/c_{12}(x) \geq 0$

$62212/c_{17}(x) - 110.6 - y_1(x) \geq 0$

$y_j(x)$, $c_j(x)$, a_j , b_j : cf. Appendix A

START: x_0 = (900 , 80 , 115 , 267 , 27)

$f(x_0)$ = -.939 (feasible)

SOLUTION: x^* = (705.1803,68.60005,102.90001,282.324999,

$f(x^*)$ = -1.90513375 ..... 37.5850413)

$r(x^*)$ = 0

$e(x^*)$ = 0

μ = 0

$I(x^*)$ = -

u^*_{max}/u^*_{min} = -

$\lambda^*_{max}/\lambda^*_{min}$ = .56E-3/.46E-6 = .12E4

PROBLEM:	86 (Colville No.1)

CLASSIFICATION:	PLR-P1-1

SOURCE: Colville [20], Himmelblau [29], Murthagh, Sargent [47]

NUMBER OF VARIABLES: $n = 5$

NUMBER OF CONSTRAINTS: $m_1 = 10(10)$, $m-m_1 = 0$, $b = 5$

OBJECTIVE FUNCTION:

$$f(x) = \sum_{j=1}^{5} e_j x_j + \sum_{i=1}^{5} \sum_{j=1}^{5} c_{ij} x_i x_j + \sum_{j=1}^{5} d_j x_j^3$$

CONSTRAINTS:

$$\sum_{j=1}^{5} a_{ij} x_j - b_i \geq 0 \quad , \quad i=1,\ldots,10$$

$$0 \leq x_i \quad , \quad i=1,\ldots,5$$

$a_{ij}, b_i, c_{ij}, d_j, e_j$: cf. Appendix A

START:	x_o	$= (0 , 0 , 0 , 0 , 1)$	(feasible)
	$f(x_o)$	$= 20$	

SOLUTION:	x^*	$= (.3,.33346761,.4,.42831010,.22396487)$
	$f(x^*)$	$= -32.34867897$
	$r(x^*)$	$= .70E-9$
	$e(x^*)$	$= .94E-8$
	μ	$= 4$
	$I(x^*)$	$= (3 , 5 , 6 , 9)$
	u^*_{max}/u^*_{min}	$= 11.84/.1039 = 113.9$
	$\lambda^*_{max}/\lambda^*_{min}$	$= 68.1/68.1 = 1$

PROBLEM:	87 (Colville No.6)
CLASSIFICATION:	GGI-P1-3
SOURCE:	Colville [20], Himmelblau [29]

NUMBER OF VARIABLES: n = 6

NUMBER OF CONSTRAINTS: $m_1 = 0$, $m-m_1 = 4$, $b = 12$

OBJECTIVE FUNCTION:

$$f(x) = f_1(x) + f_2(x)$$

$$f_1(x) = \begin{cases} 30x_1 , & 0 \leq x_1 < 300 \\ 31x_1 , & 300 \leq x_1 \leq 400 \end{cases} \qquad f_2(x) = \begin{cases} 28x_2 , & 0 \leq x_2 < 100 \\ 29x_2 , & 100 \leq x_2 < 200 \\ 30x_2 , & 200 \leq x_2 \leq 1000 \end{cases}$$

CONSTRAINTS:

$$300 - x_1 - \frac{1}{a} x_3 x_4 \cos(b - x_6) + \frac{c}{a} dx_3^2 = 0 \quad (a = 131.078)$$

$$- x_2 - \frac{1}{a} x_3 x_4 \cos(b + x_6) + \frac{c}{a} dx_4^2 = 0 \qquad (b = 1.48577)$$

$$- x_5 - \frac{1}{a} x_3 x_4 \sin(b + x_6) + \frac{c}{a} ex_4^2 = 0 \qquad (c = .90798)$$

$$\qquad\qquad\qquad\qquad\qquad\qquad\qquad (d = \cos 1.47588)$$

$$200 - \frac{1}{a} x_3 x_4 \sin(b - x_6) + \frac{c}{a} ex_3^2 = 0 \qquad (e = \sin 1.47588)$$

$$0 \leq x_1 \leq 400 \qquad 340 \leq x_3 \leq 420 \qquad -1000 \leq x_5 \leq 10000$$

$$0 \leq x_2 \leq 1000 \qquad 340 \leq x_4 \leq 420 \qquad 0 \leq x_6 \leq .5236$$

START:	x_o	=	(390,1000,419.5,340.5,198.175,.5)
	$f(x_o)$	=	42090 (not feasible)

SOLUTION:	x^*	=	(107.8119,196.3186,373.8307,420,
			213.0713,.1532920)
	$f(x^*)$	=	8927.5977
	$r(x^*)$	=	.10E-6
	$e(x^*)$	=	.74E-6
	μ	=	1
	$I(x^*)$	=	(10)
	u^*_{max}/u^*_{min}	=	30/.23E-6 = .13E9
	$\lambda^*_{max}/\lambda^*_{min}$	=	.017/.017 = 1

PROBLEM:	88 - 92 (time-optimal heat conduction)
CLASSIFICATION:	QGR-P1-(1,...,5)
SOURCE:	Schittkowski [54]
NUMBER OF VARIABLES:	$n = 2,...,6$
NUMBER OF CONSTRAINTS:	$m_1 = 1$, $m-m_1 = 0$, $b = 0$

OBJECTIVE FUNCTION:

$$f(x) = \sum_{i=1}^{n} x_i^2$$

CONSTRAINTS:

$$\epsilon^2 - h(x) \geq 0$$

$$\epsilon = .01$$

$$h(x) = \int_0^1 (\sum_{i=1}^{30} \alpha_j(s)\rho_j(x) - k_0(s))^2 ds$$

$$\alpha_j(s) = \mu_j^2 A_j \cos(\mu_j s)$$

$$\rho_j(x) = -\mu_j^{-2}(\exp(-\mu_j^2 \sum_{i=1}^{n} x_i^2) - 2\exp(-\mu_j^2 \sum_{i=2}^{n} x_i^2) + \ldots$$

$$+ (-1)^{n-1} 2\exp(-\mu_j^2 x_n^2 + (-1)^n)$$

$$k_0(s) = .5(1 - s^2)$$

$$A_j = 2\sin\mu_j / (\mu_j + \sin\mu_j \cos\mu_j) , \mu_j : \mu \tan\mu = 1$$

START:	x_0	$= (.5 , -.5 , \ldots , (-1)^{n+1}.5)$
	$f(x_0)$	$= .25n$ (not feasible)

SOLUTION:	x^*	$=$ (cf. Appendix A)
	$f(x^*)$	$= 1.36265681$
	$r(x^*)$	$\leq .30E-10$ (cf. Appendix A)
	$e(x^*)$	$\leq .16E-2$ (cf. Appendix A)
	μ	$= 1$
	$I(x^*)$	$= (1)$
	u^*_{max}/u^*_{min}	$= 1059.8/1059.8 = 1$
	$\lambda^*_{max}/\lambda^*_{min}$	$\leq .11E9$ (cf. Appendix A)

PROBLEM:	93 (transformer design)
CLASSIFICATION:	PPR-P1-6
SOURCE:	Bartholomew-Biggs [4]
NUMBER OF VARIABLES:	n = 6
NUMBER OF CONSTRAINTS:	$m_1 = 2$, $m-m_1 = 0$, $b = 6$

OBJECTIVE FUNCTION:

$$f(x) = .0204x_1x_4(x_1 + x_2 + x_3) + .0187x_2x_3(x_1 + 1.57x_2 + x_4)$$
$$+ .0607x_1x_4x_5^2(x_1 + x_2 + x_3)$$
$$+ .0437x_2x_3x_6^2(x_1 + 1.57x_2 + x_4)$$

CONSTRAINTS:

$$.001x_1x_2x_3x_4x_5x_6 - 2.07 \geq 0$$

$$1 - .00062x_1x_4x_5^2(x_1 + x_2 + x_3)$$
$$- .00058x_2x_3x_6^2(x_1 + 1.57x_2 + x_4) \geq 0$$

$$0 \leq x_i , \quad i=1,\ldots,6$$

START:	x_0	=	(5.54,4.4,12.02,11.82,.702,.852)
	$f(x_0)$	=	137.066 (feasible)

SOLUTION:	x^*	=	(5.332666,4.656744,10.43299,12.08230,
			.7526074,.87865084)
	$f(x^*)$	=	135.075961
	$r(x^*)$	=	.77E-7
	$e(x^*)$	=	.77E-6
	μ	=	2
	$I(x^*)$	=	(1 , 2)
	u^*_{max}/u^*_{min}	=	71.46/62.15 = 1.15
	$\lambda^*_{max}/\lambda^*_{min}$	=	118.9/.21 = 562.9

PROBLEM:	95 - 98
CLASSIFICATION:	LQR-P1-(1,...,4)
SOURCE:	Himmelblau [29], Holzman [32]

NUMBER OF VARIABLES: $n = 6$

NUMBER OF CONSTRAINTS: $m_1 = 4$, $m-m_1 = 0$, $b = 12$

OBJECTIVE FUNCTION:

$$f(x) = 4.3x_1 + 31.8x_2 + 63.3x_3 + 15.8x_4 + 68.5x_5 + 4.7x_6$$

CONSTRAINTS:

$$17.1x_1 + 38.2x_2 + 204.2x_3 + 212.3x_4 + 623.4x_5 + 1495.5x_6$$
$$- 169x_1x_3 - 3580x_3x_5 - 3810x_4x_5 - 18500x_4x_6 - 24300x_5x_6 \geq b_1$$

$$17.9x_1 + 36.8x_2 + 113.9x_3 + 169.7x_4 + 337.8x_5 + 1385.2x_6$$
$$- 139x_1x_3 - 2450x_4x_5 - 16600x_4x_6 - 17200x_5x_6 \geq b_2$$

$$-273x_2 - 70x_4 - 819x_5 + 26000x_4x_5 \geq b_3$$

$$159.9x_1 - 311x_2 + 587x_4 + 391x_5 + 2198x_6 - 14000x_1x_6 \geq b_4$$

$0 \leq x_1 \leq .31$, $0 \leq x_3 \leq .068$, $0 \leq x_5 \leq .028$

$0 \leq x_2 \leq .046$, $0 \leq x_4 \leq .042$, $0 \leq x_6 \leq .0134$

4 different data vectors b : cf. Appendix A

START: $x_0 = (0 , 0 , 0 , 0 , 0 , 0)$ (not feasible)

$f(x_0) = 0$

SOLUTION: $x^* = (0,0,0,0,0,.0033233033)$ (95,96)

$= (.2685649,0,0,0,.028,.0134)$ (97,98)

$f(x^*) = .015619514$ (95,96)   3.1358091 (97,98)

$r(x^*) = .21E-9$ (95,96)   0

$e(x^*) = 0$

$\mu = 6$

$I(x^*) = (1,5,6,7,8,9)$ (95,96) (1,6,7,8,15,16)

$u^*_{max}/u^*_{min} = 66.8/.003 = .2E5$ (95,96) $200/.251 = .8E3$

$\lambda^*_{max}/\lambda^*_{min} = -$

PROBLEM:	99
CLASSIFICATION:	GGR-P1-3
SOURCE:	Betts [8]
NUMBER OF VARIABLES:	$n = 7$
NUMBER OF CONSTRAINTS:	$m_1 = 0$, $m-m_1 = 2$, $b = 14$

OBJECTIVE FUNCTION:

$$f(x) = -r_8(x)^2$$

$$r_1(x) = 0 , \quad r_i(x) = a_i(t_i - t_{i-1})\cos x_{i-1} + r_{i-1}(x), \quad i=2,\ldots,8$$

CONSTRAINTS:

$$q_8(x) - 1.E5 = 0$$

$$s_8(x) - 1.E3 = 0$$

$$0 \le x_i \le 1.58 , \quad i=1,\ldots,7$$

$$q_1(x) = s_1(x) = 0$$

$$q_i(x) = .5(t_i - t_{i-1})^2(a_i\sin x_{i-1} - b) + (t_i - t_{i-1})s_{i-1}(x)$$
$$+ q_{i-1}(x)$$

$$s_i(x) = (t_i - t_{i-1})(a_i\sin x_{i-1} - b) + s_{i-1}(x) , \quad i=2,\ldots,8$$

$$a_i, t_i, b : \quad \text{cf. Appendix A}$$

START:	x_0	$= (.5 , .5 , .5 , .5 , .5 , .5 , .5)$
	$f(x_0)$	$= -.7763605E9$ (not feasible)

SOLUTION:	x^*	$= (.5424603, .5290159, .5084506, .4802693,$
		$.4512352, .4091878, .3527847)$
	$f(x^*)$	$= -.831079892E9$
	$r(x^*)$	$= .30E-7$
	$e(x^*)$	$= .31E4 , \quad \|\nabla f(x^*)\| = .32E9$
	μ	$= 0$
	$I(x^*)$	$= -$
	u^*_{max}/u^*_{min}	$= .1934E5/.4194E2 = .46E3$
	$\lambda^*_{max}/\lambda^*_{min}$	$= .50E9/.84E8 = 5.95$

PROBLEM:	100
CLASSIFICATION:	PPR-P1-7
SOURCE:	Asaadi [1], Charalambous [18], Wong [59]
NUMBER OF VARIABLES:	$n = 7$
NUMBER OF CONSTRAINTS:	$m_1 = 4$, $m-m_1 = 0$, $b = 0$

OBJECTIVE FUNCTION:

$$f(x) = (x_1 - 10)^2 + 5(x_2 - 12)^2 + x_3^4 + 3(x_4 - 11)^2$$
$$+ 10x_5^6 + 7x_6^2 + x_7^4 - 4x_6 x_7 - 10x_6 - 8x_7$$

CONSTRAINTS:

$$127 - 2x_1^2 - 3x_2^4 - x_3 - 4x_4^2 - 5x_5 \geq 0$$

$$282 - 7x_1 - 3x_2 - 10x_3^2 - x_4 + x_5 \geq 0$$

$$196 - 23x_1 - x_2^2 - 6x_6^2 + 8x_7 \geq 0$$

$$-4x_1^2 - x_2^2 + 3x_1 x_2 - 2x_3^2 - 5x_6 + 11x_7 \geq 0$$

START:	x_0	$= (1 , 2 , 0 , 4 , 0 , 1 , 1)$
	$f(x_0)$	$= 714$ (feasible)

SOLUTION:	x^*	$= (2.330499, 1.951372, -.4775414, 4.365726,$
		$-.6244870, 1.038131, 1.594227)$
	$f(x^*)$	$= 680.6300573$
	$r(x^*)$	$= .90E-7$
	$e(x^*)$	$= .36E-8$
	μ	$= 2$
	$I(x^*)$	$= (1 , 4)$
	u_{max}^*/u_{min}^*	$= 1.140/.3686 = 3.09$
	$\lambda_{max}^*/\lambda_{min}^*$	$= 46.6/4.34 = 10.7$

PROBLEM:	101 - 103
CLASSIFICATION:	PPR-P1-(8,9,10)
SOURCE:	Beck, Ecker [5], Dembo [22]
NUMBER OF VARIABLES:	n = 7
NUMBER OF CONSTRAINTS:	$m_1 = 6$, $m-m_1 = 0$, b = 14

OBJECTIVE FUNCTION: 101 : a=-.25 , 102 : a=.125 , 103 : a=.5

$$f(x) = 10x_1 x_2^{-1} x_4^2 x_6^{-3} x_7^a + 15x_1^{-1} x_2^{-2} x_3 x_4 x_5^{-1} x_7^{-.5}$$
$$+ 20x_1^{-2} x_2 x_4^{-1} x_5^{-2} x_6 + 25x_1^2 x_2^2 x_3^{-1} x_5^{.5} x_6^{-2} x_7$$

CONSTRAINTS:

$$1 - .5x_1^{.5} x_3^{-1} x_6^{-2} x_7 - .7x_1^3 x_2 x_3^{-2} x_6 x_7^{.5}$$
$$- .2x_2^{-1} x_3 x_4^{-.5} x_6^{2/3} x_7^{1/4} \geq 0$$

$$1 - 1.3x_1^{-.5} x_2 x_3^{-1} x_5^{-1} x_6 - .8x_3 x_4^{-1} x_5^{-1} x_6^2$$
$$- 3.1x_1^{-1} x_2^{.5} x_4^{-2} x_5^{-1} x_6^{1/3} \geq 0$$

$$1 - 2x_1 x_3^{-1.5} x_5 x_6^{-1} x_7^{4/3} - .1x_2 x_3^{-.5} x_5 x_6^{-1} x_7^{-.5}$$
$$- x_1^{-1} x_2 x_3^{.5} x_5 - .65x_2^{-2} x_3 x_5 x_6^{-1} x_7 \geq 0$$

$$1 - .2x_1^{-2} x_2 x_4^{-1} x_5^{.5} x_7^{1/3} - .3x_1^{.5} x_2^2 x_3 x_4^{1/3} x_7^{1/4} x_5^{-2/3}$$
$$- .4x_1^{-3} x_2^{-2} x_3 x_5 x_7^{3/4} - .5x_3^{-2} x_4 x_7^{.5} \geq 0$$

$$100 \leq f(x) \leq 3000 , .1 \leq x_1 \leq 10 , i=1,..,6, .01 \leq x_7 \leq 10$$

START:	x_o	= (6 , 6 , 6 , 6 , 6 , 6 , 6) (not feas.)
	$f(x_o)$	= 2205.868 , 2206.889 , 2208.886

SOLUTION: x* = (cf. Appendix A)

		101	102	103
f(x*)	=	1809.76476	911.880571	543.667958
r(x*)	=	.10E-10	.27E-10	.61E-11
e(x*)	=	.59E-6	.14E-6	.92E-7
μ	=	3	3	4
I(x*)	=	(2,3,13)	(1,2,3)	(1,2,3,4)
u^*_{max}/u^*_{min}	=	4567/.81E-6	2173/21.13	1287/38.71
$\lambda^*_{max}/\lambda^*_{min}$	=	.43E4/.51E2=85	.23E4/.32E2=73	.46E3/.88E2=5.2

PROBLEM:	104 (optimal reactor design)
CLASSIFICATION:	PPR-P1-11
SOURCE:	Dembo [22], Rijckaert [53]
NUMBER OF VARIABLES:	$n = 8$

NUMBER OF CONSTRAINTS: $m_1 = 6$, $m-m_1 = 0$, $b = 16$

OBJECTIVE FUNCTION:

$$f(x) = .4x_1^{.67}x_7^{-.67} + .4x_2^{.67}x_8^{-.67} + 10 - x_1 - x_2$$

CONSTRAINTS:

$$1 - .0588x_5x_7 - .1x_1 \geq 0$$

$$1 - .0588x_6x_8 - .1x_1 - .1x_2 \geq 0$$

$$1 - 4x_3x_5^{-1} - 2x_3^{-.71}x_5^{-1} - .0588x_3^{-1.3}x_7 \geq 0$$

$$1 - 4x_4x_6^{-1} - 2x_4^{-.71}x_6^{-1} - .0588x_4^{-1.3}x_8 \geq 0$$

$$1 \leq f(x) \leq 4.2$$

$$.1 \leq x_i \leq 10 \quad , \quad i=1,\ldots,8$$

START:	x_o	$=$	$(6,3,.4,.2,6,6,1,.5)$ (not feasible)
	$f(x_o)$	$=$	3.65

SOLUTION:	x^*	$=$	$(6.465114,2.232709,.6673975,.5957564,$
			$5.932676,5.527235,1.013322,.4006682)$
	$f(x^*)$	$=$	3.9511634396
	$r(x^*)$	$=$	$.58E-10$
	$e(x^*)$	$=$	$.31E-10$
	μ	$=$	4
	$I(x^*)$	$=$	$(1 , 2 , 3 , 4)$
	u^*_{max}/u^*_{min}	$=$	$6.206/.8472 = 7.32$
	$\lambda^*_{max}/\lambda^*_{min}$	$=$	$1.87/.043 = 43.2$

PROBLEM:	105 (maximum-likelihood estimation)
CLASSIFICATION:	GLR-P1-2
SOURCE:	Bracken, McCormick [13]

NUMBER OF VARIABLES: $n = 8$

NUMBER OF CONSTRAINTS: $m_1 = 1(1)$, $m-m_1 = 0$, $b = 16$

OBJECTIVE FUNCTION:

$$f(x) = -\sum_{i=1}^{235} \ln((a_i(x) + b_i(x) + c_i(x))/\sqrt{2\pi})$$

$$a_i(x) = x_1/x_6 \exp(-(y_i - x_3)^2/(2x_6^2))$$

$$b_i(x) = x_2/x_7 \exp(-(y_i - x_4)^2/(2x_7^2)) \quad , \quad i=1,\ldots,235$$

$$c_i(x) = (1 - x_2 - x_1)/x_8 \exp(-(y_i - x_5)^2/(2x_8^2))$$

y_i : cf. Appendix A

CONSTRAINTS:

$$1 - x_1 - x_2 \geq 0$$

$.001 \leq x_i \leq .499$, $i=1,2$ $\qquad 100 \leq x_3 \leq 180$

$130 \leq x_4 \leq 210 \qquad 170 \leq x_5 \leq 240 \qquad 5 \leq x_i \leq 25$, $i=6,7,8$

START:	x_0	=	$(.1,.2,100,125,175,11.2,13.2,15.8)$	
	$f(x_0)$	=	1297.6693	(feasible)

SOLUTION:	x^*	=	$(.4128928,.4033526,131.2613,164.3135,$
			$217.4222,12.28018,15.77170,20.74682)$
	$f(x^*)$	=	1138.416240
	$r(x^*)$	=	0
	$e(x^*)$	=	0
	μ	=	0
	$I(x^*)$	=	-
	u^*_{max}/u^*_{min}	=	-
	$\lambda^*_{max}/\lambda^*_{min}$	=	$.26E4/.28E-2 = .92E6$

PROBLEM:	106 (heat exchanger design)
CLASSIFICATION:	LQR-P1-5
SOURCE:	Avriel, Williams [2], Dembo [22]
NUMBER OF VARIABLES:	n = 8
NUMBER OF CONSTRAINTS:	$m_1 = 6(3)$, $m-m_1 = 0$, b = 16

OBJECTIVE FUNCTION:

$$f(x) = x_1 + x_2 + x_3$$

CONSTRAINTS:

$$1 - .0025(x_4 + x_6) \geq 0$$

$$1 - .0025(x_5 + x_7 - x_4) \geq 0$$

$$1 - .01(x_8 - x_5) \geq 0$$

$$x_1 x_6 - 833.33252 x_4 - 100 x_1 + 83333.333 \geq 0$$

$$x_2 x_7 - 1250 x_5 - x_2 x_4 + 1250 x_4 \geq 0$$

$$x_3 x_8 - 1250000 - x_3 x_5 + 2500 x_5 \geq 0$$

$$100 \leq x_1 \leq 10000$$

$$1000 \leq x_i \leq 10000 , \quad i=2,3$$

$$10 \leq x_i \leq 1000 , \quad i=4,\ldots,8$$

START:	x_o	=	(5000,5000,5000,200,350,150,225,425)
	$f(x_o)$	=	15000 (not feasible)

SOLUTION:	x^*	=	(579.3167,1359.943,5110.071,182,0174,
			295.5985,217.9799,286.4162,395,5979)
	$f(x^*)$	=	7049.330923
	$r(x^*)$	=	0
	$e(x^*)$	=	.19E-4
	μ	=	6
	$I(x^*)$	=	(1 , 2 , 3 , 4 , 5 , 6)
	u^*_{max}/u^*_{min}	=	5210/.00848 = .61E6
	$\lambda^*_{max}/\lambda^*_{min}$	=	.81E-3/.38E-3 = 2.11

PROBLEM:	107 (static power scheduling)
CLASSIFICATION:	PGR-P1-4
SOURCE:	Bartholomew-Biggs [4]
NUMBER OF VARIABLES:	n = 9
NUMBER OF CONSTRAINTS:	$m_1 = 0$, $m-m_1 = 6$, b = 8

OBJECTIVE FUNCTION:

$$f(x) = 3000x_1 + 1000x_1^3 + 2000x_2 + 666.667x_2^3$$

CONSTRAINTS:

$$.4 - x_1 + 2cx_5^2 - x_5x_6(dy_1 + cy_2) - x_5x_7(dy_3 + cy_4) = 0$$

$$.4 - x_2 + 2cx_6^2 + x_5x_6(dy_1 - cy_2) + x_6x_7(dy_5 - cy_6) = 0$$

$$.8 + 2cx_7^2 + x_5x_7(dy_3 - cy_4) - x_6x_7(dy_5 + cy_6) = 0$$

$$.2 - x_3 + 2dx_5^2 + x_5x_6(cy_1 - dy_2) + x_5x_7(cy_3 - dy_4) = 0$$

$$.2 - x_4 + 2dx_6^2 - x_5x_6(cy_1 + dy_2) - x_6x_7(cy_5 + dy_6) = 0$$

$$-.337 + 2dx_7^2 - x_5x_7(cy_3 + dy_4) + x_6x_7(cy_5 - dy_6) = 0$$

$$0 \le x_i , i=1,2 , .90909 \le x_i \le 1.0909 , i=5,6,7$$

$$y_1 = \sin x_8 , y_2 = \cos x_8 , y_3 = \sin x_9$$

$$y_4 = \cos x_9 , y_5 = \sin(x_8-x_9) , y_6 = \cos(x_8-x_9)$$

$$c = (48.4/50.176)\sin.25 , d = (48.4/50.176)\cos.25$$

START:	x_0	=	(.8,.8,.2,.2,1.0454,1.0454,0,0)
	$f(x_0)$	=	4853.3335 (not feasible)

SOLUTION:	x*	=	(.6670095,1.022388,.2282879,.1848217,
			1.090900,1.090900,1.069036,.1066126,
	f(x*)	=	5055.011803 -.3387867)
	r(x*)	=	.18E-9
	e(x*)	=	0
	μ	=	3
	I(x*)	=	(6 , 7 , 8)
	u^*_{max}/u^*_{min}	=	5208/0
	$\lambda^*_{max}/\lambda^*_{min}$	=	-

PROBLEM:	108

CLASSIFICATION:	QQR-P1-6

SOURCE:	Himmelblau [29], Pearson [49]

NUMBER OF VARIABLES:	$n = 9$

NUMBER OF CONSTRAINTS: $m_1 = 13$, $m-m_1 = 0$, $b = 1$

OBJECTIVE FUNCTION:

$$f(x) = -.5(x_1 x_4 - x_2 x_3 + x_3 x_9 - x_5 x_9 + x_5 x_8 - x_6 x_7)$$

CONSTRAINTS:

$$1 - x_3^2 - x_4^2 \geq 0 \qquad\qquad 1 - x_9^2 \geq 0$$

$$1 - x_5^2 - x_6^2 \geq 0 \qquad\qquad 1 - x_1^2 - (x_2 - x_9)^2 \geq 0$$

$$1 - (x_1 - x_5)^2 - (x_2 - x_6)^2 \geq 0$$

$$1 - (x_1 - x_7)^2 - (x_2 - x_8)^2 \geq 0$$

$$1 - (x_3 - x_5)^2 - (x_4 - x_6)^2 \geq 0$$

$$1 - (x_3 - x_7)^2 - (x_4 - x_8)^2 \geq 0$$

$$1 - x_7^2 - (x_8 - x_9)^2 \geq 0 \qquad x_1 x_4 - x_2 x_3 \geq 0$$

$$x_3 x_9 \geq 0 \qquad\qquad -x_5 x_9 \geq 0$$

$$x_5 x_8 - x_6 x_7 \geq 0 \qquad\qquad 0 \leq x_9$$

START: $x_0 = (1,1,1,1,1,1,1,1,1)$ (not feasible)

$f(x_0) = 0$

SOLUTION: $x^* = (.8841292,.4672425,.03742076,.9992996,$

$.8841292,.4672424,.03742076,.9992996,$

$.26E-19)$

$f(x^*) = -.8660254038$

$r(x^*) = .39E-9 \qquad e(x^*) = .33E-11$

$u = 9 \qquad I(x^*) = (1,3,4,6,7,9,11,$

$\qquad\qquad\qquad\qquad\qquad\qquad 12,14)$

$u^*_{max}/u^*_{min} = .1443/0$

$\lambda^*_{max}/\lambda^*_{min} = -$

PROBLEM:	109
CLASSIFICATION:	PGR-P1-5
SOURCE:	Beuneu [9]
NUMBER OF VARIABLES:	n = 9
NUMBER OF CONSTRAINTS:	$m_1 = 4(2)$, $m - m_1 = 6$, b = 16

OBJECTIVE FUNCTION:

$$f(x) = 3x_1 + 1.E-6x_1^3 + 2x_2 + .522074E-6x_2^3$$

CONSTRAINTS:

$$x_4 - x_3 + .55 \geq 0 \qquad x_3 - x_4 + .55 \geq 0$$

$$2250000 - x_1^2 - x_8^2 \geq 0 \qquad 2250000 - x_2^2 - x_9^2 \geq 0$$

$$x_5x_6\sin(-x_3 - \tfrac{1}{4}) + x_5x_7\sin(-x_4 - \tfrac{1}{4}) + 2bx_5^2 - ax_1 + 400a = 0$$

$$x_5x_6\sin(x_3 - \tfrac{1}{4}) + x_6x_7\sin(x_3 - x_4 - \tfrac{1}{4}) + 2bx_6^2 - ax_2 + 400a = 0$$

$$x_5x_7\sin(x_4 - \tfrac{1}{4}) + x_6x_7\sin(x_4 - x_3 - \tfrac{1}{4}) + 2bx_7^2 + 881.779a = 0$$

$$ax_8 + x_5x_6\cos(-x_3 - \tfrac{1}{4}) + x_5x_7\cos(-x_4 - \tfrac{1}{4}) - 200a$$
$$- 2cx_5^2 + .7533E-3ax_5^2 = 0$$

$$ax_9 + x_5x_6\cos(x_3 - \tfrac{1}{4}) + x_6x_7\cos(x_3 - x_4 - \tfrac{1}{4}) - 2cx_6^2$$
$$+ .7533E-3ax_6^2 - 200a = 0$$

$$x_5x_7\cos(x_4 - \tfrac{1}{4}) + x_6x_7\cos(x_4 - x_3 - \tfrac{1}{4}) - 2cx_7^2 + 22.938a$$
$$+ .7533E-3ax_7^2 = 0$$

$$0 \leq x_i , i=1,2 \qquad -.55 \leq x_i \leq .55 , i=3,4$$

$$196 \leq x_i \leq 252 , i=5,6,7 \qquad -400 \leq x_i \leq 800 , i=8,9$$

$$a = 50.176 , \quad b = \sin.25 , \quad c = \cos.25$$

START:	$x_0 = (0,...,0)$	$f(x_0) = 0$ (not feasible)

SOLUTION:

$$f(x^*) = 5362.06928$$

x^*	= (cf. Appendix A)	
$r(x^*)$	= .36E-7	$e(x^*) = 0$
μ	= 3	$I(x^*) = (1 , 16 , 17)$

$$u^*_{max}/u^*_{min} = 12.53/.13E-10 = .95E12$$

$$\lambda^*_{max}/\lambda^*_{min} = -$$

PROBLEM:	110
CLASSIFICATION:	GBR-P1-1
SOURCE:	Himmelblau [29], Paviani [48]
NUMBER OF VARIABLES:	n = 10
NUMBER OF CONSTRAINTS:	$m_1 = 0$, $m-m_1 = 0$, $b = 20$

OBJECTIVE FUNCTION:

$$f(x) = \sum_{i=1}^{10} [(\ln(x_i - 2))^2 + (\ln(10 - x_i))^2 - (\prod_{i=1}^{10} x_i)^{.2}$$

CONSTRAINTS:

$$2.001 \leq x_i \leq 9.999 \quad , \quad i=1,\ldots,10$$

START:	x_0	=	(9,...,9)	(feasible)
	$f(x_0)$	=	-43.134337	

SOLUTION:	x*	=	(9.35025655,...,9.35025655)
	f(x*)	=	-45.77846971
	r(x*)	=	0
	e(x*)	=	0
	μ	=	0
	I(x*)	=	-
	u^*_{max}/u^*_{min}	=	-
	$\lambda^*_{max}/\lambda^*_{min}$	=	6.92/6.52 = 1.06

PROBLEM:	111

CLASSIFICATION:	GGR-P1-4

SOURCE:	Bracken, McCormick [13], Himmelblau [29], White [58]

NUMBER OF VARIABLES:	$n = 10$

NUMBER OF CONSTRAINTS: $m_1 = 0$, $m-m_1 = 3$, $b = 20$

OBJECTIVE FUNCTION:

$$f(x) = \sum_{j=1}^{10} \exp(x_j)(c_j + x_j - \ln(\sum_{k=1}^{10} \exp(x_k)))$$

c_j : cf. Appendix A

CONSTRAINTS:

$$\exp(x_1) + 2\exp(x_2) + 2\exp(x_3) + \exp(x_6) + \exp(x_{10}) - 2 = 0$$

$$\exp(x_4) + 2\exp(x_5) + \exp(x_6) + \exp(x_7) - 1 = 0$$

$$\exp(x_3) + \exp(x_7) + \exp(x_8) + 2\exp(x_9) + \exp(x_{10}) - 1 = 0$$

$$-100 \leq x_i \leq 100 \quad , \quad i=1,\ldots,10$$

START: x_0 $= (-2.3 , \ldots ,-2.3)$ (not feasible)

          $f(x_0)$ $= -21.015$

SOLUTION: x^* $= (-3.201212,-1.912060,-.2444413,-6.537489,$

                     $-.7231524,-7.267738,-3.596711,-4.017769,$

                     $-3.287462,-2.335582)$

          $f(x^*)$ $= -47.76109026$

          $r(x^*)$ $= .34E-9$ $e(x^*) = .14E-3$

          u $= 0$ $I(x^*) = -$

          $u^*_{max}/u^*_{min} = 15.22/9.785 = 1.56$

          $\lambda^*_{max}/\lambda^*_{min} = .11/.70E-3 = 160.1$

PROBLEM:	112 (chemical equilibrium)

CLASSIFICATION: GLR-P1-3

SOURCE: Bracken, McCormick [13], Himmelblau [29], White [58]

NUMBER OF VARIABLES: $n = 10$

NUMBER OF CONSTRAINTS: $m_1 = 0$, $m-m_1 = 3(3)$, $b = 10$

OBJECTIVE FUNCTION:

$$f(x) = \sum_{j=1}^{10} x_j (c_j + \ln \frac{x_j}{x_1 + \ldots + x_{10}})$$

c_j : cf. Appendix A

CONSTRAINTS:

$$x_1 + 2x_2 + 2x_3 + x_6 + x_{10} - 2 = 0$$

$$x_4 + 2x_5 + x_6 + x_7 - 1 = 0$$

$$x_3 + x_7 + x_8 + 2x_9 + x_{10} = 0$$

$$1.E-6 \leq x_i , \quad i=1,\ldots,10$$

START: $x_o = (.1 , \ldots , .1)$ (not feasible)

$f(x_o) = -20.961$

SOLUTION: $x^* = (.01773548,.08200180,.8825646,.7233256E-3,$

$.4907851,.4335469E-3,.01727298,$

$.007765639,.01984929,.05269826)$

$f(x^*) = -47.707579$

$r(x^*) = .23E-7 \qquad e(x^*) = .43E-6$

$\mu = 2 \qquad I(x^*) = (4 , 6)$

$u^*_{max}/u^*_{min} = 15.02/.262E-3 = .57E5$

$\lambda^*_{max}/\lambda^*_{min} = 191/8.98 = 21.3$

PROBLEM:	113 (Wong No.2)

CLASSIFICATION:	QQR-P1-7

SOURCE:	Asaadi [1], Charalambous [18], Wong [59]

NUMBER OF VARIABLES: $n = 10$

NUMBER OF CONSTRAINTS: $m_1 = 8(3)$, $m-m_1 = 0$, $b = 0$

OBJECTIVE FUNCTION:

$$f(x) = x_1^2 + x_2^2 + x_1 x_2 - 14x_1 - 16x_2 + (x_3 - 10)^2$$
$$+ 4(x_4 - 5)^2 + (x_5 - 3)^2 + 2(x_6 - 1)^2 + 5x_7^2$$
$$+ 7(x_8 - 11)^2 + 2(x_9 - 10)^2 + (x_{10} - 7)^2 + 45$$

CONSTRAINTS:

$$105 - 4x_1 - 5x_2 + 3x_7 - 9x_8 \geq 0$$
$$-10x_1 + 8x_2 + 17x_7 - 2x_8 \geq 0$$
$$8x_1 - 2x_2 - 5x_9 + 2x_{10} + 12 \geq 0$$
$$-3(x_1 - 2)^2 - 4(x_2 - 3)^2 - 2x_3^2 + 7x_4 + 120 \geq 0$$
$$-5x_1^2 - 8x_2 - (x_3 - 6)^2 + 2x_4 + 40 \geq 0$$
$$-.5(x_1 - 8)^2 - 2(x_2 - 4)^2 - 3x_5^2 + x_6 + 30 \geq 0$$
$$-x_1^2 - 2(x_2 - 2)^2 + 2x_1 x_2 - 14x_5 + 6x_6 \geq 0$$
$$3x_1 - 6x_2 - 12(x_9 - 8)^2 + 7x_{10} \geq 0$$

START:	x_o	=	(2,3,5,5,1,2,7,3,6,10)	(feasible)
	$f(x_o)$	=	753	

SOLUTION:	x*	=	(2.171996,2.363683,8.773926,5.095984,
			.9906548,1.430574,1.321644,9.828726,
			8.280092,8.375927)

$f(x^*)$ = 24.3062091

$r(x^*)$ = .12E-8 $e(x^*)$ = .46E-9

μ = 6 $I(x^*)$ = (1,2,3,4,5,7)

u^*_{max}/u^*_{min} = 1.717/.02055 = 83.5

$\lambda^*_{max}/\lambda^*_{min}$ = 7.79/2.24 = 3.48

PROBLEM:	114 (alkylation process)
CLASSIFICATION:	QGR-P1-6
SOURCE:	Bracken, McCormick [13]
NUMBER OF VARIABLES:	n = 10
NUMBER OF CONSTRAINTS:	m_1 = 8(4) , $m - m_1$ = 3(1) , b = 20

OBJECTIVE FUNCTION:

$$f(x) = 5.04x_1 + .035x_2 + 10x_3 + 3.36x_5 - .063x_4x_7$$

CONSTRAINTS:

$$g_1(x) = 35.82 - .222x_{10} - bx_9 \geq 0$$

$$g_2(x) = -133 + 3x_7 - ax_{10} \geq 0$$

$$g_3(x) = -g_1(x) + x_9(1/b - b) \geq 0$$

$$g_4(x) = -g_2(x) + (1/a - a)x_{10} \geq 0$$

$$g_5(x) = 1.12x_1 + .13167x_1x_8 - .00667x_1x_8^2 - ax_4 \geq 0$$

$$g_6(x) = 57.425 + 1.098x_8 - .038x_8^2 + .325x_6 - ax_7 \geq 0$$

$$g_7(x) = -g_5(x) + (1/a - a)x_4 \geq 0$$

$$g_8(x) = -g_6(x) + (1/a - a)x_7 \geq 0$$

$$g_9(x) = 1.22x_4 - x_1 - x_5 = 0$$

$$g_{10}(x) = 98000x_3/(x_4x_9 + 1000x_3) - x_6 = 0 \qquad a = .99$$

$$g_{11}(x) = (x_2 + x_5)/x_1 - x_8 = 0 \qquad b = .9$$

bounds: cf. Appendix A

START:	x_o	=	(1745,12000,110,3048,1974,89.2,92.8,8,
	$f(x_o)$	=	-872.3872 \ 3.6,145) (not feasible)

SOLUTION:	x*	=	(1698.096,15818.73,54.10228,3031.226,
			2000,90.11537,95,10.49336,1.561636,
			153.53535)

f(x*)	=	-1768.80696		
r(x*)	=	0	e(x*) =	.16E-5
u	=	6	I(x*) =	(2,3,5,6,23,25)
u_{max}^*/u_{min}^*	=	311.8/.6778 = 460		
$\lambda_{max}^*/\lambda_{min}^*$	=	.14E-4/.14E-4 = 1		

PROBLEM:	116 (3-stage membrane separation)
CLASSIFICATION:	LQR-P1-6
SOURCE:	Dembo [21,22]
NUMBER OF VARIABLES:	n = 13
NUMBER OF CONSTRAINTS:	m_1 = 15(5) , $m-m_1$ = 0 , b = 26

OBJECTIVE FUNCTION:

$$f(x) = x_{11} + x_{12} + x_{13}$$

CONSTRAINTS:

$x_3 - x_2 \geq 0 \qquad\qquad x_2 - x_1 \geq 0$

$1 - .002x_7 + .002x_8 \geq 0 \quad 50 \leq f(x) \leq 250$

$x_{13} - 1.262626x_{10} + 1.231059x_3x_{10} \geq 0$

$x_5 - .03475x_2 - .975x_2x_5 + .00975x_2^2 \geq 0$

$x_6 - .03475x_3 - .975x_3x_6 + .00975x_3^2 \geq 0$

$x_5x_7 - x_1x_8 - x_4x_7 + x_4x_8 \geq 0$

$1 - .002(x_2x_9 + x_5x_8 - x_1x_8 - x_6x_9) - x_5 - x_6 \geq 0$

$x_2x_9 - x_3x_{10} - x_6x_9 - 500x_2 + 500x_6 + x_2x_{10} \geq 0$

$x_2 - .9 - .002(x_2x_{10} - x_3x_{10}) \geq 0$

$x_4 - .03475x_1 - .975x_1x_4 + .00975x_1^2 \geq 0$

$x_{11} - 1.262626x_8 + 1.231059x_1x_8 \geq 0$

$x_{12} - 1.262626x_9 + 1.231059x_2x_9 \geq 0$ bounds: cf. Appendix A

START: $\quad x_0 \quad = (.5,.8,.9,.1,.14,.5,489,80,650,450,150,$

$\qquad\quad f(x_0) \quad = 450 \qquad \backslash \quad 150,150)$ (not feasible)

SOLUTION: $x^* \quad = (.8037703,.8999860,.9709724,.09999952,$

$\qquad\qquad\qquad\qquad .1908154,.4605717,574.0803,74.08043,$

$\qquad\qquad\qquad\qquad 500.0162,.1,20.23413,77.34755,.00673039)$

$\qquad\quad f(x^*) \quad = 97.588409$

$\qquad\quad r(x^*) \quad = 0 \qquad\qquad e(x^*) = 0$

$\qquad\quad u \qquad = 14 \qquad\qquad I(x^*) = (3,6,\ldots,15,25,28,$

$\qquad\quad u^*_{max}/u^*_{min} = 2088/.423E\text{-}3 = .49E7 \qquad\qquad \backslash \qquad 32)$

$\qquad\quad \lambda^*_{max}/\lambda^*_{min} = -$

PROBLEM:	117 (Colville No.2, Shell Dual)
CLASSIFICATION:	PQR-P1-1
SOURCE:	Colville [20], Himmelblau [29]
NUMBER OF VARIABLES:	n = 15
NUMBER OF CONSTRAINTS:	$m_1 = 5$, $m-m_1 = 0$, $b = 15$

OBJECTIVE FUNCTION:

$$f(x) = -\sum_{j=1}^{10} b_j x_j + \sum_{j=1}^{5} \sum_{k=1}^{5} c_{kj} x_{10+k} x_{10+j} + 2\sum_{j=1}^{5} d_j x_{10+j}^{3}$$

CONSTRAINTS:

$$2\sum_{k=1}^{5} c_{kj} x_{10+k} + 3d_j x_{10+j}^{2} + e_j - \sum_{k=1}^{10} a_{kj} x_k \geq 0 \quad , \quad j=1,\ldots,5$$

$$0 \leq x_i \quad , \quad i=1,\ldots,15$$

$a_{ij}, b_j, c_{ij}, d_j, e_j$: cf. Appendix A

START:	x_0	= .001(1,1,1,1,1,1,60000,1,1,1,1,1,1,1,1)
	$f(x_0)$	= 2400.1053 (feasible)

SOLUTION: x^* = (0,0,5.174136,0,3.061093,11.83968,0,0,
.1039071,0,.2999929,.3334709,.3999910,
.4283145,.2239607)

$f(x^*)$ = 32.348679

$r(x^*)$ = 0 $e(x^*) = .35E-4$

μ = 11 $I(x^*) = (1,\ldots,7,9,12,13,$

u^*_{max}/u^*_{min} = 56.75/.2240 = 253 $\backslash$ 15)

$\lambda^*_{max}/\lambda^*_{min}$ = 3.30/.10 = 32.3

PROBLEM:	118
CLASSIFICATION:	QLR-P1-2
SOURCE:	Bartholomew-Biggs [4]
NUMBER OF VARIABLES:	n = 15

NUMBER OF CONSTRAINTS: $m_1 = 29(29)$, $m-m_1 = 0$, $b = 30$

OBJECTIVE FUNCTION:

$$f(x) = \sum_{k=0}^{4} (2.3x_{3k+1} + .0001x_{3k+1}^2 + 1.7x_{3k+2} + .0001x_{3k+2}^2 + 2.2x_{3k+3} + .00015x_{3k+3}^2)$$

CONSTRAINTS:

$$0 \le x_{3j+1} - x_{3j-2} + 7 \le 13 \qquad 0 \le x_{3j+2} - x_{3j-1} + 7 \le 14$$
$$0 \le x_{3j+3} - x_{3j} + 7 \le 13 \qquad j=1,\ldots,4$$
$$x_1 + x_2 + x_3 - 60 \ge 0 \qquad x_4 + x_5 + x_6 - 50 \ge 0$$
$$x_7 + x_8 + x_9 - 70 \ge 0 \qquad x_{10} + x_{11} + x_{12} - 85 \ge 0$$
$$x_{13} + x_{14} + x_{15} - 100 \ge 0$$

$$8 \le x_1 \le 21 \qquad 43 \le x_2 \le 57 \qquad 3 \le x_3 \le 16$$
$$0 \le x_{3k+1} \le 90 \qquad 0 \le x_{3k+2} \le 120 \qquad 0 \le x_{3k+3} \le 60$$
$$k=1,\ldots,4$$

START:	x_0	= (20,55,15,20,60,20,20,60,20,20,60, 20,20,60,20) (feasible)
	$f(x_0)$	= 664.82045000

SOLUTION:	x^*	= (8,49,3,1,56,0,1,63,6,3,70,12, 5,77,18)
	$f(x^*)$	= 664.8204500
	$r(x^*)$	= 0
	$e(x^*)$	= 0
	μ	= 15
	$I(x^*)$	= (1,17,18,19,20,22,23,24,25,27,28,29,30,
	u^*_{max}/u^*_{min}	= 2.941/.04860 = 60.5 \ 32,35)
	$\lambda^*_{max}/\lambda^*_{min}$	= -

PROBLEM:	119 (Colville No.7)

CLASSIFICATION:	PLR-P1-2

SOURCE:	Colville [20], Himmelblau [29]

NUMBER OF VARIABLES: $n = 16$

NUMBER OF CONSTRAINTS: $m_1 = 0$, $m-m_1 = 8(8)$, $b = 32$

OBJECTIVE FUNCTION:

$$f(x) = \sum_{i=1}^{16} \sum_{j=1}^{16} a_{ij}(x_i^2 + x_i + 1)(x_j^2 + x_j + 1)$$

CONSTRAINTS:

$$\sum_{j=1}^{16} b_{ij}x_j - c_i = 0 \quad , \quad i=1,\ldots,8$$

$$0 \le x_i \le 5 \quad , \quad i=1,\ldots,16$$

a_{ij}, b_{ij}, c_i : cf. Appendix A

START: x_0 = $(10,\ldots,10)$ (not feasible)

$f(x_0)$ = 566766

SOLUTION: x^* = $(.03984735,.7919832,.2028703,.8443579,$
$1.126991,.9347387,1.681962,.1553009,$
$1.567870,0,0,0,.6602041,0,.6742559,0)$

$f(x^*)$ = 244.899698

$r(x^*)$ = .26E-9 $\quad$ $e(x^*) =$ .36E-8

μ = 5 $\quad$ $I(x^*) =$ $(10,11,12,14,16)$

u_{max}^*/u_{min}^* = 95.99/4.201 = 22.9

$\lambda_{max}^*/\lambda_{min}^*$ = 39.2/25.1 = 1.56

CONSTANT DATA

This appendix summarizes constant data, parts of the definition of the problem functions, and numerical results which would break the documentation scheme used in Chapter IV to describe the test problems. The corresponding abbreviations are explained in the test problem documentations.

No. 57:

i	a_i	b_i	i	a_i	b_i
1	8	.49	23	22	.41
2	8	.49	24	22	.40
3	10	.48	25	24	.42
4	10	.47	26	24	.40
5	10	.48	27	24	.40
6	10	.47	28	26	.41
7	12	.46	29	26	.40
8	12	.46	30	26	.41
9	12	.45	31	28	.41
10	12	.43	32	28	.40
11	14	.45	33	30	.40
12	14	.43	34	30	.40
13	14	.43	35	30	.38
14	16	.44	36	32	.41
15	16	.43	37	32	.40
16	16	.43	38	34	.40
17	18	.46	39	36	.41
18	18	.45	40	36	.38
19	20	.42	41	38	.40
20	20	.42	42	38	.40
21	20	.43	43	40	.39
22	22	.41	44	42	.39

Table 5: Data for test problem no. 57.

No. 67:

Let $y_i = y_i(x)$. The functions are described by a subprogram:

$$y_2 = 1.6x_1$$
10 $y_3 = 1.22y_2 - x_1$
$$y_6 = (x_2 + y_3)/x_1$$
$$y_{2c} = .01x_1(112 + 13.167y_6 - .6667y_6^2)$$

if $|y_{2c} - y_2| \leq .001$ goto 30 else goto 20

20 $y_2 = y_{2c}$

goto 10

30 $y_4 = 93$

40 $y_5 = 86.35 + 1.098y_6 - .038y_6^2 + .325(y_4 - 89)$
$$y_8 = 3y_5 - 133$$
$$y_7 = 35.82 - .222y_8$$
$$y_{4c} = 98000x_3/(y_2y_7 + 1000x_3)$$

if $|y_{4c} - y_4| \leq .001$ goto 60 else goto 50

50 $y_4 = y_{4c}$

goto 40

60 stop

i	a_i	i	a_i
1	0	8	5000
2	0	9	2000
3	85	10	93
4	90	11	95
5	3	12	12
6	.01	13	4
7	145	14	162

Table 6: Data for test problem no. 67.

No. 70:

i	c_i	$y_{i,obs}$
1	.1	.00189
2	1	.1038
3	2	.268
4	3	.506
5	4	.577
6	5	.604
7	6	.725
8	7	.898
9	8	.947
10	9	.845
11	10	.702
12	11	.528
13	12	.385
14	13	.257
15	14	.159
16	15	.0869
17	16	.0453
18	17	.01509
19	18	.00189

Table 7: Data for test problem no. 70.

No. 83:

i	a_i	i	a_i
1	85.334407	7	.0029955
2	.0056858	8	.0021813
3	.0006262	9	9.300961
4	.0022053	10	.0047026
5	80.51249	11	.0012547
6	.0071317	12	.0019085

Table 8: Data for test problem no. 83.

No. 84:

i	a_i	i	a_i
1	−24345	11	15711.36
2	−8720288.849	12	−155011.1084
3	150512.5253	13	4360.53352
4	−156.6950325	14	12.9492344
5	476470.3222	15	10236.884
6	729482.8271	16	13176.786
7	−145421.402	17	−326669.5104
8	2931.1506	18	7390.68412
9	−40.427932	19	−27.8986976
10	5106.192	20	16643.076
		21	30988.146

Table 9: Data for test problem no. 84.

No. 85:

Let $y_i = y_i(x)$, $c_i = c_i(x)$.

$$y_1 = x_2 + x_3 + 41.6$$

$$c_1 = .024x_4 - 4.62$$

$$y_2 = 12.5/c_1 + 12$$

$$c_2 = .0003535x_1^2 + .5311x_1 + .08705y_2x_1$$

$$c_3 = .052x_1 + 78 + .002377y_2x_1$$

$$y_3 = c_2/c_3$$

$$y_4 = 19y_3$$

$$c_4 = .04782(x_1 - y_3) + .1956(x_1 - y_3)^2/x_2 + .6376y_4$$
$$+ 1.594y_3$$

$$c_5 = 100x_2$$

$$c_6 = x_1 - y_3 - y_4$$

$$c_7 = .95 - c_4/c_5$$

$$y_5 = c_6c_7$$

$$y_6 = x_1 - y_5 - y_4 - y_3$$

$$c_8 = (y_5 + y_4).995$$

$$y_7 = c_8/y_1$$

$$y_8 = c_8/3798$$

$$c_9 = y_7 - .0663y_7/y_8 - .3153$$

$$y_9 = 96.82/c_9 + .321y_1$$

$$y_{10} = 1.29y_5 + 1.258y_4 + 2.29y_3 + 1.71y_6$$

$$y_{11} = 1.71x_1 - .452y_4 + .58y_3$$

$$c_{10} = 12.3/752.3$$

$$c_{11} = (1.75y_2)(.995x_1)$$

$$c_{12} = .995y_{10} + 1998$$

$$y_{12} = c_{10}x_1 + c_{11}/c_{12}$$

$$y_{13} = c_{12} - 1.75y_2$$

$$y_{14} = 3623 + 64.4x_2 + 58.4x_3 + 146312/(y_9 + x_5)$$

$$c_{13} = .995y_{10} + 60.8x_2 + 48x_4 - .1121y_{14} - 5095$$

$$y_{15} = y_{13}/c_{13}$$

$$y_{16} = 148000 - 331000y_{15} + 40y_{13} - 61y_{15}y_{13}$$

$$c_{14} = 2324y_{10} - 28740000y_2$$

$$y_{17} = 14130000 - 1328y_{10} - 531y_{11} + c_{14}/c_{12}$$

$$c_{15} = y_{13}/y_{15} - y_{13}/.52$$

$$c_{16} = 1.104 - .72y_{15}$$

$$c_{17} = y_9 + x_5$$

i	a_i	b_i
2	17.505	1053.6667
3	11.275	35.03
4	214.228	665.585
5	7.458	584.463
6	.961	265.916
7	1.612	7.046
8	.146	.222
9	107.99	273.366
10	922.693	1286.105
11	926.832	1444.046
12	18.766	537.141
13	1072.163	3247.039
14	8961.448	26844.086
15	.063	.386
16	71084.33	140000
17	2802713	12146108

Table 10: Data for test problem no. 85.

No. 86, 117:

j	1	2	3	4	5
e_j	-15	-27	-36	-18	-12
c_{1j}	30	-20	-10	32	-10
c_{2j}	-20	39	-6	-31	32
c_{3j}	-10	-6	10	-6	-10
c_{4j}	32	-31	-6	39	-20
c_{5j}	-10	32	-10	-20	30
d_j	4	8	10	6	2
a_{1j}	-16	2	0	1	0
a_{2j}	0	-2	0	4	2
a_{3j}	-3.5	0	2	0	0
a_{4j}	0	-2	0	-4	-1
a_{5j}	0	-9	-2	1	-2.8
a_{6j}	2	0	-4	0	0
a_{7j}	-1	-1	-1	-1	-1
a_{8j}	-1	-2	-3	-2	-1
a_{9j}	1	2	3	4	5
a_{10j}	1	1	1	1	1
b_j	-40	-2	-.25	-4	-4
b_{5+j}	-1	-40	-60	5	1

Table 11: Data for test problem no. 86, 117.

No. 88 - 92:

n	x*				
2	1.074319	-.4566137			
3	1.074319	-.4566137	.30E-10		
4	.708479	.24E-4	.807600	-.456614	
5	.701893	.22E-11	.813331	.456614	.90E-11
6	.494144	-.10E-4	.614951	-.24E-5	.729259 -.456613

Table 12: Solution vectors for test problems no. 88 to 92.

n	$r(x^*)$	$e(x^*)$	$\lambda^*_{max}/\lambda^*_{min}$
2	.36E-11	.13E-6	.10E1
3	.73E-11	.94E-7	.20E2
4	.0	.14E-3	.65E8
5	.36E-11	.13E-6	.11E9
6	.0	.16E-2	.43E7

Table 13: Constraint violations, norm of Kuhn-Tucker-vector, and condition number for test problems no. 88 to 92.

No. 95 - 98:

i	b(95)	b(96)	b(97)	b(98)
1	4.97	4.97	32.97	32.97
2	-1.88	-1.88	25.12	25.12
3	-29.08	-69.08	-29.08	-124.08
4	-78.02	-118.02	-78.02	-173.02

Table 14: Data for test problems no. 95 to 92.

No. 99:

b = 32

i	a_i	t_i
1	0	0
2	50	25
3	50	50
4	75	100
5	75	150
6	75	200
7	100	290
8	100	380

Table 15: Data for test problem no. 99.

No. 101 - 103:

i	$x_i^*(101)$	$x_i^*(102)$	$x_i^*(103)$
1	2.856159	3.896253	4.394105
2	.6108230	.8093588	.8544687
3	2.150813	2.664386	2.843230
4	4.712874	4.300913	3.399979
5	.9994875	.8535549	.7229261
6	1.347508	1.095287	.8704064
7	.03165277	.02731046	.02463883

Table 16: Solution vectors for test problems no. 101 to 103.

No. 105:

i	y_i	i	y_i
1	95	168-175	175
2	105	176-181	180
3-6	110	182-187	185
7-10	115	188-194	190
11-25	120	195-198	195
26-40	125	199-201	200
41-55	130	202-204	205
56-68	135	205-212	210
69-89	140	213	215
90-101	145	214-219	220
102-118	150	220-224	230
119-122	155	225	235
123-142	160	226-232	240
143-150	165	233	245
151-167	170	234-235	250

Table 17: Data for test problem no. 105.

No. 109:

i	x_i^*	i	x_i^*	i	x_i^*
1	674.8881	4	-.3711526	7	201.465
2	1134.170	5	252.0000	8	426.661
3	.1335691	6	252.0000	9	368.494

Table 18: Solution vector for test problem no. 109

No. 111, 112:

j	c_j	j	c_j
1	−6.089	6	−14.986
2	−17.164	7	−24.100
3	−34.054	8	−10.708
4	−5.914	9	−26.662
5	−24.721	10	−22.179

Table 19: Data for test problems no. 111 and 112.

No. 114:

Bounds for test problem no. 114:

$$.00001 \leq x_1 \leq 2000$$
$$.00001 \leq x_2 \leq 16000$$
$$.00001 \leq x_3 \leq 120$$
$$.00001 \leq x_4 \leq 5000$$
$$.00001 \leq x_5 \leq 2000$$
$$85 \leq x_6 \leq 93$$
$$90 \leq x_7 \leq 95$$
$$3 \leq x_8 \leq 12$$
$$1.2 \leq x_9 \leq 4$$
$$145 \leq x_{10} \leq 162$$

No. 116:

Bounds for test problem no. 116:

$$.1 \leq x_1 \leq 1 \qquad\qquad .1 \leq x_7 \leq 1000$$
$$.1 \leq x_2 \leq 1 \qquad\qquad .1 \leq x_8 \leq 1000$$
$$.1 \leq x_3 \leq 1 \qquad\qquad 500 \leq x_9 \leq 1000$$
$$.0001 \leq x_4 \leq .1 \qquad\qquad .1 \leq x_{10} \leq 500$$
$$.1 \leq x_5 \leq .9 \qquad\qquad 1 \leq x_{11} \leq 150$$
$$.1 \leq x_6 \leq .9 \qquad\qquad .0001 \leq x_{12} \leq 150$$
$$.0001 \leq x_{13} \leq 150$$

No. 119:

j	1	2	3	4	5	6	7	8	9	10	11	12	13	14	15	16
a_{1j}	1	0	0	1	0	0	1	1	0	0	0	0	0	0	0	1
a_{2j}	0	1	1	0	0	0	1	0	0	1	0	0	0	0	0	0
a_{3j}	0	0	1	0	0	0	1	0	1	1	0	0	0	1	0	0
a_{4j}	0	0	0	1	0	0	1	0	0	0	1	0	0	0	1	0
a_{5j}	0	0	0	0	1	1	0	0	0	1	0	1	0	0	0	1
a_{6j}	0	0	0	0	0	1	0	1	0	0	0	0	0	0	1	0
a_{7j}	0	0	0	0	0	0	1	0	0	0	1	0	1	0	0	0
a_{8j}	0	0	0	0	0	0	0	1	0	1	0	0	0	0	1	0
a_{9j}	0	0	0	0	0	0	0	0	1	0	0	1	0	0	0	1
a_{10j}	0	0	0	0	0	0	0	0	0	1	0	0	0	1	0	0
a_{11j}	0	0	0	0	0	0	0	0	0	0	1	0	1	0	0	0
a_{12j}	0	0	0	0	0	0	0	0	0	0	0	1	0	1	0	0
a_{13j}	0	0	0	0	0	0	0	0	0	0	0	0	1	1	0	0
a_{14j}	0	0	0	0	0	0	0	0	0	0	0	0	0	1	0	0
a_{15j}	0	0	0	0	0	0	0	0	0	0	0	0	0	0	1	0
a_{16j}	0	0	0	0	0	0	0	0	0	0	0	0	0	0	0	1

Table 20: Data for test problem no. 119.

j	b_{1j}	b_{2j}	b_{3j}	b_{4j}	b_{5j}	b_{6j}	b_{7j}	b_{8j}	c_j
1	.22	-1.46	1.29	-1.10	.0	.0	1.12	.0	2.5
2	.20	.0	-.89	-1.06	.0	-1.72	.0	.45	1.1
3	.19	-1.30	.0	.95	.0	-.33	.0	.26	-3.1
4	.25	1.82	.0	-.54	-1.43	.0	.31	-1.10	-3.5
5	.15	-1.15	-1.16	.0	1.51	1.62	.0	.58	1.3
6	.11	.0	-.96	-1.78	.59	1.24	.0	.0	2.1
7	.12	.80	.0	-.41	-.33	.21	1.12	-1.03	2.3
8	.13	.0	-.49	.0	-.43	-.26	.0	.10	-1.5
9	1.00	.0	.0	.0	.0	.0	-.36	.0	
10	.0	1.00	.0	.0	.0	.0	.0	.0	
11	.0	.0	1.00	.0	.0	.0	.0	.0	
12	.0	.0	.0	1.00	.0	.0	.0	.0	
13	.0	.0	.0	.0	1.00	.0	.0	.0	
14	.0	.0	.0	.0	.0	1.00	.0	.0	
15	.0	.0	.0	.0	.0	.0	1.00	.0	
16	.0	.0	.0	.0	.0	.0	.0	1.00	

Table 21: Data for test problem no. 119.

SOME NUMERICAL TEST RESULTS

To give a test designer the possibility to compare his test
results with those of Hock [31], we repeat some efficiency and
accuracy results of the optimization programs listed in Table 1
of Section 2 of Chapter I. The abbreviations in the table are
the following ones:

No   : Number of the test problem.

Code : Name of the program.

ET   : Execution time in seconds.

NF   : Number of objective function evaluations.

NG   : Number of restriction function evaluations (each
         restriction counted).

NDF   : Number of gradient evaluations of the objective
         function.

NDG   : Number of gradient evaluations of the constraints
         (each restriction counted).

FV   : Objective function value.

VC   : Sum of constraint violations r(x*).

KT   : Norm of Kuhn-Tucker-vector e(x*).

An asterix indicates that a test run could not be terminated
successfully because of overflow, exceeding calculation time
(more than 10 minutes), etc.. The tests have been performed on
a Telefunken TR440 computer at the Rechenzentrum of the University
of Würzburg. All calculations within the driving programs, test
problems, and optimization codes are carried out in single precision with more than 10 correct digits (35 - 38 bit mantissa).

No	Code	ET	NF	NG	NDF	NDG	FV	VC	KT
1	VF02AD	.89	24	0	24	0	.25841789E-07	.0	
	OPRQP	.32	28	0	20	0	.15700085E-15	.0	
	GRGA	2.04	458	0	138	0	.10355110E-17	.0	
	VF01A	.30	70	0	70	0	.0	.0	
	FUNMIN	.45	118	0	26	0	.0	.0	
	FMIN	2.89	549	0	89	0	.39686225E-12	.0	
2	VF02AD	.25	16	0	16	0	.28444461E+02	.0	.0
	OPRQP	.25	18	0	13	0	.50425706E-01	.26E-05	.78E-04
	GRGA	.62	76	0	39	0	.49412293E+01	.0	.38E-06
	VF01A	.16	40	0	40	0	.49412293E+01	.0	.17E-07
	FUNMIN	1.68	402	0	92	0	.49412293E+01	.0	.47E-05
	FMIN	2.02	382	0	62	0	.50426256E-01	.0	.0
3	VF02AD	.53	10	0	10	0	.17923217E-22	.0	.27E-13
	OPRQP	.17	9	0	7	0	-.49999660E-05	.50E-05	.24E-09
	GRGA	.42	33	0	20	0	.15711625E-21	.0	.79E-13
	VF01A	.07	18	0	18	0	.29594638E-22	.0	.34E-13
	FUNMIN	.49	135	0	27	0	.89143884E-15	.0	.38E-13
	FMIN	.58	109	0	20	0	.36578482E-06	.0	.0
4	VF02AD	.11	2	0	2	0	.26666667E+01	.0	.0
	OPRQP	.20	8	0	8	0	.26666561E+01	.31E-05	.0
	GRGA	.38	14	0	12	0	.26666667E+01	.0	.0
	VF01A	.11	26	0	26	0	.26666667E+01	.13E-12	.0
	FUNMIN	.73	164	0	36	0	.26666667E+01	.34E-09	.0
	FMIN	1.33	220	0	50	0	.26666706E+01	.0	.0
5	VF02AD	.42	8	0	8	0	-.19132229E+01	.0	.0
	OPRQP	.18	9	0	7	0	-.19132230E+01	.0	.0
	GRGA	.57	36	0	50	0	-.19132229E+01	.0	.0
	VF01A	.07	16	0	16	0	-.19132230E+01	.0	.0
	FUNMIN	.19	30	0	8	0	-.19132230E+01	.0	.0
	FMIN	.94	166	0	34	0	-.19132230E+01	.0	.0
6	VF02AD	.51	10	10	10	10	.19129458E-12	.22E-04	.39E-06
	OPRQP	.22	13	13	11	11	.39299923E-12	.21E-05	.56E-06
	GRGA	.31	11	13	4	5	.41376568E+01	.20E-07	.18E+01
	VF01A	.39	82	82	82	82	.0	.0	.0
	FUNMIN	.57	149	149	33	33	.52939559E-22	.0	.0
	FMIN	1.92	236	236	37	37	.0	.0	.0
7	VF02AD	.50	12	12	12	12	-.17320508E+01	.17E-09	.35E-08
	OPRQP	.46	32	32	30	30	-.17320528E+01	.69E-05	.14E-13
	GRGA	.76	77	61	45	21	-.17320508E+01	.0	.79E-05
	VF01A	.20	43	43	43	43	-.17320510E+01	.77E-06	.63E-05
	FUNMIN	1.36	324	324	81	81	-.17320508E+01	.22E-07	.36E-08
	FMIN	.87	109	109	21	21	-.17320509E+01	.43E-06	.70E-07
8	VF02AD	.22	5	10	5	10	-.10000000E+01	.15E-02	.0
	OPRQP	.16	7	14	6	12	-.10000000E+01	.18E-05	.0
	GRGA	.66	39	144	14	20	-.10000000E+01	.58E-10	.0
	VF01A	.09	17	34	17	34	-.10000000E+01	.17E-06	.0
	FUNMIN	.35	79	158	23	46	-.10000000E+01	.85E-07	.0
	FMIN	.73	76	152	10	20	-.10000000E+01	.65E-06	.0

No	Code	ET	NF	NF	NDF	NDG	FV	VC	KT
9	VF02AD	.31	6	6	6	6	-.50000000E+00	.58E-10	.52E-05
	OPRQP	.18	11	11	7	7	-.50000002E+00	.46E-06	.85E-09
	GRGA	.33	12	8	6	6	-.64218338E-02	.0	.16E+00
	VF01A	.10	21	21	21	21	-.50000000E+00	.23E-08	.10E-06
	FUNMIN	.45	96	96	24	24	-.50000000E+00	.23E-09	.61E-07
	FMIN	.68	81	81	17	17	-.50000000E+00	.10E-07	.44E-07
10	VF02AD	.60	12	12	12	12	-.10000001E+01	.19E-06	.37E-05
	OPRQP	.45	32	32	31	31	-.10000047E+01	.93E-05	.38E-10
	GRGA	1.96	260	320	67	31	-.10000000E+01	.0	.45E-05
	VF01A	.35	70	70	70	70	-.10000000E+01	.53E-07	.48E-10
	FUNMIN	.92	225	225	52	52	-.10000000E+01	.13E-07	.22E-05
	FMIN	2.29	289	290	54	54	-.99999985E+00	.0	.0
11	VF02AD	.41	9	9	9	9	-.84984642E+01	.64E-08	.49E-05
	OPRQP	.37	24	24	24	24	-.84984844E+01	.66E-05	.79E-10
	GRGA	1.70	186	201	112	48	-.84984642E+01	.0	.32E-04
	VF01A	.18	40	40	40	40	-.84984642E+01	.49E-08	.55E-10
	FUNMIN	.50	129	129	28	28	-.84984671E+01	.94E-06	.47E-06
	FMIN	2.56	279	280	60	60	-.84984702E+01	.20E-05	.60E-05
12	VF02AD	.51	12	12	12	12	-.30000000E+02	.58E-09	.35E-07
	OPRQP	.40	40	40	26	26	-.30000004E+02	.76E-05	.15E-09
	GRGA	.92	145	89	24	19	-.30000000E+02	.0	.33E-04
	VF01A	.30	79	79	79	63	-.30000000E+02	.68E-07	.23E-05
	FUNMIN	.87	203	203	43	43	-.30000001E+02	.14E-05	.30E-05
	FMIN	1.07	117	133	28	28	-.30000003E+02	.53E-05	.28E-05
13	VF02AD	2.80	45	45	45	45	.10000001E+01	.0	.20E+01
	OPRQP	1.18	75	75	75	75	.99010346E+00	.12E-06	.0
	GRGA	.71	72	95	14	11	.10000585E+01	.0	.20E+01
	VF01A	.76	143	143	143	136	.99568269E+00	.10E-07	.0
	FUNMIN	2.08	379	379	85	85	.97718160E+00	.15E-05	.0
	FMIN	13.73	1522	2224	216	216	.83727822E+00	.15E-03	.0
14	VF02AD	.33	6	12	6	12	.13934650E+01	.87E-10	.0
	OPRQP	.37	21	42	21	42	.13934485E+01	.95E-05	.0
	GRGA	.44	22	62	8	16	.13934650E+01	.0	.0
	VF01A	.16	32	64	32	64	.13934650E+01	.39E-08	.0
	FUNMIN	.99	196	392	46	92	.13934650E+01	.36E-09	.0
	FMIN	2.49	232	465	47	94	.13934646E+01	.30E-06	.0
15	VF02AD	.26	5	10	5	10	.30650000E+03	.0	.0
	OPRQP	.43	29	58	26	52	.36037671E+03	.64E-05	.18E-07
	GRGA	1.10	114	312	46	36	.30650000E+03	.0	.0
	VF01A	.34	73	146	73	85	.30649961E+03	.57E-06	.0
	FUNMIN	.59	122	244	30	60	.30649985E+03	.15E-06	.0
	FMIN	7.76	729	1461	129	145	.30650014E+03	.0	.0
16	VF02AD	.52	6	12	6	12	.23144661E+02	.0	.0
	OPRQP	.43	23	46	22	44	.23144274E+02	.72E-05	.0
	GRGA	.39	21	50	8	16	.23144661E+02	.36E-11	.0
	VF01A	.45	89	178	89	22	.25000000E+00	.0	.51E-08
	FUNMIN	.87	166	332	33	66	.25000000E+00	.0	.17E-06
	FMIN	4.03	362	739	80	107	.24999998E+00	.0	.13E-04

No	Code	ET	NF	NG	NDF	NDG	FV	VC	KT
17	VF02AD	.89	12	24	12	24	.10000000E+01	.14E-07	.27E-05
	OPRQP	.30	19	38	15	30	.99998328E+00	.84E-05	.0
	GRGA	.84	108	128	38	30	.10000000E+01	.0	.0
	VF01A	.32	64	128	64	57	.10000000E+01	.0	.0
	FUNMIN	.38	74	148	15	30	.99999999E+00	.80E-08	.83E-06
	FMIN	7.78	541	1533	140	280	.10000001E+01	.34E-08	.0
18	VF02AD	.58	8	16	8	16	.50000000E+01	.38E-07	.18E-04
	OPRQP	.49	32	64	29	58	.49999988E+01	.62E-05	.27E-09
	GRGA	1.83	109	688	46	36	.50000000E+01	.0	.16E-05
	VF01A	.18	35	70	35	35	.50000000E+01	.16E-07	.12E-09
	FUNMIN	.54	107	214	23	46	.50000000E+01	.20E-07	.20E-10
	FMIN	4.19	450	903	51	52	.50000000E+01	.0	.0
19	VF02AD	.49	13	26	13	26	-.69618139E+04	.65E-08	.0
	OPRQP	3.55	385	770	201	402	-.70601196E+04	.84E-01	.0
	GRGA	.81	62	196	28	28	-.69618139E+04	.0	.0
	VF01A	.77	153	306	153	226	-.69618139E+04	.19E-08	.0
	FUNMIN	5.08	914	1828	199	398	-.69597506E+04	.0	.0
	FMIN	2.05	176	396	30	59	-.79509209E+04	.87E+00	.0
20	VF02AD	1.25	20	60	20	60	.38198730E+02	.0	.0
	OPRQP	.49	26	78	24	72	.40197455E+02	.80E-05	.0
	GRGA	.40	17	57	7	21	.40198730E+02	.0	.0
	VF01A	.35	64	192	64	63	.40198730E+02	.27E-09	.0
	FUNMIN	.70	151	453	31	93	.38198730E+02	.29E-10	.0
	FMIN	11.27	701	2986	116	291	.40198512E+02	.77E-07	.0
21	VF02AD	.30	4	4	4	4	-.99960000E+02	.0	.29E-10
	OPRQP	.18	7	7	7	7	-.99960000E+02	.20E-05	.10E-09
	GRGA	.77	49	6	76	41	-.99959999E+02	.0	.20E-02
	VF01A	.11	25	25	25	25	-.99960000E+02	.45E-07	.18E-05
	FUNMIN	3.11	601	601	140	140	-.99960000E+02	.28E-05	.89E-09
	FMIN	1.31	203	204	14	7	-.99989999E+02	.0	.0
22	VF02AD	.40	9	18	9	18	.10000000E+01	.0	.0
	OPRQP	.37	20	40	20	40	.99998988E+00	.15E-04	.0
	GRGA	.91	112	140	37	32	.10000000E+01	.0	.0
	VF01A	.14	23	46	23	46	.10000000E+01	.38E-08	.0
	FUNMIN	.56	134	268	32	64	.10000000E+01	.0	.0
	FMIN	1.76	174	351	36	69	.99999976E+00	.36E-06	.0
23	VF02AD	.47	7	35	7	35	.20000000E+01	.73E-11	.0
	OPRQP	.48	23	115	21	105	.19999658E+01	.17E-04	.0
	GRGA	1.00	62	475	31	75	.20000000E+01	.0	.0
	VF01A	.24	42	210	42	111	.20000001E+01	.13E-07	.0
	FUNMIN	.93	158	790	35	175	.19999999E+01	.36E-07	.0
	FMIN	8.56	423	2691	59	295	.19999819E+01	.90E-05	.0
24	VF02AD	.33	5	15	5	15	-.10000000E+01	.0	.0
	OPRQP	.29	18	54	12	36	-.10000013E+01	.18E-05	.0
	GRGA	.41	16	30	12	21	-.99998634E+00	.0	.0
	VF01A	.23	48	144	48	144	-.10000000E+01	.41E-09	.0
	FUNMIN	1.07	196	588	43	129	-.10000000E+01	.36E-07	.0
	FMIN	4.22	280	897	65	195	-.99999997E+00	.28E-07	.0

No	Code	ET	NF	NG	NDF	NDG	FV	VC	KT
25	VF02AD	.37	1	0	1	0	.32835000E+02	.0	.0
	OPRQP	.29	1	0	1	0	.32835000E+02	.0	.0
	GRGA	36.96	371	0	135	0	.48181046E-03	.0	.0
	VF01A	.73	4	0	4	0	.32835000E+02	.0	.0
	FUNMIN	13.69	186	0	36	0	.36024905E-19	.0	.0
	FMIN	54.15	731	0	142	0	.40271327E-13	.0	.0
26	VF02AD	1.34	19	19	19	19	.40485320E-07	.47E-04	.16E-04
	OPRQP	.42	45	45	20	20	.21811252E-08	.99E-05	.22E-05
	GRGA	1.03	112	146	43	19	.15904267E-17	.0	.24E-12
	VF01A	1.09	195	195	195	195	.75508673E-16	.17E-09	.44E-11
	FUNMIN	2.93	679	679	153	153	.13743264E-15	.0	.19E-08
	FMIN	1.49	182	182	43	43	.84365765E-17	.25E-08	.41E-10
27	VF02AD	1.67	25	25	25	25	.40000018E-01	.23E-06	.29E-03
	OPRQP	.66	56	56	39	39	.39999680E-01	.80E-05	.18E-07
	GRGA	3.59	584	378	175	79	.40000000E-01	.18E-10	.48E-06
	VF01A	.28	54	54	54	54	.40000000E-01	.62E-08	.80E-07
	FUNMIN	1.31	279	279	67	67	.40000000E-01	.18E-09	.70E-07
	FMIN	1.53	173	173	35	35	.39999998E-01	.43E-07	.54E-06
28	VF02AD	.30	5	5	5	5	.29778502E-20	.58E-10	.11E-09
	OPRQP	.14	6	6	4	4	.24369793E-12	.17E-07	.12E-05
	GRGA	2.22	171	6	299	153	.68956539E-12	.12E-09	.83E-06
	VF01A	.07	14	14	14	14	.0	.0	.0
	FUNMIN	.11	26	26	6	6	.0	.0	.0
	FMIN	.20	23	23	6	6	.13234890E-22	.0	.34E-11
29	VF02AD	.95	13	13	13	13	-.22627417E+02	.0	.16E-05
	OPRQP	.70	64	64	39	39	-.22627421E+02	.56E-05	.10E-05
	GRGA	2.06	310	196	84	56	-.22627417E+02	.0	.51E-04
	VF01A	.49	110	110	110	91	-.22627417E+02	.0	.0
	FUNMIN	.90	196	196	45	45	-.22627417E+02	.18E-07	.44E-06
	FMIN	1.68	159	177	39	39	-.22627416E+02	.0	.0
30	VF02AD	1.60	14	14	14	14	.10000000E+01	.0	.56E-08
	OPRQP	.44	18	18	18	18	.10000000E+01	.38E-08	.28E-09
	GRGA	.55	39	54	15	11	.10000000E+01	.0	.40E-08
	VF01A	.34	55	55	55	48	.10000000E+01	.0	.23E-06
	FUNMIN	.82	135	135	34	34	.10000000E+01	.0	.24E-07
	FMIN	10.75	1199	1340	213	213	.10001036E+01	.0	.0
31	VF02AD	1.02	10	10	10	10	.60000000E+01	.27E-09	.12E-04
	OPRQP	.44	24	24	22	22	.59999631E+01	.62E-05	.13E-06
	GRGA	.66	32	118	17	10	.60000000E+01	.0	.27E-03
	VF01A	.18	29	29	29	29	.60000000E+01	.64E-09	.15E-05
	FUNMIN	.61	108	108	22	22	.60000000E+01	.49E-08	.12E-07
	FMIN	4.48	576	577	82	81	.60000001E+01	.0	.35E-04
32	VF02AD	.33	3	6	3	6	.10000000E+01	.51E-10	.0
	OPRQP	.40	17	34	17	34	.99996106E+00	.12E-04	.0
	GRGA	.49	29	82	11	16	.10000000E+01	.0	.0
	VF01A	.26	47	94	47	49	.10000001E+01	.28E-08	.0
	FUNMIN	1.36	242	484	55	110	.10000000E+01	.44E-10	.0
	FMIN	10.41	874	1752	192	384	.10000000E+01	.10E+01	.0

No	Code	ET	NF	NG	NDF	NDG	FV	VC	KT
33	VF02AD	.57	5	10	5	10	-.40000000E+01	.0	.0
	OPRQP	.82	43	86	39	78	-.40000000E+01	.32E-10	.0
	GRGA	.41	21	40	8	16	-.40000000E+01	.0	.0
	VF01A	**							
	FUNMIN	2.03	351	702	78	156	-.39999998E+01	.0	.0
	FMIN	7.82	672	1543	112	224	-.39999985E+01	.39E-06	.0
34	VF02AD	.92	8	16	8	16	-.83403245E+00	.15E-08	.0
	OPRQP	1.00	60	120	37	74	-.83403515E+00	.73E-05	.0
	GRGA	.90	52	244	24	26	-.83403245E+00	.0	.0
	VF01A	.75	106	212	106	195	-.83403245E+00	.17E-09	.0
	FUNMIN	***							
	FMIN	7.85	579	1589	105	210	-.83403082E+00	.0	.0
35	VF02AD	.64	7	7	7	7	.11111111E+00	.0	.83E-10
	OPRQP	.19	7	7	7	7	.11111086E+00	.11E-05	.31E-06
	GRGA	.75	41	8	59	33	.11111333E+00	.0	.0
	VF01A	.19	39	39	39	39	.11111111E+00	.58E-10	.89E-08
	FUNMIN	.63	122	122	28	28	.11111111E+00	.78E-08	.26E-05
	FMIN	3.52	386	428	85	85	.11111113E+00	.0	.0
36	VF02AD	.36	4	4	4	4	-.33000000E+04	.12E-09	.0
	OPRQP	.27	10	10	10	10	-.33000007E+04	.83E-05	.0
	GRGA	.36	14	10	9	6	-.33000000E+04	.0	.0
	VF01A	.27	47	47	47	47	-.33000011E+04	.16E-04	.0
	FUNMIN	3.44	561	561	127	127	-.33000000E+04	.18E-06	.0
	FMIN	2.43	263	317	43	43	-.32999932E+04	.0	.0
37	VF02AD	1.21	12	24	12	24	-.34560000E+04	.0	.11E-07
	OPRQP	.28	12	24	12	24	-.34560000E+04	.19E-08	.12E-04
	GRGA	.50	38	18	17	24	-.34560000E+04	.0	.0
	VF01A	.26	50	100	50	100	-.34560023E+04	.16E-04	.11E-06
	FUNMIN	.59	104	208	20	40	-.34560000E+04	.0	.0
	FMIN	2.55	258	555	25	50	-.34560050E+04	.35E-04	.13E-02
38	VF02AD	15.91	109	0	109	0	.50554531E-08	.0	
	OPRQP	1.52	130	0	83	0	.69341770E-13	.0	.17E-09
	GRGA	.97	127	0	58	0	.14046987E-12	.0	
	VF01A	.71	106	0	106	0	.25397754E-20	.0	
	FUNMIN	.47	80	0	15	0	.16828624E-15	.0	
	FMIN	3.59	664	0	75	0	.29154678E-10	.0	
39	VF02AD	1.62	13	26	13	26	-.10000000E+01	.33E-08	.73E-05
	OPRQP	.55	29	58	27	54	-.10000183E+01	.18E-04	.30E-05
	GRGA	3.75	349	1392	118	86	-.10000000E+01	.32E-15	.36E-07
	VF01A	.60	74	148	74	148	-.10000000E+01	.62E-09	.23E-07
	FUNMIN	1.36	278	556	67	134	-.10000000E+01	.51E-08	.25E-13
	FMIN	4.72	421	842	86	172	-.10000001E+01	.15E-06	.78E-10
40	VF02AD	.90	6	18	6	18	-.25000000E+00	.55E-09	.84E-05
	OPRQP	.38	15	45	15	45	-.25000610E+00	.14E-04	.42E-06
	GRGA	2.65	432	675	113	135	-.25000000E+00	.0	.23E-06
	VF01A	.31	40	120	40	120	-.25000000E+00	.21E-09	.11E-08
	FUNMIN	1.14	215	645	54	162	-.25000000E+00	.44E-10	.18E-05
	FMIN	6.13	432	1296	74	222	-.25000000E+00	.37E-07	.44E-05

No	Code	ET	NF	NG	NDF	NDG	FV	VC	KT
41	VF02AD	1.34	7	7	7	7	.19259259E+01	.0	.19E-05
	OPRQP	.23	7	7	7	7	.19259259E+01	.11E-06	.11E-07
	GRGA	.34	9	9	6	6	.19259259E+01	.58E-10	.35E-04
	VF01A	.50	75	75	75	75	.19259259E+01	.11E-06	.26E-05
	FUNMIN	1.53	219	219	45	45	.19259260E+01	.62E-08	.62E-05
	FMIN	3.16	349	349	74	74	.19259259E+01	.22E-07	.64E-07
42	VF02AD	.89	10	20	10	20	.13857864E+02	.17E-09	.42E-05
	OPRQP	.44	22	44	20	40	.13857834E+02	.13E-04	.88E-08
	GRGA	4.01	787	942	209	158	.13857864E+02	.58E-10	.77E-05
	VF01A	.24	38	76	38	76	.13857864E+02	.13E-06	.18E-04
	FUNMIN	.75	141	282	36	72	.13857864E+02	.41E-09	.50E-05
	FMIN	3.08	293	586	52	104	.13857865E+02	.11E-06	.25E-04
43	VF02AD	1.47	12	36	12	36	-.44000000E+02	.35E-09	.75E-05
	OPRQP	.54	31	93	24	72	-.44000013E+02	.79E-05	.19E-06
	GRGA	2.95	426	900	101	153	-.44000000E+02	.0	.20E-04
	VF01A	.42	66	198	66	118	-.44000000E+02	.67E-08	.15E-05
	FUNMIN	1.31	211	633	47	141	-.44000000E+02	.41E-07	.55E-06
	FMIN	5.84	366	1215	92	276	-.44000000E+02	.0	.0
44	VF02AD	1.15	6	36	6	36	-.15000000E+02	.12E-09	.0
	OPRQP	.39	25	150	10	60	-.15000016E+02	.26E-05	.0
	GRGA	.55	28	102	13	60	-.15000000E+02	.0	.0
	VF01A	.62	105	630	105	630	-.15000004E+02	.94E-06	.0
	FUNMIN	2.48	284	1704	58	348	-.13066273E+02	.29E-02	.31E+01
	FMIN	21.26	1099	7042	58	348	-.30872255E+23	.0	
45	VF02AD	2.13	8	0	8	0	.10000000E+01	.0	.0
	OPRQP	.37	13	0	10	0	.99999835E+00	.26E-05	.0
	GRGA	.39	13	0	11	0	.10000000E+01	.0	.0
	VF01A	.58	97	0	97	0	.10000000E+01	.38E-08	.0
	FUNMIN	.23	40	0	4	0	-.25773834E+37	.46E+09	.0
	FMIN	2.64	369	0	82	0	.10000007E+01	.48E-06	.0
46	VF02AD	2.21	14	28	14	28	.75557031E-06	.44E-06	.47E-04
	OPRQP	.81	69	138	29	58	.30991641E-09	.60E-05	.19E-05
	GRGA	5.26	1306	518	190	308	.56686955E-10	.27E-03	.12E-04
	VF01A	1.40	148	296	148	296	.89111379E-17	.12E-09	.25E-09
	FUNMIN	2.19	332	664	76	152	.18000812E-17	.0	.11E-09
	FMIN	2.22	179	358	45	90	.67424280E-20	.17E-09	.21E-14
47	VF02AD	2.92	20	60	20	60	.24242538E-08	.27E-06	.58E-04
	OPRQP	.94	82	246	30	90	.26816447E-11	.26E-07	.29E-05
	GRGA	1.20	182	357	27	57	.52939559E-22	.22E-10	.93E-11
	VF01A	.65	72	216	72	216	.13234890E-22	.0	.69E-11
	FUNMIN	1.42	215	645	50	150	.40366414E-20	.0	.98E-10
	FMIN	1.38	100	300	18	54	.0	.0	.0
48	VF02AD	.76	7	14	7	14	.36528296E-20	.58E-10	.16E-09
	OPRQP	.28	10	20	9	18	.18533456E-10	.58E-10	.75E-05
	GRGA	.74	53	12	63	68	.0	.29E-09	.0
	VF01A	.12	17	34	17	34	.0	.0	.0
	FUNMIN	.27	37	74	8	16	.0	.0	.0
	FMIN	.42	38	76	8	16	.0	.0	.0

No	Code	ET	NF	NG	NDF	NDG	FV	VC	KT
49	VF02AD	1.15	9	18	9	18	.22835781E-04	.58E-10	.53E-03
	OPRQP	.55	25	50	22	44	.31165541E-07	.17E-09	.37E-05
	GRGA	4.27	964	12	239	308	.83660011E-13	.16E-08	.73E-09
	VF01A	.47	55	110	55	110	.10420743E-19	.0	.16E-14
	FUNMIN	.94	155	310	32	64	.68305825E-17	.0	.17E-09
	FMIN	2.11	181	362	37	74	.19476389E-20	.58E-10	.46E-15
50	VF02AD	2.87	18	54	18	54	.31208038E-08	.12E-09	.19E-03
	OPRQP	.50	23	69	17	51	.58961311E-13	.58E-10	.60E-06
	GRGA	.68	70	18	42	60	.18892858E-36	.36E-08	.87E-27
	VF01A	.27	31	93	31	93	.10720261E-20	.58E-10	.90E-10
	FUNMIN	.53	90	270	18	54	.22499313E-21	.0	.35E-10
	FMIN	2.03	159	477	21	63	.0	.0	.0
51	VF02AD	.63	5	15	5	15	.52939559E-20	.12E-09	.15E-09
	OPRQP	.20	6	18	4	12	.10292412E-09	.81E-05	.12E-04
	GRGA	.46	36	18	12	24	.13234890E-22	.0	.20E-11
	VF01A	.13	17	51	17	51	.0	.0	.0
	FUNMIN	.20	32	96	8	24	.33087225E-21	.0	.26E-10
	FMIN	.42	30	90	7	21	.16014217E-20	.58E-10	.61E-10
52	VF02AD	1.32	8	24	8	24	.53266476E+01	.10E-09	.51E-04
	OPRQP	.30	10	30	9	27	.53266459E+01	.30E-06	.82E-06
	GRGA	1.10	174	24	46	48	.53266476E+01	.36E-09	.20E-05
	VF01A	.18	23	69	23	69	.53266476E+01	.12E-09	.20E-07
	FUNMIN	1.18	196	588	47	141	.53266475E+01	.47E-08	.24E-03
	FMIN	5.17	374	1122	70	210	.53266475E+01	.12E-07	.70E-08
53	VF02AD	1.96	8	24	8	24	.40930233E+01	.87E-10	.39E-03
	OPRQP	.37	8	24	8	24	.40930210E+01	.51E-06	.14E-04
	GRGA	.46	21	24	13	24	.40930233E+01	.76E-10	.22E-09
	VF01A	.34	36	108	36	108	.40930232E+01	.25E-07	.11E-08
	FUNMIN	1.79	191	573	47	141	.40930233E+01	.16E-08	.11E-03
	FMIN	6.65	470	1410	73	219	.40930225E+01	.17E-06	.25E-07
54	VF02AD	.76	2	2	2	2	-.72239941E-33	.13E-01	.18E-30
	OPRQP	.18	3	3	3	3	-.72239493E-33	.0	.18E-30
	GRGA	1.65	273	12	76	34	-.90354712E+00	.0	.21E-04
	VF01A	1.24	135	135	135	135	-.86740884E+00	.26E-03	.41E-07
	FUNMIN	2.71	276	276	57	57	-.86740885E+00	.0	.16E-05
	FMIN	4.41	509	509	51	51	-.88533698E+00	.41E-05	.43E-03
55	VF02AD	.42	1	6	1	6	.60000000E+01	.10E+01	.55E+00
	OPRQP	.45	6	36	6	36	.66666610E+01	.14E-04	.28E+00
	GRGA	**							
	VF01A	**							
	FUNMIN	3.45	313	1878	78	468	.66666667E+01	.63E-09	.28E+00
	FMIN	13.54	581	3486	100	600	.66666664E+01	.17E-05	.28E+00
56	VF02AD	3.91	11	44	11	44	-.34560000E+01	.29E-09	.23E-06
	OPRQP	8.63	553	2212	201	804	-.34570658E+01	.74E-03	.10E-02
	GRGA	4.82	484	2792	141	240	-.34560000E+01	.0	.10E-04
	VF01A	**							
	FUNMIN	2.06	251	1004	58	232	-.34560000E+01	.15E-08	.77E-05
	FMIN	8.12	446	1784	80	320	-.34560000E+01	.25E-05	.15E-04

No	Code	ET	NF	NG	NDF	NDG	FV	VC	KT
57	VF02AD	.22	4	4	4	4	.30646306E-01	.0	.0
	OPRQP	1.13	40	40	24	24	.28459078E-01	.89E-05	.89E-06
	GRGA	.69	22	22	10	9	.30646306E-01	.0	.0
	VF01A	**							
	FUNMIN	.50	35	35	3	3	.30324805E-01	.0	.0
	FMIN	4.97	333	344	58	58	.30647619E-01	.0	.0
59	VF02AD	1.10	15	45	15	45	-.67545660E+01	.0	
	OPRQP	.30	15	45	13	39	-.67545660E+01	.0	
	GRGA	1.08	120	351	44	81	-.67545660E+01	.0	
	VF01A	.13	21	63	21	4	-.67545660E+01	.0	
	FUNMIN	9.86	1494	4482	364	1092	-.67545660E+01	.0	
	FMIN	3.33	253	815	41	83	-.78042263E+01	.0	.0
60	VF02AD	.82	9	9	9	9	.32568233E-01	.30E-05	.52E-04
	OPRQP	.37	18	18	17	17	.32568106E-01	.88E-05	.37E-11
	GRGA	2.59	221	260	303	153	.32576441E-01	.77E-03	.51E-03
	VF01A	.22	33	33	33	33	.32568201E-01	.25E-07	.80E-10
	FUNMIN	1.16	190	190	44	44	.32568200E-01	.58E-08	.15E-05
	FMIN	2.61	347	347	40	40	.32568221E-01	.20E-05	.23E-05
61	VF02AD	.74	10	20	10	20	-.14364614E+03	.29E-09	.21E-06
	OPRQP	.53	29	58	26	52	-.14364616E+03	.15E-04	.57E-09
	GRGA	.46	13	36	6	14	-.55222222E+02	.17E+01	
	VF01A	.26	40	80	40	80	-.14364613E+03	.51E-05	.34E-09
	FUNMIN	.83	178	356	43	86	-.14364614E+03	.11E-07	.20E-04
	FMIN	2.50	217	434	45	90	-.14364614E+03	.11E-05	.37E-06
62	VF02AD	1.23	20	20	20	20	-.26272514E+05	.17E-09	.39E-05
	OPRQP	.27	24	24	8	8	-.26272516E+05	.21E-06	.0
	GRGA	.54	51	7	24	16	-.26272514E+05	.0	.0
	VF01A	.44	69	69	69	69	-.26272514E+05	.83E-08	.0
	FUNMIN	1.11	170	170	44	44	-.26272514E+05	.58E-10	.0
	FMIN	11.67	1360	1360	170	170	-.26272520E+05	.94E-06	.0
63	VF02AD	.95	9	18	9	18	.96171517E+03	.93E-09	.59E-05
	OPRQP	.53	26	52	25	50	.96171516E+03	.87E-05	.35E-06
	GRGA	1.61	178	480	56	44	.96171517E+03	.0	.62E-05
	VF01A	.29	46	92	46	92	.96171518E+03	.84E-05	.65E-07
	FUNMIN	.83	147	294	38	76	.96171517E+03	.28E-08	.43E-03
	FMIN	3.22	298	596.	57	114	.96171517E+03	.10E-05	.36E-05
64	VF02AD	.16	7	7	7	7	.26603500E+06	.16E+03	
	OPRQP	95.00	32418	32418	201	201	-.34274984E+40	.10E-04	.82E+74
	GRGA	1.38	143	267	83	39	.62998426E+04	.0	.0
	VF01A	.63	104	104	104	104	.62998487E+04	.0	.0
	FUNMIN	2.05	433	433	62	62	.62998426E+04	.0	.57E-02
	FMIN	7.64	853	854	203	203	.58000020E+04	.57E+00	.11E-01
65	VF02AD	.73	11	11	11	11	.28037441E+01	.33E+01	
	OPRQP	8.49	1770	1770	201	201	.48041751E+01	.46E+00	.0
	GRGA	.79	212	21	8	8	.22978268E+01	.0	.22E+01
	VF01A	.48	81	81	81	65	.61196995E+01	.61E-02	.27E+00
	FUNMIN	5.86	1129	1129	131	131	.10268714E+01	.0	.0
	FMIN	1.17	181	182	10	1	.13085756E+01	.0	.0

No	Code	ET	NF	NG	NDF	NDG	FV	VC	KT
66	VF02AD	.85	7	14	7	14	.51816327E+00	.39E-08	.57E-06
	OPRQP	.40	18	36	17	34	.51815751E+00	.10E-04	.11E-10
	GRGA	.57	53	104	23	28	.51816327E+00	.0	.27E-07
	VF01A	.54	60	120	60	106	.51816328E+00	.69E-08	.36E-09
	FUNMIN	***	***	***	***	***	.***	***	***
	FMIN	6.00	501	1152	88	176	.51816360E+00	.0	.0
67	VF02AD	8.24	28	392	28	392	-.11620292E+04	.27E-02	.0
	OPRQP	11.52	228	3192	107	1498	-.11620348E+04	.26E-05	.0
	GRGA	6.80	217	1624	34	266	-.11620365E+04	.0	.0
	VF01A	10.59	201	2814	201	29	-.11536092E+04	.0	.0
	FUNMIN	7.42	213	2982	23	322	-.91418344E+03	.0	.0
	FMIN	157.42	578	8850	76	1064	-.11620376E+04	.24E-02	.0
68	VF02AD	6.68	39	78	39	78	-.92042506E+00	.16E-06	.35E-04
	OPRQP	32.33	402	804	201	402	-.11592745E+01	.12E-01	.39E+02
	GRGA	***	***	***	***	***	***	***	***
	VF01A	***	***	***	***	***	***	***	***
	FUNMIN	***	***	***	***	***	***	***	***
	FMIN	***	***	***	***	***	***	***	***
69	VF02AD	5.69	40	80	40	80	-.95671289E+03	.27E-07	.71E-04
	OPRQP	4.03	47	94	8	16	-.44377075E+05	.56E-01	.54E-01
	GRGA	7.42	301	220	42	48	-.95671288E+03	.0	.45E-01
	VF01A	***	***	***	***	***	***	***	***
	FUNMIN	10.07	178	356	45	90	-.95671275E+03	.27E-09	.71E-01
	FMIN	***	***	***	***	***	***	***	***
70	VF02AD	8.99	37	37	37	37	.74984705E-02	.0	.0
	OPRQP	1.30	20	20	19	19	.26908039E+00	.92E-06	.21E-05
	GRGA	15.88	521	279	121	78	.74984788E-02	.0	.0
	VF01A	3.38	66	66	66	0	.74984636E-02	.0	.0
	FUNMIN	3.85	126	126	28	28	.74984636E-02	.0	.0
	FMIN	***	***	***	***	***	***	***	***
71	VF02AD	.99	5	10	5	10	.17014017E+02	.14E-06	.70E-05
	OPRQP	.86	37	74	30	60	.17014008E+02	.11E-04	.78E-11
	GRGA	.92	49	322	18	22	.17014017E+02	.93E-09	.13E-03
	VF01A	.72	93	186	93	185	.17014017E+02	.30E-07	.46E-06
	FUNMIN	3.19	433	866	92	184	.17014017E+02	.10E-07	.71E-04
	FMIN	18.18	1846	3693	209	417	.16917050E+02	.32E+00	.47E-02
72	VF02AD	7.37	35	70	35	70	.72767936E+03	.28E-10	.27E-05
	OPRQP	1.09	66	132	45	90	.72767784E+03	.42E-07	.98E-05
	GRGA	15.35	1174	6472	645	372	.81600018E+03	.0	.0
	VF01A	1.55	191	382	191	382	.72767936E+03	.10E-09	.46E-07
	FUNMIN	3.49	468	936	92	184	.72687420E+03	.40E-04	.61E-04
	FMIN	16.53	1606	3215	198	396	.69299635E+03	.10E-02	.80E-02
73	VF02AD	.93	13	39	13	39	.29894351E+02	.66E-04	.0
	OPRQP	.76	34	102	26	78	.29894244E+02	.78E-05	.0
	GRGA	.92	64	246	39	45	.29894378E+02	.0	.0
	VF01A	1.12	150	450	150	409	.29894378E+02	.99E-10	.0
	FUNMIN	9.57	1127	3381	286	858	.30056903E+02	.36E-02	.23E+00
	FMIN	13.88	884	3036	175	525	.29894379E+02	.21E-05	.0

No	Code	ET	NF	NG	NDF	NDG	FV	VC	KT
74	VF02AD	2.26	17	85	17	85	.51264981E+04	.22E-06	.65E-05
	OPRQP	.71	25	125	23	115	.51264980E+04	.18E-04	.23E-06
	GRGA	1.02	55	390	21	65	.51264981E+04	.30E-07	.78E-06
	VF01A	**							
	FUNMIN	12.33	1303	6515	311	1555	.51264915E+04	.13E-02	.19E-04
	FMIN	8.17	461	2318	46	230	.51264983E+04	.11E+01	.54E-06
75	VF02AD	2.21	19	95	19	95	.51744127E+04	.89E-07	.0
	OPRQP	.29	9	45	7	35	.51210733E+04	.12E+01	.20E+01
	GRGA	.72	23	235	9	45	.51744129E+04	.30E-07	.0
	VF01A	**							
	FUNMIN	13.31	1336	6680	318	1590	.51743959E+04	.24E-02	.0
	FMIN	11.16	607	3120	72	360	.51744132E+04	.96E+00	.0
76	VF02AD	1.11	6	18	6	18	-.46818182E+01	.0	.27E-04
	OPRQP	.24	8	24	8	24	-.46818231E+01	.33E-05	.97E-05
	GRGA	.56	39	36	23	36	-.46818009E+01	.0	.0
	VF01A	.39	61	183	61	183	-.46818182E+01	.36E-10	.93E-07
	FUNMIN	1.13	165	495	38	114	-.46818182E+01	.49E-08	.50E-05
	FMIN	6.08	424	1312	95	285	-.46818181E+01	.0	.0
77	VF02AD	2.55	16	32	16	32	.24150513E+00	.68E-07	.35E-04
	OPRQP	.89	52	104	35	70	.24150435E+00	.11E-04	.63E-08
	GRGA	5.08	1071	620	182	204	.24150513E+00	.23E-09	.50E-05
	VF01A	.72	79	158	79	158	.24150513E+00	.28E-07	.52E-08
	FUNMIN	1.59	240	480	56	112	.24150513E+00	.35E-09	.14E-05
	FMIN	3.80	356	712	51	102	.24150513E+00	.41E-07	.45E-07
78	VF02AD	1.53	9	27	9	27	-.29197004E+01	.35E-09	.13E-05
	OPRQP	.68	27	81	24	72	-.29197077E+01	.11E-04	.47E-06
	GRGA	1.74	436	102	10	30	-.28867500E+01	.47E-09	.44E+00
	VF01A	.46	52	156	52	156	-.29197005E+01	.12E-06	.59E-07
	FUNMIN	1.22	182	546	46	138	-.29197004E+01	.24E-08	.31E-04
	FMIN	3.68	278	834	48	144	-.29197005E+01	.15E-06	.25E-05
79	VF02AD	1.79	10	30	10	30	.78776833E-01	.34E-06	.14E-03
	OPRQP	.48	17	51	17	51	.78776506E-01	.98E-05	.40E-09
	GRGA	1.90	285	354	69	99	.78776821E-01	.41E-09	.15E-05
	VF01A	.46	53	159	53	159	.78776821E-01	.19E-08	.23E-07
	FUNMIN	1.34	213	639	53	159	.78776821E-01	.16E-08	.49E-05
	FMIN	3.02	224	672	43	129	.78776814E-01	.39E-06	.47E-07
80	VF02AD	1.86	7	21	7	21	.53949847E-01	.11E-07	.15E-07
	OPRQP	.58	17	51	17	51	.53949213E-01	.17E-04	.12E-11
	GRGA	1.02	64	291	29	45	.53949848E-01	.58E-10	.42E-05
	VF01A	1.04	108	324	108	324	.53949848E-01	.20E-08	.37E-06
	FUNMIN	1.84	199	597	48	144	.53949848E-01	.52E-09	.52E-06
	FMIN	13.66	1032	3096	132	396	.53949869E-01	.61E-06	.62E-07
81	VF02AD	2.12	8	24	8	24	.53949846E-01	.43E-07	.78E-06
	OPRQP	.61	23	69	18	54	.53949284E-01	.15E-04	.23E-11
	GRGA	1.04	64	291	29	45	.53949848E-01	.23E-09	.46E-05
	VF01A	1.20	115	345	115	345	.53949848E-01	.33E-08	.28E-08
	FUNMIN	1.81	200	600	48	144	.53949847E-01	.15E-07	.31E-07
	FMIN	22.06	1662	4986	210	630	.53949892E-01	.27E-05	.31E-05

No	Code	ET	NF	NG	NDF	NDG	FV	VC	KT
83	VF02AD	1.29	4	24	4	24	-.30665539E+05	.65E-08	.0
	OPRQP	.95	22	132	22	132	-.30665546E+05	.12E-04	.0
	GRGA	1.04	54	570	23	66	-.30665539E+05	.0	.0
	VF01A	**
	FUNMIN	13.74	1190	7140	287	1722	-.30642426E+05	.0	.0
	FMIN	30.85	1287	8719	205	1230	-.40144386E+05	.11E+03	
84	VF02AD	1.70	6	36	6	36	-.52803365E+07	.63E-01	.0
	OPRQP	.40	43	258	5	30	-.55883016E+07	.68E+00	.22E+06
	GRGA	.92	36	384	13	60	-.52803351E+07	.0	.0
	VF01A	1.31	201	1206	201	145	-.30786644E+08	.25E+03	
	FUNMIN	.65	62	372	17	102	-.37331139E+07	.0	.0
	FMIN	17.78	728	4950	86	516	-.52803347E+07	.0	.0
85	VF02AD	***
	OPRQP	15.79	467	17746	201	7638	-.14375131E+01	.75E-05	.20E-02
	GRGA	12.07	98	7068	44	684	-.19051338E+01	.0	.0
	VF01A	5.59	201	7638	201	727	-.16100026E+01	.17E-01	.11E-01
	FUNMIN	***
	FMIN	***
86	VF02AD	1.26	9	90	9	90	-.32211661E+02	.17E-09	.0
	OPRQP	.39	9	90	9	90	-.31842030E+02	.39E-05	.0
	GRGA	1.81	246	350	15	100	-.32291104E+02	.58E-10	.0
	VF01A	.55	57	570	57	570	-.31862731E+02	.21E-05	.0
	FUNMIN	4.59	371	3710	89	890	-.32224850E+02	.0	.0
	FMIN	49.97	1190	14944	112	898	-.32292392E+02	.0	.0
87	VF02AD	7.59	25	100	25	100	.89275977E+04	.91E-07	.56E-06
	OPRQP	8.89	343	1372	201	804	.89275979E+04	.51E-07	.0
	GRGA	1.92	94	1244	30	60	.89276008E+04	.72E-07	.0
	VF01A	2.38	201	804	201	804	-.83892056E+01	.31E+03	
	FUNMIN	16.45	1464	5856	314	1256	.89275976E+04	.11E-04	.34E-05
	FMIN	13.94	840	3360	86	344	.89276019E+04	.19E-03	.48E-05
88	VF02AD	.27	3	3	3	3	.0	.13E+00	.0
	OPRQP	3.51	72	72	53	53	.13625202E+01	.13E-06	.17E-06
	GRGA	6.63	279	282	64	30	.13550544E+01	.74E-06	.32E-03
	VF01A	4.39	88	88	88	88	.13626566E+01	.20E-09	.93E-05
	FUNMIN	11.77	419	419	99	99	.13619869E+01	.63E-06	.16E-04
	FMIN	1.38	45	46	9	9	.32087437E-10	.13E+00	.53E-05
89	VF02AD	7.06	44	44	44	44	.26684406E+01	.11E-10	.33E+01
	OPRQP	4.66	72	72	53	53	.13626198E+01	.35E-07	.44E-04
	GRGA	8.25	194	244	50	29	.13550329E+01	.74E-05	.14E-03
	VF01A	7.17	103	103	103	103	.13626570E+01	.0	.98E-07
	FUNMIN	15.78	455	455	96	96	.13619867E+01	.63E-06	.16E-04
	FMIN	2.41	64	65	10	10	.14256270E-11	.13E+00	.24E-05
90	VF02AD	.65	3	3	3	3	.0	.13E+00	.0
	OPRQP	3.28	41	41	26	26	.12802436E-10	.13E+00	.72E-05
	GRGA	71.56	725	2311	266	104	.13626568E+01	.0	.14E-03
	VF01A	7.51	86	86	86	86	.13626638E+01	.0	.14E-03
	FUNMIN	13.15	291	291	66	66	.13619848E+01	.64E-06	.15E-03
	FMIN	2.21	47	48	9	9	.0	.13E+00	.0

No	Code	ET	NF	NG	NDF	NDG	FV	VC	KT
91	VF02AD	14.61	43	43	43	43	.13626568E+01	.73E-11	.18E-03
	OPRQP	7.47	72	72	49	49	.13625358E+01	.11E-06	.79E-05
	GRGA	53.99	508	1239	180	68	.13626568E+01	.0	.67E-03
	VF01A	11.19	95	95	95	95	.13626493E+01	.71E-08	.24E-04
	FUNMIN	35.26	574	574	131	131	.13622454E+01	.39E-06	.34E-03
	FMIN	5.84	94	95	16	16	.42345958E-10	.13E+00	.13E-04
92	VF02AD	1.27	3	3	3	3	.0	.13E+00	.0
	OPRQP	11.41	85	85	62	62	.13626182E+01	.36E-07	.26E-04
	GRGA	170.98	960	3331	416	155	.13630970E+01	.0	.70E-01
	VF01A	14.11	97	97	97	97	.13626560E+01	.80E-09	.11E-05
	FUNMIN	24.44	317	317	68	68	.13623929E+01	.25E-06	.55E-04
	FMIN	8.58	113	114	19	19	.15825515E-10	.13E+00	.79E-05
93	VF02AD	4.29	18	36	18	36	.13507596E+03	.13E-08	.45E-03
	OPRQP	.40	18	36	10	20	-.60583718E+06	.32E+00	.93E+05
	GRGA	5.39	622	1642	149	164	.13507596E+03	.0	.98E-03
	VF01A	.84	78	156	78	144	.13507595E+03	.26E-06	.34E-05
	FUNMIN	2.59	305	610	63	126	.13507596E+03	.20E-07	.24E-03
	FMIN	11.72	877	2017	175	350	.13507596E+03	.28E-08	.32E-04
95	VF02AD	1.08	2	8	2	8	.15619504E-01	.31E-06	.0
	OPRQP	1.66	33	132	33	132	.14416322E-01	.23E-04	.0
	GRGA	.85	46	208	22	48	.15619525E-01	.0	.0
	VF01A	3.14	349	1396	349	158	-.32373017E+01	.92E-01	.0
	FUNMIN	27.80	2114	8456	524	2096	.12340870E+00	.15E-02	.0
	FMIN	20.81	1213	4943	175	613	.15619487E-01	.32E-05	.0
96	VF02AD	1.10	2	8	2	8	.15619506E-01	.71E-06	.0
	OPRQP	1.72	35	140	35	140	.14847357E-01	.14E-04	.0
	GRGA	.67	44	192	22	48	.15619525E-01	.0	.0
	VF01A	3.26	363	1452	363	102	-.64055122E+00	.25E-01	.0
	FUNMIN	27.36	2108	8432	522	2088	-.40554497E-02	.12E-02	.0
	FMIN	22.97	1339	5453	195	694	.15619791E-01	.29E-08	.0
97	VF02AD	3.72	7	28	7	28	.31358091E+01	.26E-07	.0
	OPRQP	10.53	401	1604	201	804	-.19552600E+03	.41E+02	
	GRGA	1.04	73	484	31	60	.31358091E+01	.0	.0
	VF01A	2.24	201	804	201	95	-.48687755E+02	.96E+00	.0
	FUNMIN	5.91	468	1872	101	404	.35217313E+01	.21E-02	.0
	FMIN	15.92	898	3598	156	467	.40712464E+01	.14E-07	.0
98	VF02AD	3.75	7	28	7	28	.31358091E+01	.13E-09	.0
	OPRQP	4.45	164	656	84	336	-.85263714E+03	.19E+02	
	GRGA	.98	72	412	31	60	.31358091E+01	.0	.0
	VF01A	1.82	201	804	201	73	-.48625541E+02	.95E+00	.0
	FUNMIN	19.45	1510	6040	354	1416	.34682033E+01	.23E-02	.0
	FMIN	22.71	1314	5259	212	617	.31357985E+01	.70E-05	.0
99	VF02AD	1.55	2	4	2	4	-.83239119E+09	.50E+04	
	OPRQP	1.31	65	130	14	28	-.85666962E+09	.21E+05	
	GRGA	8.39	469	1422	69	82	-.83107978E+09	.45E-07	.17E+06
	VF01A	2.22	68	136	68	136	-.83107989E+09	.83E-02	.78E+02
	FUNMIN	3.86	181	362	46	92	-.83107989E+09	.67E-04	.0
	FMIN	48.92	2380	4760	206	412	-.83436612E+09	.11E+04	

No	Code	ET	NF	NG	NDF	NDG	FV	VC	KT
100	VF02AD	5.29	20	80	20	80	.68063006E+03	.76E-07	.29E-03
	OPRQP	1.09	49	196	31	124	.68063005E+03	.76E-05	.73E-08
	GRGA	1.94	213	504	33	104	.68063006E+03	.0	.24E-03
	VF01A	1.25	128	512	128	176	.68063004E+03	.24E-04	.15E-03
	FUNMIN	9.10	1037	4148	263	1052	.70530863E+03	.0	
	FMIN	10.17	544	2273	109	436	.68063006E+03	.14E-05	.73E-04
101	VF02AD	53.12	86	516	86	516	.18097648E+04	.98E-10	.37E-01
	OPRQP	13.41	386	2316	174	1044	.18097583E+04	.15E-05	.77E-02
	GRGA	36.71	1512	11706	224	756	.18097684E+04	.0	.0
	VF01A	***
	FUNMIN	13.27	529	3174	119	714	.17724429E+04	.84E-02	.18E-01
	FMIN	***
102	VF02AD	35.60	62	372	62	372	.91188057E+03	.0	.58E-03
	OPRQP	8.02	188	1128	102	612	.91187330E+03	.37E-05	.20E-02
	GRGA	32.87	928	11766	179	492	.91188059E+03	.0	.41E-01
	VF01A	***
	FUNMIN	16.20	648	3888	141	846	.91188057E+03	.42E-08	.11E-01
	FMIN	***
103	VF02AD	44.34	66	396	66	396	.54366796E+03	.65E-08	.86E-02
	OPRQP	6.56	143	858	77	462	.54366071E+03	.69E-05	.18E-03
	GRGA	32.46	879	11256	197	558	.54366797E+03	.0	.70E-02
	VF01A	***
	FUNMIN	21.22	842	5052	185	1110	.54366799E+03	.39E-06	.23E-03
	FMIN	***
104	VF02AD	26.59	19	114	19	114	.39511634E+01	.47E-09	.95E-05
	OPRQP	1.90	32	192	28	168	.39511559E+01	.17E-05	.15E-04
	GRGA	9.64	383	5010	160	372	.39511634E+01	.0	.24E-05
	VF01A	1.77	81	486	81	298	.39511603E+01	.12E-05	.18E-07
	FUNMIN	7.32	363	2178	84	504	.39511634E+01	.23E-09	.33E-04
	FMIN	35.99	1109	7019	203	1213	.39511632E+01	.11E-06	.14E-05
105	VF02AD	68.31	47	47	47	47	.11384186E+04	.0	.0
	OPRQP	27.62	64	64	36	36	.11514826E+04	.14E-13	.60E-05
	GRGA	187.13	527	19	196	119	.11384269E+04	.0	.0
	VF01A	148.78	222	222	222	222	.11384162E+04	.0	.0
	FUNMIN	146.24	569	569	112	112	.11514918E+04	.43E-08	.73E-02
	FMIN	***
106	VF02AD	44.82	44	264	44	264	.70492480E+04	.80E-04	.90E-06
	OPRQP	11.59	423	2538	201	1206	.43606073E+04	.13E+04	
	GRGA	4.04	144	3312	55	138	.70493324E+04	.0	.12E-02
	VF01A	1.52	201	1206	201	711	.29471330E+04	.60E+05	
	FUNMIN	.24	27	162	2	12	.14790334E+05	.0	.0
	FMIN	39.26	1733	10882	205	901	.95981997E+04	.52E+03	
107	VF02AD	6.80	7	42	7	42	.50550108E+04	.60E-06	.0
	OPRQP	2.05	28	168	24	144	.50549210E+04	.21E-04	.0
	GRGA	2.33	174	516	50	132	.50550118E+04	.18E-09	.0
	VF01A	4.25	227	1362	227	1362	-.81561181E+27	.98E+12	
	FUNMIN	5.57	384	2304	93	558	.50550120E+04	.12E-06	.0
	FMIN	39.52	1337	8022	210	1260	.10685045E-02	.17E+01	.14E-07

No	Code	ET	NF	NG	NDF	NDG	FV	VC	KT
108	VF02AD	14.17	9	117	9	117	-.69701242E+00	.34E-02	.64E-11
	OPRQP	2.86	51	663	39	507	-.86602552E+00	.82E-06	.57E-08
	GRGA	21.85	678	14976	176	1027	-.67498144E+00	.0	.35E-05
	VF01A	3.58	201	2613	201	893	-.86666678E+00	.47E-02	.58E-02
	FUNMIN	7.99	546	7098	123	1599	-.67498144E+00	.0	.30E-05
	FMIN	46.47	984	13566	210	1964	-.86588930E+00	.19E-03	.64E-05
109	VF02AD	*****	*****	*****	*****	*****	*****	*****	*****
	OPRQP	3.26	55	550	36	360	.53621928E+04	.16E-02	.0
	GRGA	9.92	560	5990	110	400	.53620693E+04	.36E-07	.0
	VF01A	*****	*****	*****	*****	*****	*****	*****	*****
	FUNMIN	*****	*****	*****	*****	*****	*****	*****	*****
	FMIN	71.03	1968	19683	205	2050	.53620421E+04	.24E+07	.0
110	VF02AD	9.85	9	0	9	0	-.45778470E+02	.0	.0
	OPRQP	.47	13	0	8	0	-.45778470E+02	.0	.0
	GRGA	.74	18	0	10	0	-.45778470E+02	.0	.0
	VF01A	.21	11	0	11	0	-.45778470E+02	.0	.0
	FUNMIN	.65	32	0	9	0	-.45778470E+02	.0	.0
	FMIN	1.49	124	0	25	0	-.45778470E+02	.0	.0
111	VF02AD	87.04	59	177	59	177	-.47761091E+02	.17E-07	.24E-05
	OPRQP	16.21	419	1257	201	603	-.47761088E+02	.62E-06	.38E-03
	GRGA	24.76	711	9891	171	267	-.47709717E+02	.0	.36E-05
	VF01A	7.00	223	669	223	669	-.47761088E+02	.32E-06	.32E-07
	FUNMIN	15.14	643	1929	141	423	-.47761090E+02	.35E-09	.14E-03
	FMIN	40.76	1880	5640	206	618	-.51772150E+02	.29E+00	.18E-02
112	VF02AD	4.02	11	33	11	33	-.47597034E+02	.30E-09	.12E+02
	OPRQP	22.84	2249	6747	201	603	-.47711654E+02	.72E-05	.86E-02
	GRGA	7.26	868	204	168	321	-.47725497E+02	.58E-10	.72E+00
	VF01A	2.29	201	603	201	603	-.49379780E+02	.12E+00	.12E+00
	FUNMIN	4.10	270	810	58	174	-.47711979E+02	.87E-09	.39E-01
	FMIN	32.72	1994	5982	171	513	-.47715203E+02	.77E-07	.87E-01
113	VF02AD	12.40	15	120	15	120	.24306209E+02	.16E-07	.11E-03
	OPRQP	1.94	30	240	28	224	.24306193E+02	.13E-04	.11E-08
	GRGA	3.59	336	1040	46	232	.24306209E+02	.0	.0
	VF01A	2.91	201	1608	201	860	.24285322E+02	.19E-01	.14E+00
	FUNMIN	14.57	1183	9464	269	2152	.24897161E+02	.0	.0
	FMIN	32.22	906	8089	189	1512	.24306207E+02	.56E-04	.84E-04
114	VF02AD	67.27	33	363	33	363	-.17688070E+04	.59E-06	.36E-05
	OPRQP	18.52	379	4169	201	2211	-.15605214E+04	.54E-05	.17E+00
	GRGA	5.33	133	3795	62	297	-.17684691E+04	.16E-07	.32E-02
	VF01A	*****	*****	*****	*****	*****	*****	*****	*****
	FUNMIN	*****	*****	*****	*****	*****	*****	*****	*****
	FMIN	61.22	1430	16484	205	2255	-.21802064E+04	.27E+01	
116	VF02AD	103.46	15	225	15	225	.18197689E+03	.10E+01	
	OPRQP	2.16	29	435	18	270	.17725186E+03	.27E-01	.17E+01
	GRGA	23.43	345	16605	134	870	.97588409E+02	.0	.0
	VF01A	4.03	201	3015	201	1784	.49995040E+02	.33E+00	.51E-13
	FUNMIN	*****	*****	*****	*****	*****	*****	*****	*****
	FMIN	88.00	1443	23564	205	2792	.96291888E+02	.64E-01	

No	Code	ET	NF	NG	NDF	NDG	FV	VC	KT
117	VF02AD	59.89	17	85	17	85	.32348679E+02	.36E-07	.28E-05
	OPRQP	9.00	41	205	40	200	.32348442E+02	.54E-05	.73E-06
	GRGA	17.62	1142	3080	197	710	.32348679E+02	.0	.12E-03
	VF01A	6.15	201	1005	201	180	.20640735E+01	.73E+00	.33E+01
	FUNMIN	88.68	2916	14580	727	3635	.16684781E+04	.0	.0
	FMIN	57.34	1324	6892	206	1030	.32370808E+02	.47E-02	.97E-02
118	VF02AD**								
	OPRQP	5.71	35	1015	25	725	.66482044E+03	.26E-05	.0
	GRGA	3.64	35	3422	23	377	.66537276E+03	.0	.21E-01
	VF01A **								
	FUNMIN**								
	FMIN ***								
119	VF02AD	44.06	18	144	18	144	.24489970E+03	.11E-07	.21E-02
	OPRQP	6.38	25	200	21	168	.24489970E+03	.77E-08	.14E-04
	GRGA	5.14	85	368	90	352	.24490007E+03	.15E-08	.14E+00
	VF01A **								
	FUNMIN**								
	FMIN	87.95	1574	12592	206	1648	.16841204E+03	.21E+01	.90E+01

RESTRICTION FUNCTION VALUES AND LAGRANGE-MULTIPLIERS

To allow a thorough investigation of the test problems, we enclude a list of all restriction function values

$$G := (g_1(x^*), \ldots, g_m(x^*))$$

and of all optimal Lagrange-multipliers

$$U := (u_1^*, \ldots, u_m^*).$$

The results of the subsequent table inform the reader, whether he has to expect scaling difficulties when solving a problem, how the Kuhn-Tucker-conditions are satisfied, and which constraints dominate in the Lagrange-function..

The solution x* is either the exact one or computed by one of the algorithms of Table 1 and is found in the test problem documentation of Chapter IV. The Lagrange-multipliers are obtained by the technique described in Section 2 of Chapter I. Their absolutely greatest and smallest value corresponding to the active and equality constraints have also been presented in the test problem documentation of Chapter IV. Upper and lower bounds of the variables are treated as general restrictions, cf. (2), and the succession of the constraints is defined in the following way:

I : Inequality constraints.

L : Lower bounds.

U : Upper bounds.

E : Equality constraints.

The symbols I, L, U, E follow each value for $g_j(x^*)$.

```
 1 G= (  .2500000E+01 L )
   U= (  .0              )

 2 G= (  .0           L )
   U= (  .183E+00       )

 3 G= (  .0           L )
   U= (  .100E+01        )

 4 G= (  .0           L, .0           L )
   U= (  .400E+01       ,  .100E+01        )

 5 G= (  .9528024E+00 L, .1452802E+01 L, .4547198E+01 U, .4547198E+01 U )

   U= (  .0              ,  .0            ,  .0             ,  .0             )


 6 G= (  .0           E )
   U= (  .0             )

 7 G= (  .0           E )
   U= ( -.289E+00        )

 8 G= (  .0           E, .5820766E-10 E )
   U= (  .0             ,  .0              )

 9 G= (  .0           E )
   U= (  .327E-01        )

10 G= (  .0           I )
   U= (  .500E+00        )

11 G= (  .5820766E-10 I )
   U= (  .305E+01        )

12 G= (  .0           I )
   U= (  .500E+00        )

13 G= (  .0           I, .1000000E+01 L, .0           L )
   U= (  .0             ,  .0            ,  .0              )

14 G= (  .1818989E-10 I,-.5820766E-10 E )
   U= (  .185E+01        ,-.159E+01        )

15 G= (  .0           I, .4500000E+01 I, .0           U )
   U= (  .700E+03        ,  .0            ,  .175E+04        )

16 G= (  .5625000E+00 I, .5000000E+00 I, .1000000E+01 L, .0           U,
         .7500000E+00 U )
   U= (  .0             ,  .0            ,  .0            ,  .100E+01        ,
         .0              )

17 G= (  .0           I, .0           I, .5000000E+00 L, .5000000E+00 U,
         .1000000E+01 U )
   U= (  .200E+01        ,  .0            ,  .0            ,  .0             ,
         .0              )

18 G= ( -.9313226E-09 I, .2275000E+03 I, .1381139E+02 L, .1581139E+01 L,
         .3418861E+02 U, .4841886E+02 U )
   U= (  .200E+00        ,  .0            ,  .0            ,  .0             ,
         .0              ,  .0              )
```

```
19 G= (-.9313226E-09 I, .0              I, .1095000E+01 L, .8429608E+00 L,
       .8590500E+02 U, .9915704E+02 U)
    U= ( .110E+04        , .123E+04        , .0              , .0              ,
       .0              , .0              )

20 G= ( .1250000E+01 I, .1116025E+01 I,-.3637979E-11 I, .1000000E+01 L,
       .0              U )
    U= ( .0              , .0              , .711E+02        , .0              ,
       .195E+03        )

21 G= ( .1000000E+02 I, .0              L, .5000000E+02 L, .4800000E+02 U,
       .5000000E+02 U)
    U= ( .0              , .400E-01        , .0              , .0              ,
       .0              )

22 G= ( .0              I, .0              I)
    U= ( .667E+00        , .667E+00        )

23 G= ( .1000000E+01 I, .1000000E+01 I, .1000000E+01 I, .0              I,
       .0              I, .5100000E+02 L, .5100000E+02 L, .4900000E+02 U,
       .4900000E+02 U)
    U= ( .0              , .0              , .0              , .200E+01        ,
       .200E+01        , .0              , .0              , .0              ,
       .0,             )

24 G= ( .0              I, .6000000E+01 I, .0              I, .3000000E+01 L,
       .1732051E+01 L)
    U= ( .866E+00        , .0              , .500E+00        , .0              ,
       .0              )

25 G= ( .4990000E+02 L, .2500000E+02 L, .1500000E+01 L, .5000000E+02 U,
       .6000000E+00 U, .3500000E+01 U)
    U= ( .0              , .0              , .0              , .0              ,
       .0              , .0              )

26 G= ( .0              E )
    U= ( .0              )

27 G= ( .0              E )
    U= (-.400E-01        )

28 G= ( .0              E )
    U= ( .0              )

29 G= ( .0              I )
    U= ( .707E+00        )

30 G= ( .0              I, .0              L, .1000000E+02 L, .1000000E+02 L,
       .9000000E+01 U, .1000000E+02 U, .1000000E+02 U)
    U= ( .100E+01        , .0              , .0              , .0              ,
       .0              , .0              )

31 G= ( .0              I, .1057735E+02 L, .7320508E+00 L, .1000000E+02 L,
       .9422650E+01 U, .8267949E+01 U, .1000000E+01 U)
    U= ( .600E+01        , .0              , .0              , .0              ,
       .0              , .0              )

32 G= ( .1000000E+01 I, .0              L, .0              L, .1000000E+01 L,
       .0              E )
    U= ( .0              , .0              , .400E+01        , .0              ,
       -.200E+01        )
```

```
33 G= ( .0              I, .1164153E-09 I, .0              L, .1414214E+01 L,
      .1414214E+01 L, .3585786E+01 U)
   U= ( .177E+00        , .177E+00      , .110E+02          , .0              ,
      .0              , .0              )

34 G= ( .0              I,-.1746230E-09 I, .8340324E+00 L, .2302585E+01 L,
      .1000000E+02 L, .9916597E+02 U, .9769741E+02 U, .0              U)
   U= ( .434E+00        , .434E-01      , .0                , .0              ,
      .0              , .0            , .0                , .434E-01        )

35 G= ( .5820766E-10 I, .1333333E+01 L, .7777778E+00 L, .4444444E+00 L)

   U= ( .222E+00        , .0            , .0                , .0              )


36 G= ( .0              I, .2000000E+02 L, .1100000E+02 L, .1500000E+02 L,
      .0              U, .0            U, .2700000E+02 U)
   U= ( .110E+03        , .0            , .0                , .0              ,
      .550E+02        , .800E+02      , .0                )

37 G= ( .0              I, .7200000E+02 I, .2400000E+02 L, .1200000E+02 L,
      .1200000E+02 L, .1800000E+02 U, .3000000E+02 U, .3000000E+02 U)
   U= ( .144E+03        , .0            , .0                , .0              ,
      .0              , .0            , .0                , .0              )

38 G= ( .1100000E+02 L, .1100000E+02 L, .1100000E+02 L, .1100000E+02 L,
      .9000000E+01 U, .9000000E+01 U, .9000000E+01 U, .9000000E+01 U)
   U= ( .0              , .0            , .0                , .0              ,
      .0              , .0            , .0                , .0              )

39 G= ( .0              E, .0            E)
   U= ( .100E+01        , .100E+01      )

40 G= (-.3637979E-11 E, .0            E, .3637979E-11 E)
   U= (-.500E+00        , .472E+00      ,-.354E+00          )

41 G= ( .6666667E+00 L, .3333333E+00 L, .3333333E+00 L, .2000000E+01 L,
      .3333333E+00 U, .6666667E+00 U, .6666667E+00 U, .0              U,
      .0              E)
   U= ( .0              , .0            , .0                , .0              ,
      .0              , .0            , .0                , .111E+00        ,
     -.111E+00        )

42 G= ( .0              E, .0            E)
   U= ( .200E+01        ,-.254E+01      )

43 G= ( .0              I, .1000000E+01 I, .0              I)
   U= ( .100E+01        , .0            , .200E+01          )

44 G= ( .2000000E+01 I, .9000000E+01 I, .0              I, .4000000E+01 I,
      .0              I, .1000000E+01 I, .0              L, .3000000E+01 L,
      .0              L, .4000000E+01 L)
   U= ( .0              , .0            , .125E+01          , .0              ,
      .150E+01        , .0            , .875E+01          , .0              ,
      .350E+01        , .0            )

45 G= ( .1000000E+01 L, .2000000E+01 L, .3000000E+01 L, .4000000E+01 L,
      .5000000E+01 L, .0            U, .0              U, .0              U,
      .0              U, .0            U)
   U= ( .0              , .0            , .0                , .0              ,
      .0              , .100E+01      , .500E+00          , .333E+00        ,
      .250E+00        , .200E+00      )
```

```
46 G= ( .0              E, .0              E )
   U= ( .0                , .0                )

47 G= ( .0              E, .0              E, .0              E )
   U= ( .0                , .0                , .0                )

48 G= ( .0              E, .0              E )
   U= ( .0                , .0                )

49 G= ( .0              E, .0              E )
   U= ( .0                , .0                )

50 G= ( .0              E, .0              E, .0              E )
   U= ( .0                , .0                , .0                )

51 G= ( .0              E, .0              E, .0              E )
   U= ( .0                , .0                , .0                )

52 G= ( .0              E, .0              E, .0              E )
   U= (-.328E+01          ,-.291E+01          , .775E+01          )

53 G= ( .9232558E+01 L, .1025581E+02 L, .1062791E+02 L, .9883721E+01 L,
        .1025581E+02 L, .1076744E+02 U, .9744186E+01 U, .9372093E+01 U,
        .1011628E+02 U, .9744186E+01 U, .0              E, .0              E,
        .0              E )
   U= ( .0                , .0                , .0                , .0                ,
        .0                , .0                , .0                , .0                ,
        .0                , .0                ,-.205E+01          ,-.223E+01          ,
        .595E+01          )

54 G= ( .1308571E+05 L, .1112857E+02 L, .2000000E+07 L, .1000000E+02 L,
        .1001000E+01 L, .1000000E+09 L, .6914286E+04 U, .8871429E+01 U,
        .8000000E+07 U, .1000000E+02 U, .9990000E+00 U, .1000000E+09 U,
        .0              E )
   U= ( .0                , .0                , .0                , .0                ,
        .0                , .0                , .0                , .0                ,
        .0                , .0                , .0                , .0                ,
        .486E-04          )

55 G= ( .0              L, .1333333E+01 L, .1666667E+01 L, .1000000E+01 L,
        .6666667E+00 L, .3333333E+00 L, .1000000E+01 U, .0              U,
   U= ( .667E+00          , .0                , .0                , .0                ,
        .667E+00          , .0                , .133E+01          , .0                ,

56 G= ( .5820766E-10 E, .0              E, .0              E, .5820766E-10 E )

   U= ( .681E-11          , .111E-10          , .111E-10          ,-.144E+01          )

57 G= ( .0              I, .1995267E-01 L, .5284846E+01 L )
   U= ( .667E-01          , .0                , .0                )

59 G= ( .8413345E-03 I, .5019134E+02 I, .2100057E+03 I, .1355010E+02 L,
        .5166018E+02 L, .6144990E+02 U, .1333982E+02 U )
   U= ( .114E-01          , .0                , .0                , .0                ,
        .0                , .0                , .0                )

60 G= ( .1110486E+02 L, .1119667E+02 L, .1153526E+02 L, .8895141E+01 U,
        .8803326E+01 U, .8464738E+01 U,-.2328306E-09 E )
   U= ( .0                , .0                , .0                , .0                ,
        .0                , .0                , .107E-01          )
```

```
61 G= (-.2328306E-09 E,-.5820766E-10 E)
   U= ( .888E+00        , .174E+01        )

62 G= ( .6178127E+00 L, .3282022E+00 L, .5398509E-01 L, .3821873E+00 U,
       .6717978E+00 U, .9460149E+00 U, .0            E)
      U= ( .0          , .0          , .0          , .0          ,
          .0          , .0          ,-.639E+04        )

63 G= ( .3512118E+01 L, .2169882E+00 L, .3552174E+01 L, .0            E,
       .0            E)
      U= ( .0          , .0          , .0          ,-.275E+00        ,
         -.122E+01        )

64 G= ( .7275958E-10 I, .1087347E+03 L, .8512613E+02 L, .2043247E+03 L)

   U= ( .228E+04        , .0          , .0          , .0            )

65 G= ( .0            I, .8150462E+01 L, .8150462E+01 L, .9620418E+01 L,
       .8495382E+00 U, .8495383E+00 U, .3795825E+00 U)
      U= ( .822E-01        , .0          , .0          , .0          ,
          .0          , .0          , .0            )

66 G= ( .0            I,-.5820766E-10 I, .1841265E+00 L, .1202168E+01 L,
       .3327322E+01 L, .9981587E+02 U, .9879783E+02 U, .6672678E+01 U)
      U= ( .665E+00        , .200E+00        , .0          , .0          ,
          .0          , .0          , .0          , .0            )

67 G= ( .3056042E+04 I, .2000000E+04 I, .5619544E+01 I, .4189902E+01 I,
       .7414429E+01 I, .2605525E+01 I, .4569706E+01 I, .1943958E+04 I,
       .0            I, .2380456E+01 I, .8100979E+00 I, .1585571E+01 I,
       .1384475E+01 I, .1243029E+02 I, .1728371E+04 L, .1600000E+05 L,
       .9814150E+02 L, .2716287E+03 U, .0            U, .2185849E+02 U)
      U= ( .0          , .0          , .0          , .0          ,
          .0          , .0          , .0          , .0          ,
          .313E+00        , .0          , .159E+01        , .0          ,
          .0          , .0          , .0          , .0          ,
          .0          , .0          , .340E-01        , .0            )

68 G= ( .6775875E-01 L, .3646172E+01 L, .2661752E-03 L, .8948622E+00 L,
       .9993214E+02 U, .9635383E+02 U, .1999734E+01 U, .1105138E+01 U,
      -.6074572E-09 E, .5309630E-07 E)
      U= ( .0          , .0          , .0          , .0          ,
          .0          , .0          , .0          , .0          ,
          .137E+02        ,-.777E-01        )

69 G= ( .2927142E-01 L, .1190253E+01 L, .2339468E+00 L, .7916678E+00 L,
       .9997063E+02 U, .9880975E+02 U, .1766053E+01 U, .1208332E+01 U,
       .3637979E-11 E, .4001777E-10 E)
      U= ( .0          , .0          , .0          , .0          ,
          .0          , .0          , .0          , .0          ,
          .328E+02        ,-.445E+02        )

70 G= ( .1707264E+01 I, .1227694E+02 L, .4631778E+01 L, .3128525E+00 L,
       .2029280E+01 L, .8772305E+02 U, .9536821E+02 U, .6871375E+00 U,
       .9797071E+02 U)
      U= ( .0          , .0          , .0          , .0          ,
          .0          , .0          , .0          , .0          ,
          .0            )
```

```
71 G= (  .0                I,  .0                L,  .3742999E+01 L,  .2821150E+01 L,
        .3794082E+00 L,  .4000000E+01 U,  .2570006E+00 U,  .1178850E+01 U,
        .3620592E+01 U,  .0                E )
    U= (  .552E+00          ,  .109E+01          ,  .0            ,  .0            ,
          .0                ,  .0                ,  .0            ,  .0            ,
          .0                , -.161E+00          )

72 G= (  .4092726E-11 I,  .4386038E-09 I,  .1934061E+03 L,  .1795465E+03 L,
        .1850176E+03 L,  .1687052E+03 L,  .3998066E+06 U,  .2998205E+06 U,
        .1998150E+06 U,  .9983129E+05 U )
    U= (  .769E+04          ,  .415E+05          ,  .0            ,  .0            ,
          .0                ,  .0                ,  .0            ,  .0            ,
          .0                ,  .0                )

73 G= (-.5820766E-10 I,  .0                I,  .6355216E+00 L, -.1178623E-11 L,
        .3127019E+00 L,  .5177655E-01 L, -.4001777E-10 E )
    U= (  .580E+00          ,  .411E+00          ,  .0            ,  .243E+00      ,
          .0                ,  .0                ,  .184E+02      )

74 G= (  .3489008E-01 I,  .1065110E+01 I,  .6799453E+03 L,  .1026067E+04 L,
        .6688764E+00 L,  .1537664E+00 L,  .5200547E+03 U,  .1739329E+03 U,
        .4311236E+00 U,  .9462336E+00 U,  .2980232E-07 E,  .1490116E-07 E,
        .2980232E-07 E )
    U= (  .0                ,  .0                ,  .0            ,  .0            ,
          .0                ,  .0                ,  .0            ,  .0            ,
          .0                ,  .0                , -.439E+01      , -.411E+01      ,
        -.546E+01          )

75 G= (  .6888877E-07 I,  .9599999E+00 I,  .7761592E+03 L,  .9251949E+03 L,
        .5311088E+00 L,  .5110886E-01 L,  .4238408E+03 U,  .2748051E+03 U,
        .4288912E+00 U,  .9088911E+00 U,  .0            E,  .0            E,
       -.2980232E-07 E )
    U= (  .278E+04          ,  .0                ,  .0            ,  .0            ,
          .0                ,  .0                ,  .0            ,  .0            ,
          .0                ,  .0                , -.481E+01      , -.371E+01      ,
        -.730E+01          )

76 G= (-.5820766E-10 I,  .1636364E+01 I,  .5909091E+00 I,  .2727273E+00 L,
        .2090909E+01 L, -.2633719E-10 L,  .5454545E+00 L )
    U= (  .455E+00          ,  .0                ,  .0            ,  .0            ,
          .0                ,  .173E+01          ,  .0            )

77 G= (-.5820766E-10 E, -.5820766E-10 E )
    U= (  .855E-01          ,  .319E-01          )

78 G= (  .2328306E-09 E,  .5820766E-10 E,  .5820766E-10 E )
    U= (-.744E+00          ,  .704E+00          , -.968E-01      )

79 G= (-.2910383E-09 E, -.2328306E-09 E, -.5820766E-10 E )
    U= (  .388E-01          ,  .167E-01          ,  .287E-03      )

80 G= (  .5828571E+00 L,  .3895709E+01 L,  .5027247E+01 L,  .2436359E+01 L,
        .2436355E+01 L,  .4017143E+01 U,  .7042910E+00 U,  .1372753E+01 U,
        .3963641E+01 U,  .3963645E+01 U,  .2328306E-09 E,  .5820766E-10 E,
        .1164153E-09 E )
    U= (  .0                ,  .0                ,  .0            ,  .0            ,
          .0                ,  .0                ,  .0            ,  .0            ,
          .0                ,  .0                , -.402E-01      ,  .380E-01      ,
        -.522E-02          )
```

```
81 G= ( .5828576E+00 L,  .3895708E+01 L,  .5027248E+01 L,  .2436353E+01 L,
         .2436361E+01 L,  .4017142E+01 U,  .7042917E+00 U,  .1372752E+01 U,
         .3963647E+01 U,  .3963639E+01 U,  .1164153E-09 E,  .0            E,
        -.1164153E-09 E )
    U= ( .0              ,  .0              ,  .0              ,  .0              ,
         .0              ,  .0              ,  .0              ,  .0              ,
         .0              ,  .0              , -.402E-01        ,  .380E-01        ,
        -.522E-02        )

83 G= ( .9200000E+02 I,  .8840500E+01 I,  .0            I,  .0            I,
         .1115950E+02 I,  .5000000E+01 I,  .0            L,  .0            L,
         .2995256E+01 L,  .1800000E+02 L,  .9775813E+01 L,  .2400000E+02 U,
         .1200000E+02 U,  .1500474E+02 U,  .0            U,  .8224187E+01 U )
    U= ( .0              ,  .0              ,  .809E+03        ,  .403E+03        ,
         .0              ,  .0              ,  .489E+02        ,  .843E+02        ,
         .0              ,  .0              ,  .0              ,  .0              ,
         .0              ,  .0              ,  .266E+02        ,  .0              )

84 G= ( .7556996E+05 I,  .1981571E+06 I,  .2772000E+06 I,  .2184300E+06 I,
         .9584291E+05 I,  .0            I,  .4537431E+01 L,  .1200000E+01 L,
         .4000000E+02 L,  .3000000E+00 L,  .5000000E+00 L,  .9954626E+03 U,
         .0            U,  .0            U,  .0            U,  .0            U )
    U= ( .0              ,  .0              ,  .0              ,  .0              ,
         .0              ,  .191E+02        ,  .0              ,  .0              ,
         .0              ,  .0              ,  .0              ,  .0              ,
         .412E+05        ,  .171E+04        ,  .717E+06        ,  .619E+06        )

85 G= ( .6617792E-04 I,  .6617885E-04 I,  .1921299E+03 I,  .2933116E+00 I,
         .9413438E-01 I,  .1785553E+01 I,  .3376863E+03 I,  .1316923E+03 I,
         .1008140E+01 I,  .1012132E-02 I,  .4661518E+02 I,  .4716072E+02 I,
         .1879823E+03 I,  .1393777E+00 I,  .1859694E+04 I,  .5850044E+04 I,
         .1827114E+00 I,  .6891567E+05 I,  .9275479E+07 I,  .1035868E+04 I,
         .2366087E+02 I,  .4495714E+03 I,  .2393187E+03 I,  .1332627E+03 I,
         .4425860E+01 I,  .7498787E-01 I,  .1187608E+03 I,  .3162513E+03 I,
         .3292317E+03 I,  .5182356E+03 I,  .3151816E+03 I,  .1203259E+05 I,
         .1402886E+00 I,  .6484985E-04 I,  .6791622E+05 I,  .8179076E+02 I,
         .6617885E-04 I,  .6617699E-04 I,  .7655288E+00 I,  .5294289E-04 L,
         .1029000E+03 L,  .8932500E+02 L,  .1258504E+02 L,  .2012052E+03 U,
         .2202799E+03 U,  .3184999E+02 U,  .4771601E+01 U,  .4661376E+02 U )
    U= ( .0              ,  .0              ,  .0              ,  .0              ,
         .0              ,  .0              ,  .0              ,  .0              ,
         .0              ,  .0              ,  .0              ,  .0              ,
         .0              ,  .0              ,  .0              ,  .0              ,
         .0              ,  .0              ,  .0              ,  .0              ,
         .0              ,  .0              ,  .0              ,  .0              ,
         .0              ,  .0              ,  .0              ,  .0              ,
         .0              ,  .0              ,  .0              ,  .0              ,
         .0              ,  .0              ,  .0              ,  .0              ,
         .0              ,  .0              ,  .0              ,  .0              )

86 G= ( .3629525E+02 I,  .1952319E+01 I,  .4001777E-09 I,  .1395859E+01 I,
        -.1746230E-09 I, -.5238689E-09 I,  .3831426E+02 I,  .5675248E+02 I,
         .6402843E-09 I,  .6857426E+00 I,  .3000000E+00 L,  .3334676E+00 L,
         .4000000E+00 L,  .4283101E+00 L,  .2239649E+00 L )
    U= ( .0              ,  .0              ,  .517E+01        ,  .0              ,
         .306E+01        ,  .118E+02        ,  .0              ,  .0              ,
         .104E+00        ,  .0              ,  .0              ,  .0              ,
         .0              ,  .0              ,  .0              )
```

```
87 G= (  .1078119E+03 L,  .1963186E+03 L,  .3383073E+02 L,  .8000000E+02 L,
         .1021307E+04 L,  .1532920E+00 L,  .2921881E+03 U,  .8036814E+03 U,
         .4616927E+02 U,  .0             U,  .9786929E+03 U,  .3703080E+00 U,
        -.1769513E-07 E,  .2235174E-07 E,  .4470348E-07 E,  .1490116E-07 E)
   U= (  .0             ,  .0             ,  .0             ,  .0             ,
         .0             ,  .0             ,  .0             ,  .0             ,
         .0             ,  .119E+01       ,  .0             ,  .0             ,
        -.300E+02       ,- .290E+02       ,- .226E-06       ,- .888E+00       )

88 G= (-.3637979E-11 I,  .1107432E+02 L,  .9543386E+01 L,  .8925681E+01 U,
         .1045661E+02 U)
   U= (  .106E+04       ,  .0             ,  .0             ,  .0             ,
         .0             )

89 G= (-.7275958E-11 I,  .1107432E+02 L,  .9543386E+01 L,  .1000000E+02 L,
         .8925681E+01 U,  .1045661E+02 U,  .1000000E+02 U)
   U= (  .106E+04       ,  .0             ,  .0             ,  .0             ,
         .0             ,  .0             ,  .0             )

90 G= (  .0            I,  .1070848E+02 L,  .1000002E+02 L,  .1080760E+02 L,
         .9543386E+01 L,  .9291521E+01 U,  .9999976E+01 U,  .9192400E+01 U,
         .1045661E+02 U)
   U= (  .106E+04       ,  .0             ,  .0             ,  .0             ,
         .0             ,  .0             ,  .0             ,  .0             ,
         .0             )

91 G= (-.3637979E-11 I,  .1070189E+02 L,  .1000000E+02 L,  .1081333E+02 L,
         .1045661E+02 L,  .1000000E+02 L,  .9298107E+01 U,  .1000000E+02 U,
         .9186669E+01 U,  .9543386E+01 U,  .1000000E+02 U)
   U= (  .106E+04       ,  .0             ,  .0             ,  .0             ,
         .0             ,  .0             ,  .0             ,  .0             ,
         .0             ,  .0             ,  .0             )

92 G= (  .0            I,  .1049414E+02 L,  .9999990E+01 L,  .1061495E+02 L,
         .9999998E+01 L,  .1072926E+02 L,  .9543387E+01 L,  .9505856E+01 U,
         .1000001E+02 U,  .9385049E+01 U,  .1000000E+02 U,  .9270741E+01 U,
         .1045661E+02 U)
   U= (  .106E+04       ,  .0             ,  .0             ,  .0             ,
         .0             ,  .0             ,  .0             ,  .0             ,
         .0             ,  .0             ,  .0             ,  .0             ,
         .0             )

93 G= (-.7741619E-07 I,  .6317350E-07 I,  .5332666E+01 L,  .4656744E+01 L,
         .1043299E+02 L,  .1208231E+02 L,  .7526074E+00 L,  .8786508E+00 L)
   U= (  .715E+02       ,  .622E+02       ,  .0             ,  .0             ,
         .0             ,  .0             ,  .0             ,  .0             )

95 G= (  .5820766E-10 I,  .6483440E+01 I,  .2908000E+02 I,  .8532462E+02 I,
        -.4761493E-11 L,- .3552394E-10 L,- .7026110E-10 L,- .1718565E-10 L,
        -.7489936E-10 L,  .3323303E-02 L,  .3100000E+00 U,  .4600000E-01 U,
         .6800000E-01 U,  .4200000E-01 U,  .2800000E-01 U,  .1007670E-01 U)
   U= (  .314E-02       ,  .0             ,  .0             ,  .0             ,
         .425E+01       ,  .317E+02       ,  .627E+02       ,  .153E+02       ,
         .668E+02       ,  .0             ,  .0             ,  .0             ,
         .0             ,  .0             ,  .0             ,  .0             )
```

```
 96 G= (  .0                 I, .6483440E+01 I, .6908000E+02 I, .1253246E+03 I,
           -.5197228E-11 L, -.3877482E-10 L, -.7669086E-10 L, -.1875834E-10 L,
           -.8175356E-10 L,  .3323303E-02 L,  .3100000E+00 U,  .4600000E-01 U,
            .6800000E-01 U,  .4200000E-01 U,  .2800000E-01 U,  .1007670E-01 U)
        U= (  .314E-02       ,  .0            ,  .0            ,  .0            ,
              .425E+01       ,  .317E+02      ,  .627E+02      ,  .153E+02      ,
              .668E+02       ,  .0            ,  .0            ,  .0            ,
              .0             ,  .0            ,  .0            ,  .0            )

 97 G= (  .0                 I, .1253952E+01 I, .6148000E+01 I, .1109820E+03 I,
            .2685649E+00 L,  .0            L,  .0            L,  .0            L,
            .2800000E-01 L,  .1340000E-01 L,  .4143509E-01 U,  .4600000E-01 U,
            .6800000E-01 U,  .4200000E-01 U,  .0            U,  .0            U)
        U= (  .251E+00       ,  .0            ,  .0            ,  .0            ,
              .0             ,  .222E+02      ,  .486E+02      ,  .516E+02      ,
              .0             ,  .0            ,  .0            ,  .0            ,
              .0             ,  .0            ,  .638E+01      ,  .200E+03      )

 98 G= (  .0                 I, .1253952E+01 I, .1011480E+03 I, .2059820E+03 I,
            .2685649E+00 L,  .0            L,  .0            L,  .0            L,
            .2800000E-01 L,  .1340000E-01 L,  .4143509E-01 U,  .4600000E-01 U,
            .6800000E-01 U,  .4200000E-01 U,  .0            U,  .0            U)
        U= (  .251E+00       ,  .0            ,  .0            ,  .0            ,
              .0             ,  .222E+02      ,  .486E+02      ,  .516E+02      ,
              .0             ,  .0            ,  .0            ,  .0            ,
              .0             ,  .0            ,  .638E+01      ,  .200E+03      )

 99 G= (  .5424603E+00 L,  .5290159E+00 L,  .5084506E+00 L,  .4802693E+00 L,
            .4512352E+00 L,  .4091878E+00 L,  .3527847E+00 L,  .1037540E+01 U,
            .1050984E+01 U,  .1071549E+01 U,  .1099731E+01 U,  .1128765E+01 U,
            .1170812E+01 U,  .1227215E+01 U,  .0            E,  .2980232E-07 E)
        U= (  .0            ,  .0            ,  .0            ,  .0            ,
              .0            ,  .0            ,  .0            ,  .0            ,
              .0            ,  .0            ,  .0            ,  .0            ,
              .0            ,  .0            ,  .419E+02      ,  .193E+05      )

100 G= (-.6891787E-07 I,  .2525617E+03 I,  .1448782E+03 I, -.2142042E-07 I)

        U= (  .114E+01       ,  .0            ,  .0            ,  .369E+00      )

101 G= (  .3099342E+00 I, -.1000444E-10 I,  .3637979E-11 I,  .6131223E+00 I,
            .1709765E+04 I,  .1190235E+04 I,  .2756159E+01 L,  .5108230E+00 L,
            .2050813E+01 L,  .4612874E+01 L,  .8994875E+00 L,  .1247508E+01 L,
            .2165277E-01 L,  .7143841E+01 U,  .9389177E+01 U,  .7849187E+01 U,
            .5287126E+01 U,  .9000512E+01 U,  .8652492E+01 U,  .9968347E+01 U)
        U= (  .0            ,  .376E+04      ,  .457E+04      ,  .0            ,
              .0            ,  .0            ,  .0            ,  .0            ,
              .0            ,  .0            ,  .0            ,  .0            ,
              .809E-06      ,  .0            ,  .0            ,  .0            ,
              .0            ,  .0            ,  .0            ,  .0            )

102 G= (  .2182787E-10 I, -.2432898E-10 I, -.2955858E-11 I,  .1883271E+00 I,
            .8118806E+03 I,  .2088119E+04 I,  .3796253E+01 L,  .7093588E+00 L,
            .2564386E+01 L,  .4200913E+01 L,  .7535549E+00 L,  .9952874E+00 L,
            .1731046E-01 L,  .6103747E+01 U,  .9190641E+01 U,  .7335614E+01 U,
            .5699087E+01 U,  .9146445E+01 U,  .8904713E+01 U,  .9972690E+01 U)
        U= (  .211E+02       ,  .170E+04      ,  .217E+04      ,  .0            ,
              .0            ,  .0            ,  .0            ,  .0            ,
              .0            ,  .0            ,  .0            ,  .0            ,
              .0            ,  .0            ,  .0            ,  .0            ,
              .0            ,  .0            ,  .0            ,  .0            )
```

```
103 G= ( .1091394E-10 I, .3637979E-11 I,-.6139089E-11 I, .6593837E-11 I,
          .4436680E+03 I, .2456332E+04 I, .4294105E+01 L, .7544687E+00 L,
          .2743230E+01 L, .3299979E+01 L, .6229261E+00 L, .7704064E+00 L,
          .1463883E-01 L, .5605895E+01 U, .9145531E+01 U, .7156770E+01 U,
          .6600021E+01 U, .9277074E+01 U, .9129594E+01 U, .9975361E+01 U)
      U= ( .387E+02      , .834E+03      , .129E+04      , .868E+02      ,
          .0            , .0            , .0            , .0            ,
          .0            , .0            , .0            , .0            ,
          .0            , .0            , .0            , .0            ,
          .0            , .0            , .0            , .0            )

104 G= ( .0            I,-.5820766E-10 I, .7275958E-11 I, .1455192E-10 I,
          .2951163E+01 I, .2488366E+00 I, .6365114E+01 L, .2132709E+01 L,
          .5673975E+00 L, .4957564E+00 L, .5832676E+01 L, .5427235E+01 L,
          .9133220E+00 L, .3006682E+00 L, .3534886E+01 U, .7767291E+01 U,
          .9332603E+01 U, .9404244E+01 U, .4067324E+01 U, .4472765E+01 U,
          .8986678E+01 U, .9599332E+01 U)
      U= ( .236E+01      , .621E+01      , .928E+00      , .847E+00      ,
          .0            , .0            , .0            , .0            ,
          .0            , .0            , .0            , .0            ,
          .0            , .0            , .0            , .0            ,
          .0            , .0            )

105 G= ( .1837546E+00 I, .4118928E+00 L, .4023527E+00 L, .3126131E+02 L,
          .3431351E+02 L, .4742222E+02 L, .7280178E+01 L, .1077170E+02 L,
          .1574682E+02 L, .8610725E-01 U, .9564734E-01 U, .4873869E+02 U,
          .4568649E+02 U, .2257778E+02 U, .1271982E+02 U, .9228301E+01 U,
          .4253175E+01 U)
      U= ( .0            , .0            , .0            , .0            ,
          .0            , .0            , .0            , .0            ,
          .0            , .0            , .0            , .0            ,
          .0            , .0            , .0            , .0            ,
          .0            )

106 G= ( .6748400E-05 I, .6748327E-05 I, .6748440E-05 I, .7629395E-05 I,
          .7629395E-05 I, .0            I, .4793167E+03 L, .3599429E+03 L,
          .4110071E+04 L, .1720174E+03 L, .2855985E+03 L, .2079799E+03 L,
          .2764162E+03 L, .3855979E+03 L, .9420683E+04 U, .8640057E+04 U,
          .4889929E+04 U, .8179826E+03 U, .7044015E+03 U, .7820201E+03 U,
          .7135838E+03 U, .6044021E+03 U)
      U= ( .196E+04      , .521E+04      , .511E+04      , .848E-02      ,
          .958E-02      , .100E-01      , .0            , .0            ,
          .0            , .0            , .0            , .0            ,
          .0            , .0            , .0            , .0            ,
          .0            , .0            )

107 G= ( .6670095E+00 L, .1022388E+01 L, .1818100E+00 L, .1818100E+00 L,
          .1599459E+00 L, .0            U, .0            U, .2186407E-01 U,
          .0            E,-.3637979E-11 E, .6912160E-10 E,-.5820766E-10 E,
          .0            E, .5093170E-10 E)
      U= ( .0            , .0            , .0            , .0            ,
          .0            , .279E+03      , .569E+03      , .151E+01      ,
         -.433E+04      ,-.409E+04      ,-.521E+04      ,-.200E-06      ,
          .0            , .761E+00      )
```

```
108 G= (-.6548362E-10 I, .1000000E+01 I,-.6184564E-10 I,-.6548362E-10 I,
        .1000000E+01 I,-.6912160E-10 I,-.6548362E-10 I, .1000000E+01 I,
       -.6548362E-10 I, .8660254E+00 I, .9803664E-21 I,-.2316283E-19 I,
        .8660254E+00 I, .2619846E-19 L)
    U= ( .144E+00        , .0            , .144E+00      , .144E+00      ,
         .0             , .144E+00       , .144E+00      , .0            ,
         .144E+00       , .0             , .0            , .468E-12      ,
         .0             , .0             )


109 G= ( .4527835E-01 I, .1054722E+01 I, .1612487E+07 I, .8278696E+06 I,
         .6748881E+03 L, .1134170E+04 L, .6835691E+00 L, .1788474E+00 L,
         .5600000E+02 L, .5600000E+02 L, .5464535E+01 L, .8266608E+03 L,
         .7684941E+03 L, .4164309E+00 U, .9211526E+00 U, .0           U,
         .0           U, .5053546E+02 U, .3733392E+03 U, .4315059E+03 U,
         .1490116E-07 E, .0            E,-.1490116E-07 E,-.1862645E-08 E,
         .3725290E-08 E, .9313226E-09 E)
    U= ( .125E+02        , .0            , .0            , .0            ,
         .0             , .0            , .0            , .0            ,
         .0             , .0            , .0            , .0            ,
         .0             , .0            , .0            , .389E+01      ,
         .594E+01       , .0            , .0            , .0            ,
        -.437E+01       ,-.401E+01      ,-.608E+01      ,-.146E-10      ,
         .132E-10       , .906E+00      )


110 G= ( .7349257E+01 L, .7349257E+01 L, .7349257E+01 L, .7349257E+01 L,
         .7349257E+01 L, .7349257E+01 L, .7349257E+01 L, .7349257E+01 L,
         .7349257E+01 L, .7349257E+01 L, .6487435E+00 U, .6487435E+00 U,
         .6487435E+00 U, .6487435E+00 U, .6487435E+00 U, .6487435E+00 U,
         .6487435E+00 U, .6487435E+00 U, .6487435E+00 U, .6487435E+00 U)
    U= ( .0             , .0            , .0            , .0            ,
         .0             , .0            , .0            , .0            ,
         .0             , .0            , .0            , .0            ,
         .0             , .0            , .0            , .0            ,
         .0             , .0            , .0            , .0            )


111 G= ( .9679879E+02 L, .9808794E+02 L, .9975556E+02 L, .9346251E+02 L,
         .9927685E+02 L, .9273226E+02 L, .9640329E+02 L, .9598223E+02 L,
         .9671254E+02 L, .9766442E+02 L, .1032012E+03 U, .1019121E+03 U,
         .1002444E+03 U, .1065375E+03 U, .1007232E+03 U, .1072677E+03 U,
         .1035967E+03 U, .1040178E+03 U, .1032875E+03 U, .1023356E+03 U,
        -.1164153E-09 E, .5820766E-10 E, .1746230E-09 E)
    U= ( .0             , .0            , .0            , .0            ,
         .0             , .0            , .0            , .0            ,
         .0             , .0            , .0            , .0            ,
         .0             , .0            , .0            , .0            ,
         .0             , .0            , .0            , .0            ,
        -.978E+01       ,-.130E+02      ,-.152E+02      )


112 G= ( .1773448E-01 L, .8200080E-01 L, .8825636E+00 L, .7223256E-03 L,
         .4907841E+00 L, .4325469E-03 L, .1727198E-01 L, .7764639E-02 L,
         .1984829E-01 L, .5269726E-01 L, .5820766E-08 E, .7974450E-08 E,
         .9429641E-08 E)
    U= ( .0             , .0            , .0            , .262E-03      ,
         .0             , .130E-02      , .0            , .0            ,
         .0             , .0            ,-.958E+01      ,-.126E+02      ,
        -.150E+02       )


113 G= (-.9313226E-09 I, .0           I, .0           I, .0           I,
         .9313226E-09 I, .6148503E+01 I,-.2328306E-09 I, .5002396E+02 I)
    U= ( .172E+01        , .475E+00      , .138E+01      , .205E-01      ,
         .312E+00       , .0            , .287E+00      , .0            )
```

```
114 G= ( .3296788E+00 I,  .0              I,  .0              I,  .3086216E+01 I,
            .0              I,  .0              I,  .6093070E+02 I,  .1909596E+01 I,
            .1698096E+04 L,  .1581873E+05 L,  .5410227E+02 L,  .3031226E+04 L,
            .2000000E+04 L,  .5115367E+01 L,  .5000000E+01 L,  .7493358E+01 L,
            .3616364E+00 L,  .8535354E+01 L,  .3019044E+03 U,  .1812743E+03 U,
            .6589772E+02 U,  .1968774E+04 U,  .0              U,  .2884633E+01 U,
            .0              U,  .1506642E+01 U,  .2438364E+01 U,  .8464646E+01 U,
            .0              E,  .0              E,  .0              E )
     U= ( .0                 ,  .699E+02         ,  .312E+03         ,  .0              ,
            .678E+00           ,  .230E+03         ,  .0              ,  .0              ,
            .0                 ,  .0              ,  .0              ,  .0              ,
            .0                 ,  .0              ,  .0              ,  .0              ,
            .0                 ,  .0              ,  .0              ,  .0              ,
            .0                 ,  .0              ,  .884E+00         ,  .0              ,
            .173E+03           ,  .0              ,  .0              ,  .0              ,
           -.421E+01           ,  .746E+02         ,  .594E+02         )

116 G= ( .7098639E-01 I,  .9621576E-01 I,  .2309389E-06 I,  .4758841E+02 I,
            .1524116E+03 I,  .2309462E-06 I,  .2309444E-06 I,  .2309457E-06 I,
            .2296874E-06 I,  .2309243E-06 I,  .2314664E-06 I,  .2309456E-06 I,
            .2309407E-06 I,  .2318993E-06 I,  .2384186E-06 I,  .7037703E+00 L,
            .7999860E+00 L,  .8709724E+00 L,  .9989952E-01 L,  .9081545E-01 L,
            .3605717E+00 L,  .5739803E+03 L,  .7398043E+02 L,  .1615532E-01 L,
            .0              L,  .1923413E+02 L,  .7734745E+02 L,  .6630397E-02 L,
            .1962297E+00 U,  .1000140E+00 U,  .2902758E-01 U,  .4837857E-06 U,
            .7091846E+00 U,  .4394283E+00 U,  .4259197E+03 U,  .9259196E+03 U,
            .4999838E+03 U,  .4999000E+03 U,  .1297659E+03 U,  .7265245E+02 U,
            .1499933E+03 U )
     U= ( .0                 ,  .0              ,  .209E+02         ,  .0              ,
            .0                 ,  .100E+01         ,  .209E+04         ,  .107E+00         ,
            .461E+00           ,  .453E+03         ,  .126E+01         ,  .262E+03         ,
            .107E+04           ,  .100E+01         ,  .100E+01         ,  .0              ,
            .0                 ,  .0              ,  .0              ,  .0              ,
            .0                 ,  .0              ,  .0              ,  .0              ,
            .119E+00           ,  .0              ,  .0              ,  .423E-03         ,
            .0                 ,  .0              ,  .0              ,  .0              ,
            .0                 ,  .0              ,  .0              ,  .0              ,
            .0                 ,  .0              ,  .0              ,  .0              ,
            .0                 )

117 G= ( .7217750E-08 I,  .6519258E-08 I,  .6519258E-08 I,  .8789357E-08 I,
            .6693881E-08 I,  .0              L,  .0              L,  .5174136E+01 L,
            .0              L,  .3061093E+01 L,  .1183968E+02 L,  .0              L,
            .0              L,  .1039071E+00 L,  .0              L,  .2999929E+00 L,
            .3334709E+00 L,  .3999910E+00 L,  .4283145E+00 L,  .2239607E+00 L )
     U= ( .300E+00           ,  .333E+00         ,  .400E+00         ,  .428E+00         ,
            .224E+00           ,  .363E+02         ,  .195E+01         ,  .0              ,
            .140E+01           ,  .0              ,  .0              ,  .383E+02         ,
            .568E+02           ,  .0              ,  .686E+00         ,  .0              ,
            .0                 ,  .0              ,  .0              ,  .0              )
```

```
118 G= (  .0              I, .7000000E+01 I, .9000000E+01 I, .9000000E+01 I,
        .1400000E+02 I, .1400000E+02 I, .1400000E+02 I, .1400000E+02 I,
        .4000000E+01 I, .1300000E+02 I, .1300000E+02 I, .1300000E+02 I,
        .1300000E+02 I, .6000000E+01 I, .4000000E+01 I, .4000000E+01 I,
        .0              I, .0              I, .0              I, .0              I,
        .9000000E+01 I, .0              I, .0              I, .0              I,
        .0              I, .7000000E+01 I, .0              I, .0              I,
        .0              I, .0              L, .6000000E+01 L, .0              L,
        .1000000E+01 L, .5600000E+02 L, .0              L, .1000000E+01 L,
        .6300000E+02 L, .6000000E+01 L, .3000000E+01 L, .7000000E+02 L,
        .1200000E+02 L, .5000000E+01 L, .7700000E+02 L, .1800000E+02 L,
        .1300000E+02 U, .8000000E+01 U, .1300000E+02 U, .8900000E+02 U,
        .6400000E+02 U, .6000000E+02 U, .8900000E+02 U, .5700000E+02 U,
        .5400000E+02 U, .8700000E+02 U, .5000000E+02 U, .4800000E+02 U,
        .8500000E+02 U, .4300000E+02 U, .4200000E+02 U )
   U= (  .230E+01         ,  .0              ,  .0              ,  .0              ,
        .0              ,  .0              ,  .0              ,  .0              ,
        .0              ,  .0              ,  .0              ,  .0              ,
        .0              ,  .0              ,  .0              ,  .0              ,
        .486E-01        ,  .176E+01        ,  .117E+01        ,  .586E+00        ,
        .0              ,  .291E+00        ,  .193E+00        ,  .956E-01        ,
        .166E+01        ,  .0              ,  .230E+01        ,  .230E+01        ,
        .230E+01        ,  .294E+01        ,  .0              ,  .540E+00        ,
        .0              ,  .0              ,  .191E+01        ,  .0              ,
        .0              ,  .0              ,  .0              ,  .0              ,
        .0              ,  .0              ,  .0              ,  .0              ,
        .0              ,  .0              ,  .0              ,  .0              ,
        .0              ,  .0              ,  .0              ,  .0              ,
        .0              ,  .0              ,  .0              )

119 G= (  .3984735E-01 L, .7919832E+00 L, .2028703E+00 L, .8443579E+00 L,
        .1269906E+01 L, .9347387E+00 L, .1681962E+01 L, .1553009E+00 L,
        .1567870E+01 L,-.3590212E-11 L,-.6129009E-11 L,-.8867949E-12 L,
        .6602041E+00 L,-.2543407E-11 L, .6742559E+00 L,-.1104337E-10 L,
        .4960153E+01 U, .4208017E+01 U, .4797130E+01 U, .4155642E+01 U,
        .3730094E+01 U, .4065261E+01 U, .3318038E+01 U, .4844699E+01 U,
        .3432130E+01 U, .5000000E+01 U, .5000000E+01 U, .5000000E+01 U,
        .4339796E+01 U, .5000000E+01 U, .4325744E+01 U, .5000000E+01 U,
        .0              E, .0              E,-.5820766E-10 E,-.5820766E-10 E,
       -.5820766E-10 E, .5820766E-10 E, .0              E, .0              E )
   U= (  .0              ,  .0              ,  .0              ,  .0              ,
        .0              ,  .0              ,  .0              ,  .0              ,
        .0              ,  .312E+02        ,  .533E+02        ,  .771E+01        ,
        .0              ,  .221E+02        ,  .0              ,  .960E+02        ,
        .0              ,  .0              ,  .0              ,  .0              ,
        .0              ,  .0              ,  .0              ,  .0              ,
        .0              ,  .0              ,  .0              ,  .0              ,
        .641E+02        ,-.195E+02        ,-.411E+02        ,  .420E+01        ,
        .272E+02        ,-.148E+02        ,  .254E+02        ,-.840E+02        )
```

References

[1]   J. Asaadi, A computational comparison of some nonlinear
        programs, Mathematical Programming, Vol.4 (1973), 144-154.

[2]   M. Avriel, A.C. Williams, An extension of geometric
        programming with applications in engineering optimization,
        Journal of Engineering Mathematics, Vol.5, No.3 (1971),
        187-194.

[3]   G.K. Barnes, M.S. Thesis, The University of Texas,
        Austin, Texas, 1967.

[4]   M.C. Bartholomew-Biggs, A numerical comparison between
        two approaches to nonlinear programming problems, Tech-
        nical Report No.77, Numerical Optimisation Centre,
        Hatfield, England, 1976.

[5]   P.A. Beck, I.G. Ecker, A modified concave simplex algo-
        rithm for geometric programming, Journal of Optimization
        Theory and Applications, Vol.15, No.2 (1975), 189-202.

[6]   E.J. Beltrami, A comparison of some recent iterative
        methods for the numerical solution of nonlinear programs,
        in: Proceedings of the Second International Conference
        on Computing Methods in Optimization Problems, San Remo,
        1968, Springer-Verlag, Berlin, Heidelberg, New York, 1969.

[7]   M.J. Best, A feasible conjugate-direction method to solve
        linearly constrained minimization problems, Journal of
        Optimization Theory and Applications, Vol.16, No.1/2
        (1975), 25-38.

[8]   J.T. Betts, An accelerated multiplier method for nonlinear
        programming, Journal of Optimization Theory and Applica-
        tions, Vol.21, No.2 (1977), 137-174.

[9]   J. Beuneu, Adaption de la methode des centres linearisée
      a un probléme de dispatching économique, Report du Labo-
      ratoire de Calcul de la Faculté des Sciences de l'Uni-
      versité de Lille, 1972.

[10] M.C. Biggs, Computational experience with Murray's algo-
      rithm for constrained minimization, Technical Report No.23,
      Numerical Optimisation Centre, Hatfield, England, 1971.

[11] M.J. Box, A new method of constrained optimization and a
      comparison with other methods, Computer Journal, Vol.8,
      No.1 (1965), 42-51.

[12] M.J. Box, A comparison of several current optimization
      methods and the use of transformation in constrained
      problems, Computer Journal, Vol.9 (1966), 67-77.

[13] J. Bracken, G.P. McCormick, Selected applications of
      nonlinear programming, John Wiley & Sons, Inc., New York,
      1968.

[14] R.G. Brusch, A rapidly convergent method for equality
      constrained function minimization, IEEE Conference of
      Decision and Control, San Diego, California, 1973.

[15] R.G. Brusch, A numerical comparison of several multiplier
      methods for equality constrained function minimization,
      Paper No. WA2.6, Convair Division of General Dynamics
      Corporation.

[16] J.C.P. Bus, A proposal for the classification and documen-
      tation of test problems in the field of nonlinear pro-
      gramming, Reprint, Mathematisch Centrum, Amsterdam, 1977.

[17] C.W. Caroll, The created response surface technique for
      optimizing nonlinear restrained systems, Operations Re-
      search, No.9 (1961), 169.

[18] C. Charalambous, Nonlinear least path optimization and
      nonlinear programming, Mathematical Programming, Vol.12,
      No.2 (1977), 195-225.

[19]   E. von Collani, Kostenoptimale Prüfpläne bei laufender
         Kontrolle eines normalverteilten Merkmals, Dissertation,
         Institut für Angewandte Mathematik und Statistik, Univer-
         sität Würzburg, 1978.

[20]   A.R. Colville, A comparative study on nonlinear programming
         codes, IBM Scientific Center Report 320-2949, New York,
         1968.

[21]   R.S. Dembo, Solution of complementary geometric programming
         problems, M.Sc. Thesis, Technion, Haifa, 1972.

[22]   R.S. Dembo, A set of geometric programming test problems
         and their solutions, Mathematical Programming, Vol.10,
         No.2 (1976), 192-213.

[23]   V. Dimitru, S. Moga, Testing the efficiency of the se-
         quential optimizing technique, Economic Computation and
         Economic Cybernetics Studies and Research, No.4 (1973),
         55-62.

[24]   U. Eckhardt, Pseudo-complementary algorithms for mathe-
         matical programming, in: Numerical Methods for Nonlinear
         Optimization, F.A. Lootsma ed., Academic Press, New York,
         1972.

[25]   Y. Evtushenko, Generalized Lagrange multiplier technique
         for nonlinear programming, Journal of Optimization Theory
         and Applications, Vol.21, No.2 (1977), 121-136.

[26]   R. Fletcher, S.A. Lill, A class of methods for nonlinear
         programming. II: computational experience, in: Nonlinear
         Programming, J.B. Rosen, O.L. Mangasarian, K. Ritter eds.,
         Academic Press, New York, 1970.

[27]   F.J. Gould, Nonlinear tolerance programming, in: Numerical
         Methods for Nonlinear Optimization, F.A Lootsma ed., Aca-
         demic Press, New York, 1972.

[28]   J.K. Hartman, Iterative determination of parameters for
         an exact penalty function, Journal of Optimization Theory
         and Applications, Vol.16, No.1/2 (1975), 49-66

[29]   D.M. Himmelblau, Applied nonlinear programming, McGraw-
        Hill Book-Company, New York, 1972.

[30]   D.M. Himmelblau, R.V. Yates, A new method of flow routing,
        Water Resources Research, Vol.4 (1968), 1193.

[31]   W. Hock, Testing nonlinear programming codes, submitted
        for publication.

[32]   A.G. Holzman, Comparative analysis of nonlinear programming
        codes with the Weisman algorithm, SRCC Report No.113,
        University of Pittsburgh, Pittsburgh, 1969.

[33]   W.S. Hsia, Decomposition of the convex simplex method,
        Journal of Optimization Theory and Applications, Vol.16,
        No.5/6 (1975), 399-408.

[34]   H.Y. Huang, A.K. Aggerwal, A class of quadratically con-
        vergent algorithms for constrained function minimization,
        Journal of Optimization Theory and Applications, Vol.16,
        No.5/6 (1975), 447-485.

[35]   J.P. Indusi, A computer algorithm for constrained minimi-
        zation, in: Minimization Algorithms, Mathematical Theories
        and Computer Results, G.P. Szegö ed., Academic Press,
        New York, 1972.

[36]   A.P. Jones, The chemical equilibrium problem: an appli-
        cation of SUMT, Report RAC-TP-272, Research Analysis
        Corporation, McLean, Virginia, 1967.

[37]   H. Konno, A cutting plane algorithm for solving bilinear
        programs, Mathematical Programming, Vol.11, No.1 (1976),
        14-27.

[38]   H.W. Kuhn, A.W. Tucker, Nonlinear programming, in: Pro-
        ceedings of the Second Berkeley Symposium on Mathematical
        Statistics and Programming, University of California Press,
        Berkeley, 1951.

[39]   C.L. Lawson, R.J. Hanson, Solving least squares problems,
        Prentice Hall, Englewood Cliffs, New Jersey, 1974.

[40]   G.P. McCormick, Second order conditions for constrained
        minima, SIAM Journal on Applied Mathematics, Vol.15,
        No.3 (1967), 641-652.

[41]   G.P. McCormick, Computability of global solutions to fac-
        torable nonconvex programs: Part I - Convex underesti-
        mating problems, Mathematical Programming, Vol.10, No.2
        (1976), 147-175.

[42]   A. Miele, E.E. Cragg, R.R. Iyer, A.V. Levy, Use of the
        augmented penalty function in mathematical programming
        problems, part 2, Journal of Optimization Theory and
        Applications, Vol.8, No.2 (1971), 115-130.

[43]   A. Miele, H.Y. Huang, J.C. Heideman, Sequential gradient-
        restoration algorithm for the minimization of constrained
        functions, ordinary and conjugate gradient versions,
        Journal of Optimization Theory and Applications, Vol.4,
        No.4 (1969), 213-243.

[44]   A. Miele, P.E. Mosaley, A.V. Levy, G.M. Coggins, On the
        method of multipliers for mathematical programming prob-
        lems, Journal of Optimization Theory and Applications,
        Vol.10, No.1 (1972), 1-33.

[45]   A. Miele, J.L. Tietze, A.V. Levy, Comparison of several
        gradient algorithms for mathematical programming prob-
        lems, Aero-Astronautics Report No.94, Rice University,
        Houston, Texas, 1972.

[46]   H. Mine, K. Ohno, M. Fukushima, A conjugate interior
        penalty method for certain convex programs, SIAM Journal
        on Control and Optimization, Vol.15, No.5 (1977), 747-755.

[47]   B.A. Murthagh, R.W. Sargent, A constrained minimization
        method with quadratic convergence, in: Optimization,
        R. Fletcher ed., Academic Press, New York, 1970.

[48]   D.A. Paviani, A new method for the solution of the general
        nonlinear programming problem, Ph.D. Dissertation, The
        University of Texas, Austin, Texas, 1969.

[49] J.D. Pearson, On variable metric methods of minimization,
      Report RAC-TP-302, Research Analysis Corporation, McLean,
      Virginia, 1968.

[50] H.E. Pickett, A contribution to the thaumaturgy of nonli-
      near programming, Report No. ATR-71 (S9990)-1, The
      Aerospace Corporation, San Bernardino, California, 1970.

[51] M.J.D. Powell, A method for nonlinear constraints in
      minimization problems, in: Optimization, R. Fletcher ed.,
      Academic Press, New York, 1969.

[52] M.J.D. Powell, Algorithms for nonlinear constraints that
      use Lagrangian functions, Mathematical Programming, Vol.14,
      No.2 (1978), 224-248.

[53] M.J. Rijckaert, Engineering applications of geometric
      programming, in: Optimization and Design, M. Avriel,
      M.J. Rijckaert, M. Wilde, eds., Prentice Hall, Englewood
      Cliffs, New Jersey, 1973.

[54] K. Schittkowski, An adaptive precision method for the
      numerical solution of constrained optimization problems
      applied to a time-optimal heating process, Proceedings of
      the 8-th IFIP Conference on Optimization Techniques,
      Springer-Verlag, Berlin, Heidelber, New York, 1978.

[55] K. Schittkowski, Nonlinear programming codes - Information,
      tests, performance, Lecture Notes in Economics and Mathe-
      matical Systems, No.183, Springer-Verlag, Berlin, Heidel-
      berg, New York, 1980.

[56] S.B. Schuldt, A method of multipliers for mathematical
      programming problems with equality and inequality con-
      straints, Journal of Optimization Theory and Applications,
      Vol.17, No.1/2 (1975), 155-161.

[57] B.V. Sheela, P. Ramamoorthy, Swift - a new constrained
      optimization technique, Computer Methods in Applied Me-
      chanics and Engineering, Vol.6, No.3 (1975), 309-318.

[58]   W.B. White, S.H. Johnson, G.B. Dantzig, Chemical equi-
       librium in complex mixtures, Journal of Chemical Physics,
       Vol.28 (1958).

[59]   K.P. Wong, Decentralization planning by vertical decompo-
       sition of an economic system: A nonlinear approach,
       Ph.D. Thesis in National Economic Planning, University of
       Birmingham, Birmingham, England.

Name   ....

Institution   ....

Mailing address   ....

                      ....

                      ....

Prof. J. Stoer

Institut für Angewandte Mathematik und Statistik

Universität Würzburg

Am Hubland

D-87 Würzburg, Germany (F.R.)

ORDER FORM

Please send me a copy of FORTRAN subroutines for nonlinear programming test examples on magnetic tape.

Magnetic tape format:

	Proposed format	Other format requested
Label	labelled *)	
No. of tracks	9	xxxxxxxxxxxx
Density in bpi	800	xxxxxxxxxxxx
Parity	odd	xxxxxxxxxxxx
Character code	EBCDIC	
Bytes per record	80	
Records per block	20	

Enclosed is my payment (money check, payable to Prof. Stoer, above address) or a copy of a bank remittance (Universität Würzburg, No. 50 120, Städtische Sparkasse Würzburg, Germany, F.R., BLZ 790 500 00; note down: Verwahrungen Prof. Stoer) in the amount of

                 70,- DM .   **)

                               ....
                               Signature

*)   IBM or ECMA standard.

**) The equivalent amount in any other currency can be used.

Vol. 83: NTG/GI-Gesellschaft für Informatik, Nachrichtentechnische Gesellschaft. Fachtagung „Cognitive Verfahren und Systeme", Hamburg, 11.–13. April 1973. Herausgegeben im Auftrag der NTG/GI von Th. Einsele, W. Giloi und H.-H. Nagel. VIII, 373 Seiten. 1973.

Vol. 84: A. V. Balakrishnan, Stochastic Differential Systems I. Filtering and Control. A Function Space Approach. V, 252 pages. 1973.

Vol. 85: T. Page, Economics of Involuntary Transfers: A Unified Approach to Pollution and Congestion Externalities. XI, 159 pages. 1973.

Vol. 86: Symposium on the Theory of Scheduling and its Applications. Edited by S. E. Elmaghraby. VIII, 437 pages. 1973.

Vol. 87: G. F. Newell, Approximate Stochastic Behavior of n-Server Service Systems with Large n. VII, 118 pages. 1973.

Vol. 88: H. Steckhan, Güterströme in Netzen. VII, 134 Seiten. 1973.

Vol. 89: J. P. Wallace and A. Sherret, Estimation of Product. Attributes and Their Importances. V, 94 pages. 1973.

Vol. 90: J.-F. Richard, Posterior and Predictive Densities for Simultaneous Equation Models. VI, 226 pages. 1973.

Vol. 91: Th. Marschak and R. Selten, General Equilibrium with Price-Making Firms. XI, 246 pages. 1974.

Vol. 92: E. Dierker, Topological Methods in Walrasian Economics. IV, 130 pages. 1974.

Vol. 93: 4th IFAC/IFIP International Conference on Digital Computer Applications to Process Control, Part I. Zürich/Switzerland, March 19–22, 1974. Edited by M. Mansour and W. Schaufelberger. XVIII, 544 pages. 1974.

Vol. 94: 4th IFAC/IFIP International Conference on Digital Computer Applications to Process Control, Part II. Zürich/Switzerland, March 19–22, 1974. Edited by M. Mansour and W. Schaufelberger. XVIII, 546 pages. 1974.

Vol. 95: M. Zeleny, Linear Multiobjective Programming. X, 220 pages. 1974.

Vol. 96: O. Moeschlin, Zur Theorie von Neumannscher Wachstumsmodelle. XI, 115 Seiten. 1974.

Vol. 97: G. Schmidt, Über die Stabilität des einfachen Bedienungskanals. VII, 147 Seiten. 1974.

Vol. 98: Mathematical Methods in Queueing Theory. Proceedings 1973. Edited by A. B. Clarke. VII, 374 pages. 1974.

Vol. 99: Production Theory. Edited by W. Eichhorn, R. Henn, O. Opitz, and R. W. Shephard. VIII, 386 pages. 1974.

Vol. 100: B. S. Duran and P. L. Odell, Cluster Analysis. A Survey. VI, 137 pages. 1974.

Vol. 101: W. M. Wonham, Linear Multivariable Control. A Geometric Approach. X, 344 pages. 1974.

Vol. 102: Analyse Convexe et Ses Applications. Comptes Rendus, Janvier 1974. Edited by J.-P. Aubin. IV, 244 pages. 1974.

Vol. 103: D. E. Boyce, A. Farhi, R. Weischedel, Optimal Subset Selection. Multiple Regression, Interdependence and Optimal Network Algorithms. XIII, 187 pages. 1974.

Vol. 104: S. Fujino, A Neo-Keynesian Theory of Inflation and Economic Growth. V, 96 pages. 1974.

Vol. 105: Optimal Control Theory and its Applications. Part I. Proceedings 1973. Edited by B. J. Kirby. VI, 425 pages. 1974.

Vol. 106: Optimal Control Theory and its Applications. Part II. Proceedings 1973. Edited by B. J. Kirby. VI, 403 pages. 1974.

Vol. 107: Control Theory, Numerical Methods and Computer Systems Modeling. International Symposium, Rocquencourt, June 17–21, 1974. Edited by A. Bensoussan and J. L. Lions. VIII, 757 pages. 1975.

Vol. 108: F. Bauer et al., Supercritical Wing Sections II. A Handbook. V, 296 pages. 1975.

Vol. 109: R. von Randow, Introduction to the Theory of Matroids. IX, 102 pages. 1975.

Vol. 110: C. Striebel, Optimal Control of Discrete Time Stochastic Systems. III. 208 pages. 1975.

Vol. 111: Variable Structure Systems with Application to Economics and Biology. Proceedings 1974. Edited by A. Ruberti and R. R. Mohler. VI, 321 pages. 1975.

Vol. 112: J. Wilhelm, Objectives and Multi-Objective Decision Making Under Uncertainty. IV, 111 pages. 1975.

Vol. 113: G. A. Aschinger, Stabilitätsaussagen über Klassen von Matrizen mit verschwindenden Zeilensummen. V, 102 Seiten. 1975.

Vol. 114: G. Uebe, Produktionstheorie. XVII, 301 Seiten. 1976.

Vol. 115: Anderson et al., Foundations of System Theory: Finitary and Infinitary Conditions. VII, 93 pages. 1976

Vol. 116: K. Miyazawa, Input-Output Analysis and the Structure of Income Distribution. IX, 135 pages. 1976.

Vol. 117: Optimization and Operations Research. Proceedings 1975. Edited by W. Oettli and K. Ritter. IV, 316 pages. 1976.

Vol. 118: Traffic Equilibrium Methods, Proceedings 1974. Edited by M. A. Florian. XXIII, 432 pages. 1976.

Vol. 119: Inflation in Small Countries. Proceedings 1974. Edited by H. Frisch. VI, 356 pages. 1976.

Vol. 120: G. Hasenkamp, Specification and Estimation of Multiple-Output Production Functions. VII, 151 pages. 1976.

Vol. 121: J. W. Cohen, On Regenerative Processes in Queueing Theory. IX, 93 pages. 1976.

Vol. 122: M. S. Bazaraa, and C. M. Shetty,Foundations of Optimization VI. 193 pages. 1976

Vol. 123: Multiple Criteria Decision Making. Kyoto 1975. Edited by M. Zeleny. XXVII, 345 pages. 1976.

Vol. 124: M. J. Todd. The Computation of Fixed Points and Applications. VII, 129 pages. 1976.

Vol. 125: Karl C. Mosler. Optimale Transportnetze. Zur Bestimmung ihres kostengünstigsten Standorts bei gegebener Nachfrage. VI, 142 Seiten. 1976.

Vol. 126: Energy, Regional Science and Public Policy. Energy and Environment I. Proceedings 1975. Edited by M. Chatterji and P. Van Rompuy. VIII, 316 pages. 1976.

Vol. 127: Environment, Regional Science and Interregional Modeling. Energy and Environment II. Proceedings 1975. Edited by M. Chatterji and P. Van Rompuy. IX, 211 pages. 1976.

Vol. 128: Integer Programming and Related Areas. A Classified Bibliography. Edited by C. Kastning. XII, 495 pages. 1976.

Vol. 129: H.-J. Lüthi, Komplementaritäts- und Fixpunktalgorithmen in der mathematischen Programmierung. Spieltheorie und Ökonomie. VII, 145 Seiten. 1976.

Vol. 130: Multiple Criteria Decision Making, Jouy-en-Josas, France. Proceedings 1975. Edited by H. Thiriez and S. Zionts. VI, 409 pages. 1976.

Vol. 131: Mathematical Systems Theory. Proceedings 1975. Edited by G. Marchesini and S. K. Mitter. X, 408 pages. 1976.

Vol. 132: U. H. Funke, Mathematical Models in Marketing. A Collection of Abstracts. XX, 514 pages. 1976.

Vol. 133: Warsaw Fall Seminars in Mathematical Economics 1975. Edited by M. W. Loś, J. Loś, and A. Wieczorek. V. 159 pages. 1976.

Vol. 134: Computing Methods in Applied Sciences and Engineering. Proceedings 1975. VIII, 390 pages. 1976.

Vol. 135: H. Haga, A Disequilibrium – Equilibrium Model with Money and Bonds. A Keynesian – Walrasian Synthesis. VI, 119 pages. 1976.

Vol.136: E. Kofler und G. Menges, Entscheidungen bei unvollständiger Information. XII, 357 Seiten. 1976.

Vol. 137: R. Wets, Grundlagen Konvexer Optimierung. VI, 146 Seiten. 1976.

Vol. 138: K. Okuguchi, Expectations and Stability in Oligopoly Models. VI, 103 pages. 1976.

Vol. 139: Production Theory and Its Applications. Proceedings. Edited by H. Albach and G. Bergendahl. VIII, 193 pages. 1977.

Vol. 140: W. Eichhorn and J. Voeller, Theory of the Price Index. Fisher's Test Approach and Generalizations. VII, 95 pages. 1976.

Vol. 141: Mathematical Economics and Game Theory. Essays in Honor of Oskar Morgenstern. Edited by R. Henn and O. Moeschlin. XIV, 703 pages. 1977.

Vol. 142: J. S. Lane, On Optimal Population Paths. V, 123 pages. 1977.

Vol. 143: B. Näslund, An Analysis of Economic Size Distributions. XV, 100 pages. 1977.

Vol. 144: Convex Analysis and Its Applications. Proceedings 1976. Edited by A. Auslender. VI, 219 pages. 1977.

Vol. 145: J. Rosenmüller, Extreme Games and Their Solutions. IV, 126 pages. 1977.

Vol. 146: In Search of Economic Indicators. Edited by W. H. Strigel. XVI, 198 pages. 1977.

Vol. 147: Resource Allocation and Division of Space. Proceedings. Edited by T. Fujii and R. Sato. VIII, 184 pages. 1977.

Vol. 148: C. E. Mandl, Simulationstechnik und Simulationsmodelle in den Sozial- und Wirtschaftswissenschaften. IX, 173 Seiten. 1977.

Vol. 149: Stationäre und schrumpfende Bevölkerungen: Demographisches Null- und Negativwachstum in Österreich. Herausgegeben von G. Feichtinger. VI, 262 Seiten. 1977.

Vol. 150: Bauer et al., Supercritical Wing Sections III. VI, 179 pages. 1977.

Vol. 151: C. A. Schneeweiß, Inventory-Production Theory. VI, 116 pages. 1977.

Vol. 152: Kirsch et al., Notwendige Optimalitätsbedingungen und ihre Anwendung. VI, 157 Seiten. 1978.

Vol. 153: Kombinatorische Entscheidungsprobleme: Methoden und Anwendungen. Herausgegeben von T. M. Liebling und M. Rössler. VIII, 206 Seiten. 1978.

Vol. 154: Problems and Instruments of Business Cycle Analysis. Proceedings 1977. Edited by W. H. Strigel. VI, 442 pages. 1978.

Vol. 155: Multiple Criteria Problem Solving. Proceedings 1977. Edited by S. Zionts. VIII, 567 pages. 1978.

Vol. 156: B. Näslund and B. Sellstedt, Neo-Ricardian Theory. With Applications to Some Current Economic Problems. VI, 165 pages. 1978.

Vol. 157: Optimization and Operations Research. Proceedings 1977. Edited by R. Henn, B. Korte, and W. Oettli. VI, 270 pages. 1978.

Vol. 158: L. J. Cherene, Set Valued Dynamical Systems and Economic Flow. VIII, 83 pages. 1978.

Vol. 159: Some Aspects of the Foundations of General Equilibrium Theory: The Posthumous Papers of Peter J. Kalman. Edited by J. Green. VI, 167 pages. 1978.

Vol. 160: Integer Programming and Related Areas. A Classified Bibliography. Edited by D. Hausmann. XIV, 314 pages. 1978.

Vol. 161: M. J. Beckmann, Rank in Organizations. VIII, 164 pages. 1978.

Vol. 162: Recent Developments in Variable Structure Systems, Economics and Biology. Proceedings 1977. Edited by R. R. Mohler and A. Ruberti. VI, 326 pages. 1978.

Vol. 163: G. Fandel, Optimale Entscheidungen in Organisationen. VI, 143 Seiten. 1979.

Vol. 164: C. L. Hwang and A. S. M. Masud, Multiple Objective Decision Making – Methods and Applications. A State-of-the-Art Survey. XII, 351 pages. 1979.

Vol. 165: A. Maravall, Identification in Dynamic Shock-Error Models. VIII, 158 pages. 1979.

Vol. 166: R. Cuninghame-Green, Minimax Algebra. XI, 258 pages. 1979.

Vol. 167: M. Faber, Introduction to Modern Austrian Capital Theory. X, 196 pages. 1979.

Vol. 168: Convex Analysis and Mathematical Economics. Proceedings 1978. Edited by J. Kriens. V, 136 pages. 1979.

Vol. 169: A. Rapoport et al., Coalition Formation by Sophisticated Players. VII, 170 pages. 1979.

Vol. 170: A. E. Roth, Axiomatic Models of Bargaining. V, 121 pages. 1979.

Vol. 171: G. F. Newell, Approximate Behavior of Tandem Queues. XI, 410 pages. 1979.

Vol. 172: K. Neumann and U. Steinhardt, GERT Networks and the Time-Oriented Evaluation of Projects. 268 pages. 1979.

Vol. 173: S. Erlander, Optimal Spatial Interaction and the Gravity Model. VII, 107 pages. 1980.

Vol. 174: Extremal Methods and Systems Analysis. Edited by A. V. Fiacco and K. O. Kortanek. XI, 545 pages. 1980.

Vol. 175: S. K. Srinivasan and R. Subramanian, Probabilistic Analysis of Redundant Systems. VII, 356 pages. 1980.

Vol. 176: R. Färe, Laws of Diminishing Returns. VIII, 97 pages. 1980.

Vol. 177: Multiple Criteria Decision Making-Theory and Application. Proceedings, 1979. Edited by G. Fandel and T. Gal. XVI, 570 pages. 1980.

Vol. 178: M. N. Bhattacharyya, Comparison of Box-Jenkins and Bonn Monetary Model Prediction Performance. VII, 146 pages. 1980.

Vol. 179: Recent Results in Stochastic Programming. Proceedings, 1979. Edited by P. Kall and A. Prékopa. IX, 237 pages. 1980.

Vol. 180: J. F. Brotchie, J. W. Dickey and R. Sharpe, TOPAZ – General Planning Technique and its Applications at the Regional, Urban, and Facility Planning Levels. VII, 356 pages. 1980.

Vol. 181: H. D. Sherali and C. M. Shetty, Optimization with Disjunctive Constraints. VIII, 156 pages. 1980.

Vol. 182: J. Wolters, Stochastic Dynamic Properties of Linear Econometric Models. VIII, 154 pages. 1980.

Vol. 183: K. Schittkowski, Nonlinear Programming Codes. VIII, 242 pages. 1980.

Vol. 184: R. E. Burkard and U. Derigs, Assignment and Matching Problems: Solution Methods with FORTRAN-Programs. VIII, 148 pages. 1980.

Vol. 185: C. C. von Weizsäcker, Barriers to Entry. VI, 220 pages. 1980.

Vol. 186: Ch.-L. Hwang and K. Yoon, Multiple Attribute Decision Making – Methods and Applications. A State-of-the-Art-Survey. XI, 259 pages. 1981.

Vol. 187: W. Hock, K. Schittkowski, Test Examples for Nonlinear Programming Codes. V. 178 pages. 1981.

Ökonometrie und Unternehmensforschung
Econometrics and Operations Research